"Up! Flee! Out into broad and open land!
And this book full of mystery,
From **NOSTRADAMUS'** own very hand,
Is it not sufficient company?
The stars' course then you'll understand
And Nature, teaching you, will then expand
The power of your soul, as when
One **SPIRIT** to another **SPEAKS.**"

Faust, act 1, scene 1.

NOSTRADAMUS

A rare woodcut from the Henry C. Roberts Collection.

THE
COMPLETE
PROPHECIES OF
NOSTRADAMUS

Translated, Edited and Interpreted

BY

HENRY C. ROBERTS

Published by

NOSTRADAMUS, INC.

380 CANAL STREET, N. Y. C. 13, N. Y.

Copyright, 1949, by
HENRY C. ROBERTS

All rights reserved

Eighth Printing

INTRODUCTION

Nearly everyone, at one time or another, has heard or read something about Nostradamus and his prophecies. Yet, the astonishing fact is that not since 1672 has there been printed an English edition of his complete quatrains. As a bookseller, I was struck by this lack because of the great number of people, interested in predictions and other phenomena of this nature, who had come to me over a period of years, inquiring for the complete works of Nostradamus in English. As a student of the occult, always seeking materials on the subject, I too was anxious to procure the unabridged work of the man who is acknowledged as one of the greatest seers in the history of occult science.

Spurred on by these incentives, I began to search the field for all books, old and new, pertaining to Nostradamus. The reward was scanty. The current available books on Nostradamus dealt with but a few of his more noted quatrains, discussing them at length, but making no attempt to bring to light more than a few hundred out of the thousand he had purportedly written.

At long last I obtained, at an almost prohibitive price, a copy of the afore-mentioned 1672 edition: *The True Prophecies or Prognostications of Michael Nostradamus*, translated and annotated by Theophilus de Garencieres. I had perused but a few pages when I was struck by the sense of familiarity that these verses seemed to hold for me. Words that the author claimed held no significance for him, took on for me a definite meaning, became clearly focused into patterns of events—past, present and future. Here, I felt, was my book.

Such being the case, I determined to start the long and arduous task of making available, a new complete edition of Nostradamus, using all the materials at hand, bringing to them new interpretations in the light of recent events, taking as much as possible the same position as if Nostradamus were alive today—speaking with both our voices.

Avoiding the hitherto lengthy explanations that, I felt, bewildered rather than enlightened the reader, I have tried to make the interpretations concise and simple; I have also, as much as was feasible, tried to preserve the spirit and cadence of the original quatrains. The present text is the result, and I believe it to be clean and true. At all times, where there were discrepancies or ambiguities in the French text, I have accepted the oldest versions, especially considering Garencieres' book as the most authoritative.

From the time of the Delphic Sibyl it has been the characteristic of occult prophecies and utterances, often to seem unintelligible and garbled to the uninitiate. The strange, broken, and often incoherent nature of the quatrains, both in French and English, is the hallmark of prophetic media.

Nevertheless, at this point, I feel that a few words of explanation are necessary with regard to certain questions that may arise in the reader's mind. Primarily, we must clear up the fact that the word "prophecy" does not, in its literal sense, apply to every one of these quatrains. A good number of the verses have reference to events of the days before and during the time of Nostradamus—events that distressed, pleased, or shocked him, and which he considered important enough to record for posterity. But the bulk of his work was based upon his awesome gift of prognostication, and it is this that we are mainly concerned with. Even after deep study and wide consultation of occult materials, it was not always possible to assign these predictions to definite places or people. It would have been an easy matter to lightly attribute certain doings to certain people, but that would have taken on the nature of "guessing," and we say, in closing, that we prefer to leave that to the reader; for he will inevitably attempt to do so, and we urge him so to do—with "our" blessing.

HENRY C. ROBERTS

New York, N. Y.
November, 1946

INTRODUCTION TO SECOND EDITION

Beyond a shadow of doubt, the methods employed and results obtained by Nostradamus in looking into the future were outside of the physical framework.

What to the contemporary critics of his day, for want of a better term they chose to call magic or occult, we today now recognize as the operation of certain tenuous and imponderable laws that permeate the entire Cosmos. These intangible but all pervading forces we group today under the general title of "Extra Sensory Perception."

Such startling and apparently miraculous phenomena as mediumism, telepathy, telekinesis, etc., are today the serious subject of study by such accredited scientists as Dr. Rhine of Duke University and Prof. Gardner Murphy of New York University. An entirely new line of investigation is in progress in this new science of "Para-psychology" which promises rich rewards for mankind.

Who knows? Perhaps some day this new line of scientific activity may be developed to a point where it will have a practical application to our every day life and make possible a revolutionary concept of nature's forces.

HENRY C. ROBERTS

New York, N. Y.
March 2, 1949

PREFACE TO FIRST EDITION

A Letter of Dedication to his son, Caesar Nostradamus

Thy late coming, Caesar Nostradamus, my son, hath caused me to bestow much time in continual and nocturnal watchings, that I might leave a memorial of me after my death, to the common benefit of mankind, concerning the things which the Divine Essence hath revealed to me by astronomical revolutions. Since it hath pleased the immortal God that thou art come late into this world, and canst say that thy years are but few, and thy months incapable to receive into thy weak understanding what I am forced to define of futurity; since it is not possible to leave thee in writing what might be obliterated by the injury of time, for the hereditary gift of occult prediction shall be locked up in my breast; considering also that events are definitely uncertain, and that all is governed by the power of God who inspired us not by a Bacchic fury nor yet by Lymphatic motion, but by astronomical effects—"*Soli numine divino afflati praesagiunt et spirito prophetico particularia.*" *

Although I have often foretold long before what hath afterwards come to pass, and in particular regions, acknowledging all to have been done by divine virtue and inspiration, I was willing to hold my peace by reason of the injury—not only of the present time, but also of the future—because to put them in writing, the Kingdoms, Sects, and Regions shall be so diametrically opposed, that if I should relate what shall happen hereafter, those of the present Reign, Sect, Religion and Faith, would find it so disagreeing with their fancies, that they would condemn that which future ages shall find and know to be true. Consider also the saying of our Saviour, "*Nolite sanctum dare canibus neque mittatis margaritas vestras ante porcos, ne forte conculcent eas pedibus suis, et conversi dirumpant vos.*" (Matt. vii. 6)

For this reason I have withheld my tongue from the vulgar, and my pen from paper. But, afterwards, I was willing for the common good to enlarge myself in dark and abstruse sentences, declaring the future events, chiefly the most urgent and those which I foresaw (whatever human mutation happened) would not offend the hearers, all under dark figures

---

* "Such alone as are inspired by the divine power can predict particular events in a spirit of prophecy."

3

more than prophetical. Although "*Abscondidisti hoec à sapientibus, et prudentibus, id est, potentibus et regibus, et enucleasti ea exiguis et tenuibus.*" * The prophets, by means only of the immortal God and good Angels, have received the spirit of vaticination, by which they foresee things, and foretell future events. For nothing is perfect without Him, whose power and goodness are so great to His creatures, that though they are but men, nevertheless by the likeness of their good genius to the Angels, this heat and prophetical power draws near us, as do the rays of the sun, which cast their influence alike upon bodies that are elementary and non-elementary. As for us, who are but men, we cannot attain anything by our natural knowledge, of the secrets of God our Creator. "*Quia non est nostrum noscere tempora, nec momenta,*" etc. (Acts i. 7)

There are, or may come some persons, to whom God Almighty will reveal by impressions made on their understanding some secrets of the future, according to judicial astrology, as it hath happened in former times, when a certain power and voluntary faculty possessed them as a flame of fire. So by His inspiration, they were able to judge of divine and human things, for the divine works that are absolutely necessary, God will complete.

But, my son, I speak to thee a little too obscurely. There are secrets that are received by the subtle spirit of fire, by which the understanding is moved to contemplate the highest celestial bodies, being active and vigilant to the very pronunciation without fear or any shameful loquacity; all of which proceeded from the divine power of the Eternal God, from whom all goodness flows.

Now, my son, although I have inserted the name of prophet here, I will not attribute to myself so sublime a title, for "*Propheta dicitur hodie, olim vocabatur videns,*" ** and prophets are those properly, my son, that see things remote from the natural knowledge of mankind. Or, to put the case, the prophets, by the means of the perfect light of prophecy, may see divine things as well as human (which cannot but be seeing the effects of future predictions) and do extend a great distance, for the secrets of God are incomprehensible, and their efficient power is far remote from the natural knowledge, taking their origin in the free will, causing those things to appear which otherwise could not be known, neither by human auguries nor by any hidden knowledge or secret virtue under Heaven. Only by the means of some indivisible eternal being, and by Herculean agitation the causes come to be known by the celestial motion.

I say, therefore, my son, that you may not understand me well, because

---

* Thou hast hidden these things from the wise and prudent and hast revealed them to the small and weak."

** "He who is called prophet now, once was called seer."

the knowledge of this matter cannot yet be imprinted in thy weak brain. Future causes afar off are subject to the knowledge of human creatures, if (notwithstanding the Creator) things present and future were neither obscure nor hidden from the intellectual seal; but the perfect knowledge of the cause of things cannot be acquired without the divine inspiration, seeing that all prophetical inspiration received hath its original principle from God the Creator, next, from good luck, and afterwards from nature. Therefore, causes, independently produced or not produced, the prophecy partly happens where it hath been foretold, for the understanding being intellectually created cannot see occult things, unless it be by the voice coming from the limbo, by the means of the thin flame, to which the knowledge of future causes is inclined. And, also, my son, I entreat thee not to bestow thy understanding on such fopperies which dry up the body and damn the soul, and bring vexation to the senses. Chiefly abhor the vanity of the execrable magic forbidden by the Sacred Scriptures and by the Canons of the Church; except from this judicial astrology by which, and by the means of divine inspiration, with continual calculations, we have put in writing, our prophecies.

Although this occult philosophy was not forbidden, I could never be persuaded to meddle with it, although many volumes concerning that art, which hath been concealed a great while, were presented to me. But fearing what might happen, after I had read them, I presented them to Vulcan and, while he was devouring them, the flame mixed with the air, there was an unwonted light more bright than the usual flame and it was, as if there were lightning, shining all the house over, as if it had been all in a flame. Therefore, that henceforth you might not be abused in the search of the perfect transformation, as much lunar as solar, and to seek in the waters uncorruptible metal, I have burnt them all to ashes. But as to the judgment which cometh to be perfected by the help of the celestial judgment, that I will manifest to you that you may have knowledge of future things; rejecting the fantastic imaginations that may arise, and limiting the particularity of places which were arrived at by divine and supernatural inspiration, according to the celestial figures, by an occult property, and by a divine virtue, power and faculty—in the presence of which the three aspects of time are comprehended by eternity, an evolution that ties into one the cause that is past, present, and future; "quia omnia sunt nuda et aperta. . ." *

Therefore, my son, thou mayst, notwithstanding thy tender brain, comprehend things that shall happen hereafter, and may be foretold by celestial natural lights, and by the spirit of prophecy, not that I will attribute to myself the name of a prophet, but as a mortal man, being no

---

* "For all things are naked and open."

farther from Heaven by my sense than I am from Earth by my feet. "*Possum non errare, falli, decipi,*" * (albeit) I am the greatest sinner of the world subject to all human afflictions. But being surprised sometimes by a prophetical mood, and by a long calculation, pleasing myself in my study, I have made Books of Prophecies, each one containing a hundred Astronomical Stanzas, which I have joined obscurely, and are perpetual prophecies from this year to the year 3797, at which some perhaps will frown, seeing so large an extension of time, and that I treat of everything under the Moon. If thou livest the natural age of a man thou shalt see in thy climate, and under the Heaven of thy nativity, the future things that have been foretold.

God only knoweth the eternity of the light proceeding from Himself, and I say freely to those to whom His incomprehensible greatness hath by a long melancholic inspiration revealed, that by the means of this occult cause, divinely manifested, chiefly by two principal causes, there is comprehension and understanding in him that is inspired and prophetic. One is that which cleareth the supernatural light and foretelleth by the doctrine of the planets, and the other forecasts by inspired revelation, which is a kind of participation in the divine eternity, by means of Him, of God the Creator. And by these means he knows that what is predicted is true, and hath taken its original from above, and such light and small flame is of all efficacy and sublimity, no less than the natural light makes the philosophers so secure, that by the means of the principles of the first cause, they have attained the greatest depth of the profoundest sciences.

But I must not wander too far, my son, from the capacity of thy sense. I find that learning shall be at a great loss, and that before the universal conflagration shall happen so many great inundations, that there shall scarce be any land that shall not be covered with water, and this shall last so long, that except for Ethnographies and Topographies all shall perish. Before and after these inundations in many countries there shall be such scarcity of rain and such a great deal of fire, and burning stones shall fall from Heaven, that nothing unconsumed shall be left. All this shall happen a little while before the great conflagration.

Although the planet Mars makes an end of his course, and is come to the end of his last period, nevertheless he shall begin it again. Some shall be gathered in Aquarius for many years, others in Cancer also for many years. Now we are governed by the Moon, under the power of Almighty God; which Moon before she hath finished her circuit, the Sun shall come, and then Saturn. According to the celestial signs, the reign of Saturn shall come again, so that all being calculated, the world draws near to its anaragonic revolution (death-dealing).

---

* "I am able not to err, be deceived nor fail."

From this present time that I write this, before 177 years, three months, eleven days, through pestilence, famine, war, and for the most part, inundations, the world between this and that prefixed time, before and after, for several times shall be so diminished, and the people shall be so few, that they shall not find enough to till the ground, so that they shall remain fallow as long as they had once been tilled. We are now in the seventh millenary, which ends all and brings us near the eighth, where the firmament of the eighth sphere is, which, in a latitudinary dimension, is the place where the Great God shall make an end of this revolution, where the celestial bodies shall move again, and the superior motion that maketh the Earth firm and stable, *"non inclinabitur in seculum seculorum,"* * unless His will be accomplished and not otherwise.

Although by ambiguous opinions exceeding all natural reasons by Mahometical dreams, also sometimes God the Creator by the ministers of His messengers of fire and flame, shows to our external senses, and chiefly to our eyes, the causes of future predictions, signifying the future event, that will manifest to him that prophesies. For the prophecy that is made by the internal light, comes to judge of the thing partly with and by the means of external light, although the part which seemeth to come by the eye of understanding, comes only from the lesion of its imaginative sense. The reason is evident why what he foretelleth comes by divine inspiration, or by the means of an angelical spirit, inspired into the prophetic person, anointing him with vaticinations, moving the fore part of his fancy, by divers nocturnal apparitions, so that by astronomical administrations, he prophesies with a divine certitude, joined to the holy prediction of the future, having no other regard than to the freedom of his mind.

Come now, my son, and understand that I find by my revelations (astrological), which agree with the divine inspiration, that the swords draw near to us now, and the plague and the war more horrid than hath been seen in the life of three men before, and also famine, which shall return often, for the stars agree with the revolution, *"Visitabo in virga ferrea iniquitates eorum, et in verberibus percutiam eos."* ** For the mercies of God shall not be spread for a while, my son, before most of my prophecies shall come to pass, thus oftentimes shall happen sinister storms. *"Conteram ego, et confringam,"* (said the Lord) *"et non miserebor."* † And a thousand other accidents shall happen by waters and continual rains, as I have more fully at large declared in my other Prophecies, written *in soluta oratione,* limiting the places, times and prefixed terms, that men coming after, may

---

* "Whence it shall not deviate from age to age."
** "I will visit their iniquities with a rod of iron, and with blows will strike them."
† "I will trample them and break them, and not show pity."

see and know that those accidents are certainly come to pass, as we have marked in other places, speaking more clearly, although the explication be involved in obscurity: "*Sed quando submoventa erit ignorantia*"; * the case shall be made more clear. Making an end here, my son, accept this gift of thy father, Michael Nostradamus, hoping to expound to thee every prophecy of these quatrains, praying to the Immortal God that he will grant thee a long life in felicity.

---

* "When the time arrives for the removal of ignorance."

From Salon, this 1st of March, 1555.

CENTURY I

1

Estant assis, de nuit secrette estude,
Seul, repose sur la selle d'airain,
Flambe exigue, sortant de solitude,
Fait proferer qui n'est a croire vain.

Seated at night in my secret study,
Alone, reposing over the brass tripod,
A slender flame leaps out of the solitude,
Making me pronounce that which is not in vain.

Nostradamus clearly shows his method of preparing for a nocturnal visitation from divine sources, from which he shall gain the knowledge of future events for the benefit of Posterity.

2

La verge en main, mise au milieu
des branches,
De l'onae je mouille & le limbe
& le pied,
En peur j'escris fremissant par les
manches;
Splendeur Divine; le Divine prez
s'assied.

With divining rod in hand, I wet the limb and foot,
Set in the middle of the branches.
Fearsome awe trembles my hand, I await,
Heavenly Splendor! The Divine Genius sitteth by.

Evidently our author employed an instrument similar to the present forked, divining rod, now used for locating water. In a large brass bowl filled with water, various segments were marked off and, as the rod dipped to the proper significant areas, messages would emanate.

3

Quand la littiere du tourbillon versee,	When the litter shall be overthrown by a gust of wind,
Et seront faces de leurs manteaux couvers,	And faces shall be covered with cloaks,
La Republique par gens nouveaux vexee,	The Republic shall be vexed by new people,
Lors blancs & rouges jugeront a L'envers.	Then shall White and Red judge wrongly.

During a period of transition, a temporary group, which will be neither Red nor White, shall be in power over the Republic.

4

Par l'Univers sera fait un Monarque,	In the world shall be a Monarch,
Qu'en paix & vie ne sera longuement,	Who will not leave peace, nor be long alive,
Lors se perdra la Piscature Barque,	Then will be lost the Fishing Boat,
Sera regie en plus grand detriment.	And shall be governed to its great detriment.

The Roman Catholic Church is often compared to a ship or boat, by Nostradamus. At a time when a Temporal Ruler shall reign over the entire earth, the Church shall be conspicuous by its absence.

5

Chassez seront sans faire long combat,	They shall be driven away without great fighting,
Par le pais seront plus fort grevez,	Those of the country shall be greatly grieved,
Bourg & Cite auront plus grand debat,	Town and City shall have a mighty debate,
Carcas, Narbonne auront coeurs esprouvez.	Carcassone, Narbonne shall prove their heart.

Here is nothing mysterious. It must be borne in mind that Nostradamus was a devout Catholic, and in keeping with the then current struggle between the Protestants and Catholics for power, he foretells a fraternal melee, centering about Carcassone and Narbonne in Languedoc.

6

L'oeil de Ravenne sera destitue,
Quand a ses pieds les aisles sailli-
ront;
Les deux de Bresse auront consti-
tue,
Turin, Verceil, que Gaulois foule-
ront.

The eye of Ravenna shall be desti-
tute,
When the wings shall rise at his
feet.
The two of Brescia shall have established Turin and Venice,
Which the French shall have trod
upon.

One who lives in Ravenna shall not find time for the pursuit of riches
when the wings of inspiration arise.
The French shall ultimately have sovereignty.

7

Tard arrive, l'execution faite,
Le vent contrare, lettres au che-
min prinses,
Les conjurez quatorze d'une secte,
Par le Rousseau seront les entre-
prinses.

One arriving too late, the execution will take place,
The wind being contrary, and letters intercepted on the way.
The conspirators fourteen of a
separate body,
By the Red One, the enterprise
shall be undertaken.

The Red One will be the leader of a conspiracy involving fourteen
members, terminating in an execution, previously delayed.

8

Combien de fois prinse cite solaire,
Seras, changeant les loix barbares
& vaines,
Ton mal s'approche, plus seras tributaire,
Le grand Adrie recouvrira tes
veines.

How often taken, O city of the Sun
shall thou be?
Changing thy vain and barbarous
laws,
Thy Evil groweth nigh, Thou shalt
be more tributary,
The great Venice shall recover thy
veins.

Heliopolis, or Baalbec, an ancient city in Syria near Damascus, famous
for its ruins, is used symbolically by Nostradamus to indicate the growing
evil in the world.

9

De l'Orient viendra le coeur punique,
Fascher Adrie, & les hoirs Romu-
lides,
Accompagne de la classe Libique
Trembler Melites, & proches Isles
vuides.

From the East of Africa shall come
the Lion-Heart,
To vex Venice and the heirs of
Romulus,
Accompanied by the Libian Tribe,
Malta shall tremble and the neigh-
boring islands shall be empty.

A remarkably prophetic description of the role of Emperor Haile
Selassie, in World War II, who reconquered Ethiopia, in East Africa,
and sent an expedition to aid the Allied Cause, eventually defeating the
Fascists of Italy, self-styled "Heirs of Romulus."

10

Sergens transmis dans la Cage de
Fer,
Ou les enfans septains du Roy
sont pris,
Les vieux & peres sortiront bas
d'enfer,
Ains mourir voir de son fruit mort
& cris.

Sergeants sent into the Cage of
Iron,
Where the seven children of the
King are,
The old men and fathers shall see
the death and cries of their first
fruit,
And before they die, shall go
through Hell.

A description of the incidents that came to pass during the "Reign of
Terror" in the French Revolution. The daily roll calls of those proscribed
for the guillotine are graphically portrayed.

11

Le mouvement de sens, coeur,
pieds, & mains,
Seront d'accord, Naples, Leon, Si-
cile,
Glaives, Feux, Eaux, puis au Noble
Romains,
Plongez, Tuez, Morts, par cerveau
debile.

Naples, Spain and Sicily shall agree
To the movement with heart, feet
hands and sense,
Swords, Fires, Water, then to the
Noble Romans,
Plunged into death by a weak
brain.

The active cooperation of Fascist Italy and Falangist Spain is foretold,
predicting dire results to both Mussolini and his cohorts.

12

Dans peu ira fauce brute fragile,
De bas en haut ensleve promptement,
Puis en estant desloyal & labile,
Qui de Verone aura gouvernment.

In a little while a treacherous brute shall be raised,
Quickly from a low to high estate,
Unfaithfully and swiftly,
He shall have the government of Italy.

A continuation of the previous quatrain, this depicts the rise of Mussolini from an insignificant rabble rouser to Duce, or Leader of the Italian State.

13

Les exiles, par ire, haine intestine,
Feront au Roy grand conjuration,
Secret mettront ennemis par la mine,
Et les vieux siens, contre eux sedition.

The exiles, by anger, shall spread internal strife,
And make against the King a great conspiracy,
Secret enemies shall they put in the mine,
And raise the old ones against them by sedition.

The progress of the Italian conspiracy is indicated—the rise of a fifth column rife with internal dissensions, culminating with a plot against King Victor Emmanuel.

14

De gens esclave, chansons, chants, & requestes,
Captifs par Princes, & Seigneurs aux prisons,
A l'aduenir par idiots sans testes,
Seront receus par divins oraisons.

Being kept prisoners, by Princes and Lords,
The slavish people petition for songs and books,
For the future, idiots without heads
Shall be received by divine prayers.

The forecast of a revolution in Russia. The Russian, or Slavonic, people, held in subjection by their rulers, will seek enlightenment and surcease from oppression.

15

Mars nous menace par la force bellique,
Septante fois fera le sang respandre,
Auge & ruine de l'Ecclesiastique,
Et par ceux qui d'eux rien ne voudront entendre.

Mars threatens us with a warlike force,
Seventy times he shall cause blood to be shed,
Causing the ruin of the Clergy
And those who will hear nothing from them.

The Damoclean Sword of War shall hang over Humanity for a period of Seventy Great Wars, eventually causing a debacle among the heedless mortals as well as the Church.

16

Faux a l'Estang, joint vers la Sagittaire,
En son haut auge de l'exaltation,
Peste, Famine, Mort de main militaire,
Le Siecle approcher de renovation.

When a fish pond that was a meadow shall be mowed,
Sagittarius being in the ascendant,
Plague, Famine, Death by the military hand,
The Century approaches renewal.

In 1999, as the old century is about to expire, between November 23rd and December 21st, the climactic War of Wars shall be unleashed.

17

Par quarante ans l'Iris n'apparoistra,
Par quarante ans tous les jours sera veu,
La Terre aride en siccite croistra,
Et grand deluge quand sera apparceu.

For forty years the rainbow shall not appear,
For forty years it shall be seen every day,
The parched earth shall wax drier and drier,
And a great flood when it shall appear.

A continuation of the preceding stanza—the prediction depicts conditions during the Armageddon.

18

Par la discorde, negligence Gau-
  loise,
Sera passage a Mahomet ouvert,
De sang trempe la terre & mer
  Senoise,
Le Port Phocen de voiles & nefs
  couvert.

Through the discord and negligence of the French,
A passage shall be opened to Mahomet,
The land and sea of Italy shall be
  bloody,
And the harbor of Marseilles shall
  be covered with sails and ships.

The Arab Mohammedan Confederacy, dominated by the Mohammedan Church, shall find an entering wedge into geo-politics largely through French aid.

19

Lors que serpens viendront circuir
  l'air,
Le sang Troien verse par les Espagnes,
Par eux; grand nombre en sera fait
  tare,
Chef fuit, cache aux marets dans
  les saignes.

When the serpents shall come to
  encompass the air,
The French blood shall be angered
  by Spain,
By them, a great number shall perish,
The chief flies, and hides in the
  rushes of the marshes.

At the beginning of World War II, the air superiority of the Nazis was clearly demonstrated much to the chagrin of the French, who, threatened by Spain, were forced to maintain a strong force at their border. Eventually, the French President and his entourage were forced to fly from Paris.

20

Tours, Orleans, Blois, Angers,
  Renes & Nantes,
Cites vexees par soudain change-
  ment,
Par langues estranges seront ten-
  dues tentes,
Fleuves, Darts, Rennes, Terre &
  Mer tremblement.

Tours, Orleans, Blois, Angers,
  Reims and Nantes,
Cities vexed by sudden change,
By strange languages tents shall be
  set up,
Rivers, Darts, Rennes, Land and
  Sea shall tremble.

The German Invasion continues, and the above-named cities are quickly changed over to Nazi rule. The strange German language becomes the official speech, and the rest of France trembles under bombardment from the air.

21

Profonde argile blanche nourrit rocher,
Qui d'un abysme istra l'acticineuse,
En vain troublez ne l'seront toucher,
Ignorant estre au fond terre argileuse.

A deep white clay a rock supports,
Which shall break out of the deep like milk,
In vain people shall be troubled, not daring to touch it,
Being ignorant that in the bottom there is a milky clay.

A prediction of a new and as yet undiscovered method of utilization of Nature's resources, producing powerful actinic properties.

22

Ce qui vivra & n'aura aucen sens,
Viendra le fer a mort son artifice,
Autun, Chalons, Langres, & les deux Sens,
La guerre & la glasse fera grand malefice.

That which shall live shall leave no direction,
Its destruction and death will come by stratagem,
Autun, Chalons, Langres, and from both sides,
The war and ice shall do great harm.

A forecast of the use of supersonic weapons, traveling in the near absolute zero temperature above the stratosphere.

23

Au mois troisiesme se levant le Soleil,
Sanglier, Leopard, aux champs Mars pour combatre,
Leopard lasse au Ciel esttena son oeil,
Un Aigle autour du Soleil voit sesbatre.

In the third month at the rising of the sun,
The Wild Boar and Leopard in the fields of Mars battle,
The Leopard weary, lifts his eyes to Heaven
And seeth an eagle playing about the Sun.

The English Lion, or Leopard, doggedly holds off the German Boar, as the American Eagle gains altitude for his fateful swoop.

24

A Cite Nevue pensif pour condam-
    ner,
Loisel de Proie au ciel se vient off-
    rir,
Apres Victoire a captifs pardonner
Cremone & Mantoue grands maux
    auront ouffert.

In the New City, to condemn an
    idea,
The Bird of Prey shall offer himself
    to the sky,
After Victory the prisoners shall
    be forgiven,
After Cremona and Mantua have
    suffered much.

After many cities have received severe damage, and victory is achieved, a trial shall be held in New City (Nu-Rem-Burg). Most of the prisoners shall be given light sentences.

25

Perdu, trouve cache de si long sie-
    cle
Sera Pasteur demy-Dieu honore,
Ains que la Lune acheve son grand
    Siecle,
Par autre vents fera dishonore.

Lost, found again, hidden so great
    a while,
A Pasteur as Demi-God shall be
    honored,
But before the moon her great
    cycle ends,
By other ancient ones shall be dis-
    honored.

Louis Pasteur, the great French physician, is shown here to be worshipped almost as a demi-god for his discoveries, until a resurgence of an older school.

26

Le grande du Fondre tomb d'heure
    diurne,
Mal & predit par porteur popu-
    laire,
Suivant presage tombe d'heure
    nocturne,
Conflict Rheims, Londres, Etrus-
    que, Pestifere.

The great man falleth by lightning
    in the day,
An evil foretold by the postulant
    one,
According to the forecast, another
    falls in hours of the night,
A conflict at Rheims and London,
    and a plague in Tuscany.

The taking over of Czechoslovakia by Hitler, the resignation of President Benes, the dissensions over the matter between France and England, and the dire warning of the consequences of this betrayal, are all remarkably outlined in this prophecy.

27

Des soubs le chesne Guyen du ciel
frappe,
Non loin de la est cache le thresor,
Qui par long siecles avoir este
grappe,
Trouve mourra, l'oeil creve de res-
sor.

Underneath the cord, Guien struck
from the sky,
Near where is hid a great treasure,
Which has been many years a
gathering,
Being found, he shall die, the eye
put out by a spring.

Paratroopers alight near the Nazi's plunder hoard and, captured, they
are executed.

28

La Tour de Bouk craindra fuste
barbare,
Un temps, long temps apres barque
Hesperique,
Bestial, gens, meubles tous deux
feront grand tare,
Taurus & Libra quelle mortelle
pique.

The Tower of Bouk shall be in awe
of barbarous musty odor,
For a while, and a long time after
afraid of Spanish craft,
Cattle, people and goods, both
shall receive a great damage,
Taurus and Libra, oh, what a
deadly feud!

The Tower of Bouk is a fortified place at the mouth of the Rhone. It
shall be attacked by gas, discharged from craft flying the Spanish flag,
sometime in April or October.

29

Quand le poisson, terrestre &
aquatique,
Par forte vague au gravier sera mis,
Sa forme estrange suave & horri-
fique,
Par mer aux murs bien tost enemies.

When the fish, that is both ter-
restrial and aquatic,
By a strong wave shall be cast upon
the shore,
With his strange, fearful, horrid
form,
Soon after the enemy shall come
to the walls by the sea.

A clear account of the D-Day Invasion of the Normandy beaches, with
an exact description of the amphibious tanks and ducks employed by
the Allies.

30

La Nef estrange par le tourment Marin,
Abordera pres le port incognu,
Nonobstant signs due remeau palmerin.
Apres mort, pille, bon advis tard venu.

The strange ship by the Seas torment,
Shall come near the unknown port,
Notwithstanding the signs given to it of the bows and palms,
It shall die, be plundered, a good advice come too late.

A prophetic description of France in the days preceding the War, when the Ship of State was sabotaged and plundered by avaricious, selfish, factional disputes.

31

Tant d'ans les guerras, en Gaule dureont,
Outre la course du Castulon Monarque,
Victoire incerte trois grands couroneront,
Aigle, Coq, Lune, Lion Soleil en Marque.

So many years the wars shall last in France,
Beyond the course of the Castillian monarch,
An uncertain victory three great ones shall crown
The Eagle, the Cock, the Moon, the Lion leaving the sun in its mark.

At the conclusion of the war, an insecure truce is declared between the victors—United States, France, China, and England—all of whom will exact a penalty from the Land of the Rising Sun, or Japan.

32

La grand Empire sera tost translate,
En lieu petit qui bien tost viendra coistre,
Lieu bien infime d'exigue comte,
Ou au milieu viendra poser son scepter.

The great Empire shall soon be translated
Which shall grow soon into an inferior place of small account,
In the middle of which he shall come,
To lay down his scepter.

A continuation of the previous stanza. Great Japan will degenerate into a minor power, with the Emperor abdicating the throne.

33

Pres d'un grand pont de plaine spa-
cieuse,
Le grand Lion par force, Cesarees,
Fera abatre hors cite, rigoureuse,
Par effroy portes luy seront reser-
rees.

At a great bridge, near a spacious
plain,
The great Lion, by Caesarous
forces,
Shall come to be pulled down before the rigorous city,
The gates which shall be shut to
him.

Winston Churchill will re-enter English politics to save the Tory
Party from Labor, but, by a coalition, shall be defeated.

34

L'oiseau de proye volant a la fe-
nestre,
Avant conflict, fait au Francois
parure,
L'un bon prendra, l'autre ambigue
sinistre,
La partie foible tiendra pour bonne
augure.

The bird of prey flying to the win-
dow,
Before battle shall appear to the
French,
One shall take good omen of it, the
other, an ambiguous one,
The weaker party shall hold it a
good sign.

A foreign Demagogue will cause intrigue by dividing the various
parties, and the faction weakest in numbers will be spurred to action.

35

Le Lion jeune le vieux surmontera,
En champ bellique par singulier
duelle,
Dans cage d'or loeil il lui crevera,
Deux plays une puis mourir mort
cruelle.

The young Lion shall overcome
the old one
In martial field by a single duel,
In a golden cage he shall put out
his eye,
Two wounds from one, then he
shall die a cruel death.

One of the most famous of Nostradamus' prophecies:—The Young
Lion, a Scottish Knight, in a tournament with King Henry II, the Old Lion,
accidentally pierced his golden helmet with a splinter of his wooden lance,
putting out his eye and penetrating his brain, causing the King to die "a
cruel death."

36

Tard le Monarque se viendra re-
  pentir.
De navior mis a mort son adver-
  saire,
Mais viendra bien a plus haut con-
  sentir,
Que tout son sang par mort fera
  deffaire.
	The Monarch shall repent too late,
	That he has not put his adversary
	  to death,
	But he shall give his consent to a
	  greater thing than that,
	Which is, to kill all his adversary's
	  kindred.

Toussaint L'Overture, the great leader of the Negroes of Haiti, and his connection with Napoleon I, is here foreseen. Despite his fight on the side of the French, L'Overture was eventually deposed as Governor of Haiti by Napoleon, and brought to France where he died in prison.

37

Un peu devant que le Soleil saba-
  conse
Conflict donne, grand peuple du-
  bieux,
Profligez, port-marin ne fait re-
  sponce,
Pont & sepulchre en deux es-
  tranges lieux.
	A little before the sun sets,
	A battle shall be given, a great peo-
	  ple shall be doubtful,
	Of being foiled, the sea port makes
	  no answer,
	A bridge and sepulchre shall be in
	  two strange places.

One of the numerous prophecies that refer to the events in the great Armageddon.

38

Le sol & l'aigle victeur parois-
  stront,
Response vain au vaincu lon as-
  seure,
Par Cor ne cris, harnois n'arreste-
  ront,
Vindicte paix, par mort lacheve a
  l'heure.
	The sun and eagle shall appear to
	  be victorious,
	A vain answer shall be made good
	  to the vanquished,
	By no means, arms shall not be
	  stopped,
	Peace, prosecuted by death, it shall
	  be achieved.

A movement shall arise for the suppression of armament and wars. War in itself will become so terrible that nations will achieve peace through fear of Universal Death.

39

De nuit le lit le supresme estrange,
Pour avoir trop suborne blonde
   esleu,
Partrois l'Empire subroge exancle,
A mort metra, carte ne pacquet
   leu.

By night, in the bed, the chief one
   shall be strangled,
For having corrupted too much the
   fair elect,
By three the Empire subrogate
   exancle.
He, devoted to death, reading
   neither card nor packet.

The author purposely obscured this prophecy in the third line, because the persons concerned were then alive, viz., King Phillip II of Spain, who caused his only son, Don Carlos, to be strangled in bed, for suspicion of being intimate with his wife, Elizabeth of France and daughter of Henry II.

40

La tourbe fausse dissimilant folie
Fera Bizance un changement de
   loix,
Istra d'Egypt qui veus que l'on de-
   slie,
Edict, changant monnoys & alloys.

The false troupe dissembling their
   folly,
Shall make in Constantinople, a
   change of laws,
One shall come out of Egypt who
   will have untied the edict,
Changing the money and the
   standards.

At a convention held in the Near East, the Nations will attempt to draw up an economic and financial formula for the free flow of world trade.

41

Siege a cite & de nuit assaille,
Peu eschapez non loing de Mer
   conflict,
Femme de joys, retour fils, de faillie
Poison & lettres cache dedans le
   plic.

A siege laid to a city, and assaulted
   by night,
A few shall escape to fight not far
   from the sea,
A woman swoons for joy to see her
   son returned,
A poison hidden in the fold of
   letters.

A local incident which meant much to contemporary Provençals, but which now, from our distant point of view, has lost its importance.

42

Les dix Calendes d'Avril de fait Gothique,	The tenth of the Calends of April, Gothic account,
Rescuscite encor par gens malins,	Raised up again by malicious persons,
Le feu estaint, assemblee diabolique,	The light put out, a diabolical assembly,
Cherchand les os de d'amant & Psellin.	Seek for the bones of the lovers and Psellus.

An account of a witches' assembly, on the twenty-third of April, old style—evil persons assemble and various diabolical acts are performed in the dark, all according to Psellus, a famed Byzantine writer on Black Magic.

43

Avant qu'avien le changement d'Empire,	Before the change of Empire comes,
Ill adviendra un cas bien merveilleux,	There shall be a strange accident,
Le champ mue, le pilier de Porphyre,	A field shall be changed, and a pillar of Porphyry
Mis, translate sur le Rocher Noileux.	Shall be transported upon the chalky cliffs.

England will change its course of Empire, when upon the chalky cliffs of Dover, shall appear a pillar, or adherent, of Porphyry (a famous anti-Christian philosopher of ancient Rome, A.D. 233–305).

44

En bref seront de retour sacrifices,	In a short time sacrifices shall return again,
Contrevenans seront mis a martyre,	Opposers shall be put to martyrdom,
Plus ne seront moins, abbez ne novices,	There shall be no more monks, abbots, nor novices,
Le miel sera beaucoup plus cher que cire.	Honey shall be dearer than wax.

A period of persecution against the Catholic Church is foretold, when Protestants will forbid the use of wax candles used in the Catholic ritual.

45

Secteur de Sectes, grand paine au delateur,
Beste en theatre, dresse le jeu scenique,
Du fait antique ennobly l'inventeur,
Par sectes, monde confus & schismatique.

Followers of Sects, great pains to the informer,
A beast on the stage prepares the scenes,
The inventor of that iniquitous fact shall be famous,
By sects the world shall be confused and schismatic.

Nostradamus, a confirmed Catholic, and a believer in the infallibility of the Church, releases a blast of condemnation at Martin Luther, whose appearance divided the Christian World into innumerable Sects.

46

Tout aupres d'Auch, de Lectoure & Mirande,
Grande feu du ciel en trois nuits tombera,
Chose adviendra bien stupende & mirande,
Bien peu apres al terre tremblera.

Near Auch, Lectoure and Mirande,
A great fire shall from the sky for three nights fall,
A thing shall happen stupendous and wonderful,
And shortly after the ground shall quake.

Auch, Lectoure, and Mirande are towns in Guyenne, a Province of France, in the vicinity of Bordeaux. This area, Nostradamus informs us, will bear watching.

47

Du Lac Lemans les sermons fascheront,
Des jours seront reduit par des sepmains,
Puis mois, puis an, puis tous dafalliront,
Les Magistrats damneront leurs Loix vaines.

The sermons of the Leman Lake shall be troublesome,
Some of the days shall be extended weeks,
Then into months, then into years, when they shall fail,
The magistrates shall condemn their own inept laws.

Lake Leman is the ancient name for Geneva. Here is clearly foretold the efforts and final failure of the League of Nations.

48

Vingt ans du regne de la lune passez,	Twenty years of the reign of the moon having passed,
Sept mil ans autre tiendra sa monarchie,	Seven thousand years another shall hold his monarchy,
Quand le soleil prendra ses jours laissez,	When the sun shall resume his days past,
Lors accomplit a fine ma Prophecie.	Then is fulfilled and ends my prophecy.

The end of the world is here explicitly prophesied by Nostradamus. In the year 7000 the Sun will destroy the Earth and again resume its undisputed sway.

49

Beaucoup, beaucoup avant telles menees,	Much, very much before these doings happen,
Ceux d'Orient par la vertu Lunaire,	Those of the East by virtue of the Moon,
L'An mil sept cens feront grands emmenees,	In the year 1700, shall carry away great multitudes,
Subjugant presque le coin Aquilonaire.	And shall subdue almost the whole northern section.

In the year 2025, by ritual, China, having completed her industrial and economic expansions, will absorb almost the whole of Northern Russia and Scandinavia.

50

De l'aquatique triplicite naistra,	From the aquatic triplicity shall be born,
Un qui fera Feudy pour sa feste,	One who shall make Thursday his holiday,
Son bruit, loz, regne & puissance croistra,	His fame, praise, rule, and power shall grow,
Par Terre & Mer, aux Orients tempeste.	By Land and Sea to become a tempest to the east.

A triple alliance shall bring forth one who is a follower of Thor, God of Thunder, bringing much grief to the East.

51

Chef d'Aries, Jupiter and Saturn,
Dieu Eternal quelles mutations!
Puis apres long siecle son malin
   temps retourne,
Gaule & Italy quelles emotions!

Heads of Aries, Jupiter and Saturn,
O Eternal God, What changes
   there shall be!
After an era his evil time returns,
Gaule and Italy, what commotion!

A period of unrest in Italy shall culminate in the intervention of the French and a complete change in the social order.

52

Les deux malin de Scorpion conjoint,
Le Grand Seigneur meurtry dedans
   sa salle,
Peste a l'Eglise par le nouveau Roy
   jonts,
L'Europe basse & Septentrioanle.

The two evils of Scorpion being
   joined,
The Grand Seignior murdered in
   his hall,
Plague to the Church by a King
   joined to it,
Europe in the depths and dismem-
   bered.

The Church, as well as all Europe, is to be cut up by one born a member of the Catholic Church.

53

Las qu'on verra grand peuple tour-
   mente,
Et la Loy Saincte en totale ruyne,
Par autres loix toute la Chrestiente,
Quand d'or, d'argent trouve nou-
   velle mine.

Alas, how a great people shall be
   tormented
And the Holy Laws in total ruin,
By other laws, all Christianity
   troubled,
When new mines of gold and silver will be found.

The industrial revolution, the discovery of gold mines in Africa, Australia, etc., the rise of the God of Mammon, shall bring grief to all of Christendom.

54

Deux revolts faits du malin falci-
 gere
De regne & siecles fait permutation
Le mobil signe en son endroit s'in-
 gere,
Aux deux esgaux & d'inclination.

Two revolts shall be made by the
 evil torch bearer,
Which shall make a change of the
 reign and age,
The mobile sign to right shall meddle,
And shall have an inclination to
 the two equals.

The evil genius of the age shall instigate two revolts, in the name of
enlightenment; the Swastika shall make concessions to the right and to
both leaders.

55

Soubz l'opposite climat Babylo-
 nique,
Grande sera de sang effusion,
Que terre & mer, air. ciel sera
 inique,
Sectes, faim, regnes, pestes, confusion.

In the climate opposite to the
 Babylonian,
There shall be a great effusion of
 blood,
So that the land and sea, air and
 heaven shall seem unjust,
Sects and famine shall rule over
 plague and confusion.

Cataclysmic destruction, with great loss of life, is promised to the land
of the Pacific, far in the East (the antipodes of the Near East or Baby-
lonia).

56

Vous verrez tost & tard faire grand
 change
Horreurs extresmes & vindications,
Que si la lune conduite par son
 ange,
Le ciel s'approche des inclinations.

Sooner or later, you shall see great
 changes,
Extreme horrors and persecutions,
The moon led by her angel,
The heaven draws near its inclina-
 tion.

This quatrain reflects, as do so many of Nostradamus' prophecies, his
repeated prophetical conviction of the great changes to take place in the
future, most of which will lead to strife among humans and the ultimate
destruction of the Earth.

57

Par grand discord la trombe tremblera,	By great discord, the trumpet shall vibrate,
Accord rompu, dressant la teste au ciel,	Agreement broken, lifting the head to heaven,
Bouche sanglante dans le sang nagera,	A bloody mouth shall swim in blood,
Au sol sa face oingte de laict & miel.	The face turned to the sun anointed with milk and honey.

A clear and forthright prediction. Japan will treacherously break her agreement with the United States and, plunging into the bloody war, she will embark on her East Asia Co-Prosperity scheme, promising a future land of milk and honey to her cohorts.

58

Trenche le ventre, naistra avec deux testes	Slit in the belly, it shall be born with two heads,
Et quatre bras, quelques ans entiers viura,	And four arms, and shall live a few years,
Jour qui Aquilare celebrera ses festes,	The day that Aquila shall celebrate his feasts,
Foussan, Thurin, chef Ferrare suyura.	Fossan, Turin, the chief of Ferrara shall run away.

A monstrous thing shall be brought into being, but shall not exist long. When Aquila (a Jewish Proselyte who literally translated the Hebrew Scriptures into Greek) celebrates his feast, the Italians shall have much sorrow.

59

Les exilez deportez dans les Isles,	The exiles that were carried into the Isles,
Au changement d'un plus cruel Monarque,	At the whim of a most cruel monarch,
Seront meurtris, & mis deux des scintilles	Shall be murdered, and put in the sparks of fire,
Qui de parler ne seront este parques.	Because they had not been sparing of their tongues.

Hitler's wholesale extermination of the Jews and Poles, followed by the infamous cremation of their bodies, is indicated in this quatrain.

60

Un Empereur naistra pres d'Italie,	An Emperor shall be born in Italy.
Qui a l'Empire sera vendu bien cher,	Who shall cost the Empire dear,
Diront avec quels gens il se ralie	They shall say, with what peoples he keeps company!
Qu'on trouvera moins Prince que boucher.	He shall be found less a Prince than a butcher.

A presage of the coming of Napoleon, born in Corsica (then an Italian possession), and the subsequent wars and destruction he will bring to Europe.

61

La republique miserable infelice,	The miserable and unhappy republic
Sera vastee du nouveau Magistrat,	Shall be wasted by the new Magistrate,
Leur grand amas de l'exil malefice,	Their great number of broken refugees,
Fera Sueve ravir leur grand contract.	Shall cause Sweden to break her contract.

This refers to the dissipation of the resources of France, and the repudiation by Sweden of her treaty with France in favor of a Russian alliance, on December 3, 1804.

62

La grande perte las! que feront les lettres	Alas, what a great loss shall learning suffer
Avant le cicle de laton a parfaict,	Before the cycle of the moon is accomplished,
Feu, grand deluge, plus par ignares sceptres	By fire, great flood, and ignorant scepters,
Que de long siecle ne se verra refaict.	More than can be made good again in a long age.

The cycle of the moon shall end when, on the last cataclysmic day, it shall fall on the earth; until then much misery shall happen due to the ignorance of men.

63

Les fleaux passees diminue le monde,
Long-temps la paix, terres inhabitees,
Seur marchera par le ceil, terre, mer & Onde,
Puis de nouveau les guerres suscitees.

The scourge being past, the world shall be made smaller,
Peace for a long time, lands inhabited,
Everyone safe shall go by air, land and sea,
And then the wars shall begin anew.

In the period after the great influenza epidemic, that followed World War I, great progress was made in air travel, etc.; then after a brief time, World War was renewed.

64

De nuict soleil penseront auoir veu,
Quand le porceau demy homme on verra,
Bruit, chant, bataille au Ciel battre apperceu
Et bestes brutes a parler on orra.

They shall think to have seen the sun in the night,
When the hog half a man shall be seen,
Noise, singing, battles in the sky shall be perceived,
And brute beasts shall be heard to speak.

This presages modern mechanized warfare: searchlights, baby tanks, whistling bombs, dog fights in the air, and radio equipment.

65

Enfant sans mains, jamais veu si grand foudre
L'enfant Royal au jeu d'esteuf blesse,
Au puy brisez, fulgures allant moudre,
Trois sur le chaines par le milieu trousse.

A child without hands, lightning never so great was seen,
The Royal child, wounded at the tennis court,
Bruised at the well, lightning going to the ground,
Three in the midst of the field shall be struck thereby.

An allegorical attempt to show that when the "Oath of the Tennis Court" was taken by the French Revolutionists, the Royal Three were irretrievably struck down, viz; Louis XVI, Marie Antoinette, and the Dauphin.

66

Celuy qui lors portera les nouvelles,	He that then shall carry the news,
Apres un peu il viendra respirer,	A little while after shall draw his breath,
Vivers, Tournon, Montferrant & Pradelles,	Viviers, Tournon, Montserrant, and Pradelles,
Gresle & tempeste, les fera souspirer.	Hail and storm shall make them sigh.

A continuation of the preceding quatrain—the mounting storm of the Revolution rolls over all France.

67

La grand famine que je sens approcher,	The great famine do I see drawing near,
Aouvent tourner puis estre universelle,	Turning from one way to another and then becoming universal,
Si grande & longue qu'on viendra arracher,	So great and long, that they shall come to pluck
Du bois racine, & l'enfant de mamelle.	The root from the wood and the child from the breast.

The French Revolution continues and a period of famine and exhaustion follows.

68

O quel horrible & malheureux tourment!	O what a horrid and sad torment
Trois innocens qu'on viendra a livrer,	Shall be put to three innocents,
Poison suspecte, mal garde tradiment	Poison shall be suspected, evil guards shall betray them.
Mis en horreur par bourreaux enyvrez.	They shall be put to horror by drunken executioners.

Three innocent persons shall be suspected of a poison plot, and they shall be tortured and put to death by drunken executioners.

69

La grand montagne ronde de sept
estades,
Apres paix, guerre, faim, inonda-
tion,
Roulera loing, abysmant grand con-
tades,
Mesmes antiques, & grand fonda-
tion.

The great mountain encompasses
seven stadia,
After peace, war, famine, and
inundation,
Shall tumble a great way, sinking
great countries,
Even ancient houses and their great
foundations.

Great institutions, after surviving the vicissitudes of war, etc., shall
go down, carrying with them the long established order and the ruling
castes.

70

Pluys, faim, guerre, en Perse non
cessee,
La foy trop grande trahira le Monarque,
Par la finie en Gaule commencee,
Secret augure pour a un estre
parque.

Rain, famine, war in Persia hav-
ing not ceased,
Too great credulity shall betray the
Monarch,
Being ended there, it shall com-
mence in France,
A secret omen to one that he shall
die.

The weak, vacillating policy of Louis XVI, and his too great faith in
advisers, bring France to the brink of disaster, and an unheeded omen to
the King himself.

71

La tour marins trois fois prinse &
reprinse
Par Espagnols, Barbares, Ligurins,
Marseille & Aix, Arles par ceux de
Pise
Vast, feu, fer, pille, Avignon des
Thurins.

The sea tower three times taken
and retaken,
By Spaniards, Barbarians, and Italians,
Marseilles, and Aix, Arles by those
of Pisa,
Waste, fire, iron, pillage, Avignon
by Piedmont.

Confirmation of Quatrain 28, Century One—wherein France is attacked by the Axis.

72

Du tout Marseille des habitans changee	Marseilles shall wholly change her inhabitants,
Course & pour fuitte jusques pres de Lyon,	These shall run and be pursued as far as Lyons,
Narbon, Tholoze par Bordeaux outragee,	Narbonne, Toulouse shall wrong Bordeaux,
Tuez, captifs, presque d'un million.	Killed and prisoners shall be almost a million.

The Vichy Regime of Marshal Petain occupied the territory of Toulouse, Lyons, and Narbonne. German troops entered Paris (June 14, 1940) and the government fled to Bordeaux.

73

France a cinq parts par neglect assaillie	France by neglect shall be assaulted by five sides,
Tunys, Argiels esmeuz par Persiens,	Tunis and Algiers shall be stirred by the Persians,
Leon, Seville, Barcelone faillie	Leon, Seville, Barcelona shall be missed,
N'aura la classe par les Venitiens.	And not be pursued by the Venetians.

By the pettiness of her political parties, France will be invaded, and in French Africa the Italians will cause unrest, while the cities of Spain remain untouched.

74

Apres sejourne vogueront en Epire	After a stay, they shall sail toward Epirus,
Le grand secours viendra vers Antioche,	The great aids shall come toward Antioch.
Le noir poil crespe tendra fort a l'Empire,	The black hair curled, shall aim much to the Empire,
Barbe d'airain le rostira en broche.	The brazen beard shall be roasted on a spit.

An Axis expedition will be sent to Epirus (Greece) and the Mediterranean. Mussolini, the Black One, will aim at expansion of the Italian Empire.

75

Le tyran Siene occupera Savone,
Le fort gaigne tiendra classe ma-
   rine,
Les deux armees par la marque
   d'Ancone
Par effrayeur le chef s'en examine.

The tyrant of Sienna shall occupy
   Savone,
The fort being won, shall hold a
   fleet,
The two armies shall go by the
   way of Ancona,
Where by fear the chief shall be
   examined.

The tyrant of Italy shall occupy French Savoy, thereby tying up the
British fleet on the coast. Two Italian armies will proceed east, past
Ancona, on the Adriatic Sea. Marshal Balbo will be executed.

76

D'un nom farouche tel profere sera,
Que les trois soeurs auront fato le
   Nom
Puis grand peuple par langue & fait
   dira,
Plus que nul autre aura bruit &
   renom.

By a wild name one shall be called,
So that three sisters shall have the
   name of Fate
Afterward a great people by tongue
   and deeds shall say,
He shall have fame and renown
   more than any other.

One of the more obscure of Nostradamus' stanzas. Quite evidently it
refers to the Three Fates and their influence upon the lives of men; but a
specific explication cannot be gathered from it.

77

Entre deux mers dressera promontoire
Que puis mourra par le mords du
   cheval,
Le sien Neptune pliera voille noire,
Par Calpre & classe supres de Rocheval.

Between two seas shall a promontory be raised,
By him, who shall die by the biting
   of the horse,
The proud Neptune shall fold the
   black sail,
Through Calpre, and a fleet shall
   be near Rocheval.

In Greek legend, according to the history of Theseus, the Greeks, in
order to please the Minotaur, sent him a tribute of Athenian children in a
ship with black sails.

78

D'un chef vieillard naistra sens he-
bete,
Degenerant par scavoir & par
armes,
Le chef de France par sa soeur re-
doute,
Champs divisez, concedez aux gens
L'armes.

An old head shall beget an idiot,
Who shall degenerate in learning
and in arms,
The head of France shall be feared
by his sister,
The fields divided and granted to
the people's army.

An explication that the corrupt oligarchy of France will so degenerate that the social and economic order will collapse of its own weight.

79

Bazax, Lectore, Condon, Ausch,
Agine,
Esmeus par loix, querelles & mono-
pole,
Car Bourd, Tholouse, Bay mettra
en ruyne,
Renouveller voulant leur tauropole.

Bazax, Lectore, Condon, Auch,
Agine,
Being moved by laws, quarrels and
monopoly,
They shall put to ruin Bordeaux,
Toulouse, Bayonne,
Going about to renew their Tauro-
pole.

The Northern industrial districts of France will try to exploit the agricultural regions.

80

De la sixiesme claire splendeur ce-
leste,
Viendra tonner si fort eu la Bour-
gongne,
Puis naistra monstre de tres-hy-
deuse beste,
Mars, Avril, May, Juin grand char-
pin & rongne.

From the sixth bright celestial
splendor,
Shall come very great lightning to
Burgundy,
After which shall be born a monster of a most hideous beast,
In March, April, May and June
shall be great quarrelling and
muttering.

The sixth planet from the Sun, or Saturn, shall shed a clear light on horrific events to occur in the above-named months.

81

D'humain troupeau neuf seront mis a part;
De jugement & conseil separees,
Leur sort sera divise en depart,
Kappa, Theta, Lambda, morts, bannis, egarez.

Of the human flock, nine shall be set aside,
Being divided in judgment and counsel,
Their destiny shall be to be divided,
Kappa, Theta, Lambda, dead, banished, scattered.

The Supreme Court of the United States, consisting of nine members, is here indicated.

82

Quand les colomnes de bois grande tremblee,
D'auster conduicte couverte de rubriche,
Tant vuidera dehors une grand assemblee,
Trembler Vienne & le pays d'Austriche.

When the wooden columns shall be shaken
By the stern wind and covered by a ruby hue,
Then shall go out a great assembly,
And Vienna and the land of Austria shall tremble.

The weak foundations are shaken by the rising Red Storm, which will make strong progress in Austria.

83

La gent estrange divisera butins
Saturne & Mars son regard furieux,
Horrible estrange aux Toscans & Latins,
Grec qui seront a frapper curieux.

The alien agent shall divide booties,
Saturn and Mars shall have his aspect furious,
Horrid and strange to the Tuscans and Latins,
The Grecians shall be curious to strike.

Enemy alien agents shall loot occupied countries to feed the ravenous maw of the military octopus, to the horror of the easy-going Latins, who are about to be attacked by the Greeks.

84

Lune obscur cie aux profondes te-
nebres,
Son frere passe de couleur ferrigine;
Le grand cache long temps soubs
les tenebres,
Tiendra fer dans la pluie sanguine.

The moon shall be obscured in the
deepest darkness,
Her brother shall pass being of a
ferruginous colour;
The great one long hidden under
shadows,
Shall make his iron lukewarm in
the bloody rain.

At a time when vision is obscured, the Sun shall take on a tinge of
red, or iron rust, and this will be the signal for the great one to rise and
whet his sword.

85

Par la response de dame, roy
trouble,
Ambassadeurs mespriseront leur
vie,
Les grand ses freres contrefera double,
Par deux mourront ire, hain envie.

A king shall be troubled by the
answer of a lady,
Ambassadors shall despise their
lives,
The great one being undecided,
shall counterfeit his brothers,
They shall die by two, anger,
hatred, and envy.

Another of Nostradamus' obscure quatrains and, according to his own
interpretation, merely denoting "there shall be anger, hatred and envy."

86

Le grande Royne quand se verra
vaincue
Fera excez de masculin courage;
Sur cheval fleuve passera toute nue,
Suitte par fer, a foy fera outrage.

When the queen shall see herself
vanquished,
She shall do a deed of masculine
courage,
Upon a horse, she shall pass over
the river naked,
Followed by iron she shall do
wrong to her faith.

Marie Antoinette, seeing herself vanquished, flees imprisonment
stripped naked of all wealth, and denies her identity to her captors.

87

Ennosigee, feu du centre de terre,
Fera trembler autour de Cite Neu-
    fue;
Deux grands rocher long temps
    ferot la guerre,
Puis Arethusa rougira nouveau
    Fleuve.

Ennosigee, fire of the center of the
    earth,
Shall make an earthquake of the
    New City,
Two great rocks shall long time
    war against each other,
After that, Arethusa shall color red
    the fresh river.

A terrific fire, of the same nature as that at the center of the earth,
shall make a shambles of "New ——— City." (Arethusa was an everflow-
ing classic spring.)

88

Le divin mal surprendra le grand
    Prince,
Un peu devant aura femme es-
    pousee;
Son puy & credit a un coup viendra
    mince,
Conseil mourra pour la teste rasee.

The divine sickness shall surprise
    a great prince,
A little while after he hath married
    a woman,
His support and credit shall at
    once become slender,
Council shall die for the shaven
    head.

Napoleon's desire to found an empire led to his marriage to Marie
Louise, who bore him an heir. His quarrels with the Pope are also indicated here.

89

Tous ceux de Ilerde seront dedans
    Moselle
Mettans a mort tous ceux de Loyre
    & Seine,
Secours marin viendra pres d'haute
    velle.
Quand l'Espagnol ouvrira toute
    viene.

All those of l'Isle shall be in the
    Moselle,
Putting to death all those of Loire
    and Seine,
The sea chase shall come near the
    high city
When the Spaniard shall open all
    veins.

Quarrels and warfare among the provinces of France are here referred
to.

90

Bourdeaux, Poitiers, au son de la campane,	Bordeaux, Poitiers, at the sound of the bell,
A grand classe ira jusques a l'Angon,	With a great navy shall go as far as Langon,
Contre Gaulois sera leur tramontane,	Against the French shall their Tramontane be,
Quand monstre hideux naistra pres d'Orgon.	When a hideous monster shall be born near Orgon.

Tramontane, in Italian, is the North Wind; Orgon is a town in Gascony.—An implication that France will be pitted against Northern adversaries and native quislings.

91

Les Dieux feront aux humains apparence,	The Gods shall make it appear to mankind,
Ce qu'ile seront autheurs de grand conflit.	That they are the authors of a great war,
Avant ciel veu serain, espee & lance,	The sky that was serene shall show sword and lance,
Que vers main gauche sera plus grand affliction.	On the left hand the affliction shall be greater.

Predestined by the Gods, war shall make its appearance without warning, largely in the air.

92

Sous un la paix par tout sera clemence	Under one shall be peace, and everywhere clemency,
Mais non long temps, pille & rebellion	But not for a long while, then shall be plundering and rebellion,
Par refus, ville, terre & mer entammee,	By a denial shall town, land and sea be assaulted,
Morts & captifs, le tiers d'un million.	Dead and taken prisoner shall be the third part of a million.

The sneak attack on Pearl Harbor, by the Japanese, ushered the United States into World War II, resulting in 350,000 American casualties.

93

Terre Italique pres des monts trem-
blera,
Lyon & Coq, non trop confererez,
En lieu de peur, l'un l'autre s'ai-
dera,
Seul Castulon & Celtes moderez.

The Italian land of the mountains
shall tremble,
The Lion and the Cock shall not
agree very well together,
And for fear shall help one another,
Only Spain and the Celts shall be
neutral.

The old animosities between the French and the English will be wiped
out during their mutual engagement in a war of world-wide proportions.
The neutrality of Spain and Ireland during this conflict is indicated.

94

Au port Selim le tryan mis a mort
La liberte non pourtant recouvree
Le nouveau Mars par vindicte &
remort.
Dame par force de frayeur hon-
oree.

In the port, Selim the tyrant shall
be put to death,
And yet, liberty shall not be recovered,
The new War by vengeance and
remorse begun,
A lady by force of fear shall be
honored.

The reference here is to Selim II of Turkey, under whose leadership the
great naval battle of Lepanto was fought.

95

Devant Moustier trouve enfant
besson
D'heroicq sang de moyne vestu-
tisque,
Son bruit par secte, langue & Puissance son,
Qu'on dira soit efleue le Vospique.

Before the monastery shall one
twin be found
From heroic blood of a monk and
ancient,
His fame by sect, tongue and power
shall be founded,
So that they shall say, Vopisk is
highly raised.

One of a pair of illegitimate twins, found deserted in a church, shall
rise to great heights.

96

Celuy qu'aura la charge de destruire	He that shall be in charge to de-
Temples & sectes changees par fan-	stroy
tasie,	Churches and sects changed by fan-
Plus aux rochers qu'aux vivans	tasy,
viendra nuyre,	Shall do more harm to the stones
Par langue ornee d'oreilles ressai-	than to the living,
sies.	By a smooth tongue filling up the
	ears.

One shall undertake a campaign to destroy the Churches, but will not succeed, due to the firmness of the faithful, more durable than stone.

97

Ce que fer, flamme, n'a sceu para-	What neither iron nor fire could
cheuer,	achieve,
La douce langue au conseil viendra	Shall be done by a smooth tongue
faire	in a council,
Par repos, songe, le roy fera resuer,	In sleep a dream shall make the
Plus l'ennemy en feu, sang mili-	king to think,
taire.	The more the enemy in fire and
	military blood.

The propaganda and infiltration tactics of native traitors shall accomplish as much for the enemy as actual military operations.

98

Le chef qu'aura conduit peuple in-	The leader who shall lead an in-
finy	finite number of people,
Loing de son ciel, de moeurs &	Far from their country to one of
langue estrange,	strange manners and language,
Cinq mil en, Crete, & Thessale	Five thousand in Candia and Thes-
finy,	saly finished,
Le chef fuyant sauve en la marine	The leader escaping, shall be safe
grange.	in a barn on the sea.

The Axis fiasco in attempting to invade on all fronts is foretold, as well as the escape of the chief criminal, Hitler, in a submarine.

99

Le Grand Monarque qui fera compagnie,
Avec deux Roys unis par amitie,
O quel souspir sera la grande mes-
nie,
Enfant Narbon a l'entour quel
pitie.

Le Grand Monarque shall keep
company,
With two kings united in friendship,
Oh what fights shall be made by
their followers,
Children, O what a pity about Narbonne,

Le Grand Monarque refers to Louis XIV. He exhausted France by his desires of conquest, preparing the way for the Revolution.

100

Long temps au ciel veu gris oyseau,
Aupres de Dole & de Tosquane
terre,
Tenant au bec un verdoyant rameau
Mourra tost grand, & finira la
guerre.

For a long while shall be seen in
the air a gray bird,
Near Dola and the Tuscan land,
Holding in his beak a green bough,
Then a great one shall die and the
war be finished.

The role of Franklin D. Roosevelt is here clearly prophesied, indicating his untimely and tragic death just a few weeks before the close of the war in Europe.

1

Vers Aquitaine par insuls Britaniques
Et par aux mesmes grandes incursions
Pluyes, gelees feront terroir iniques
Port Selyn fortes fera invasions.

Towards Gascony by English assaults
By the same shall be made great incursions,
Rains, frosts shall make the ground unrighteous,
Port Selyn shall make strong invasions.

The English shall invade Gascony at a time of rain and frost and the Turks shall make a great incursion.

2

La teste bleue fera la teste blanche,
Autant de mal que France a fait leur bien,
Mort a l'anthenne, grande pendu sur la branche
Quand des prins siens le Roy dira combien.

The blue law shall do the white law
As much harm, as France has done it good,
Dead on the antenna, a great one hanged on a branch,
When a king taken by his own shall say "How much?"

The one wearing the blue beret shall prevail over the aged white one, and a ruler shall be held for ransom as the radio remains silent.

3

Pour la chaleur solaire sur la mer	By the heat of the sun upon the sea,
De Negrepont les poissons demy cuits,	At Black Bridge, the fishes shall be half broiled,
Les habitans les viendront entemer	The inhabitants shall come to cut them up,
Quand Rhod & Gennes leur faudra le biscuit.	When Rhodes and Genoa shall want biscuits.

A terrific heat will be engendered in the sea, destroying marine life, and the lands near the Mediterranean shall lack luxuries.

4

Depuis Monach jusqu'au pres de Sicile,	From Monaco as far as Sicily,
Toute la plage demourra desolee	All the sea coast shall be left desolate,
Il n'y aura faux-bourgs, cite, ne ville,	There shall not be suburbs, cities nor towns,
Que par Barbares, pille soit & vollee.	Which shall not be pillaged and plundered by Barbarians.

The western Italian Sea Coast from Monaco to Sicily will be invaded and sacked by barbarians.

5

Quand dans poissin fer & lettre enfermee,	When in an iron fish, a letter shall be shut up,
Hors sortira qui pis fera la guerre,	He shall go out, that shall afterwards make war,
Aura par mer sa classe bien ramee,	He shall have his fleet by the sea well provided,
Apparoissant pres de Latine terre.	Appearing by the Roman Land.

In a submarine, one bearing an important letter and military secrets shall land and afterwards lead a nation to victory. Gen. Clark's daring feat —culminating in the North African campaign—is clearly foreshadowed.

6

Aupres des portes & dedans deux citez
Seront deux fleaux onc n'apperceu yn tel,
Faim dedans peste, de fer hors gens boutez,
Crier secours au grand Dieu immortel.

Near the gates and within two cities,
Shall be two scourges, I never saw the like,
Famine, within plague, people thrust out by the sword,
Shall cry for help to the great God immortal.

This prognosticates conditions in Budapest, one of the Axis satellites, in the closing days of the War.

7

Entre plusieurs aux iles deportes
L'un estre nay a deux dents en la gorge
Mourront de faim, les arbres esbroutez.
Pour eux neuf Roy nouvel edict leur forge.

Among many that shall be transported into the islands,
One shall be born with two teeth in his mouth,
They shall die of hunger, the trees shall be eaten,
They shall have a new king, who shall make new laws for them.

The Australian Islands, after much travail, shall produce a strong leader, under whose leadership independence shall be achieved.

8

Temples sacrez prime facon Romaine,
Reietteront les goffes fondemens,
Prenant leurs loix premieres & humaines
Chassant, non tout, des saincts les cultemens.

Temples consecrated and the early Roman way,
Shall reject the tottering foundations,
Sticking to their first humane laws,
Expelling, but not altogether, the worshipping of saints.

The rise of the Reformation and split from the Catholic Church is here predicted; and the retaining in Protestant litany of only a few of the Saints.

9

Neuf ans le regne le maigre en paix
  tiendra
Puis il cherra en soif si sanguinaire
Pour luy grand peuple sans foy &
  loy mourra,
Tue par un beaucoup plus debon-
  naire.

Nine years shall the lean one keep
  the kingdom in peace,
Then he will fall into such a bloody
  thirst,
That a great people shall die without faith or law,
He shall be killed by one much
  wilder than himself.

The references here point to the reign of Louis XVI—the short period
of peace at the start of his kingship, the bloody and lawless revolution, and
his eventual execution before the eyes of the roaring mobs of Paris.

10

Avant long temps le tout sera range
Nous esperons un siecle bien senes-
  tre
L'estat des masques & des seule
  bien change,
Peu trouveront qu'a son rang vue-
  ille estre.

Before long, all shall be arranged,
We look for an era most sinister,
The state of the masks and they
  alone shall be changed,
They shall find few that will keep
  their rank.

A continuation of the preceding prophecy, describing the chaotic conditions to prevail during the Revolution.

11

Le prochain, fils de l'asnier paru-
  iendra
Tant esleve jusques au regne des
  forts
Son aspre gloire un chacun la
  eraindra,
Mais ses enfans du regne jettez
  hors.

The eldest son of L'Aisnier shall
  prosper,
Being raised to the degree for the
  great ones,
Everyone shall fear his high glory,
But his children shall be cast out.

This is the famous prediction Nostradamus sent to the Lord of
L'Aisnier, who had written him to know of his children's future.

12

Yeux clos ouverts d'antique fantasie
L'habit des seules seront mis a neant;
Le grand monarque chastira leur frenaisie,
Ravir des temples le thresor par devant.

Eyes shut, shall be opened by an antique fancy,
The clothes of the solitary shall be brought to nothing,
The great monarch shall punish their frenzy,
For having ravished the treasure of the temple before.

The Goddess of Justice, with blindfolded eyes, will be resurrected, and shall mete out punishment to the ravishers of the people and the temple.

13

Le corps sans ame plus n'estre en sacrifice,
Jour de la mort mis en nativite,
L'esprit divin fera l'ame felice
Voyant le verbe en son eternite.

The body without soul shall be no more admitted in sacrifice,
The day of death placed on the birthday,
The divine spirit shall make the soul happy,
By seeing the voice in its eternity.

A prophecy of the reformation of the ceremony of the Mass, and the Sacrament of the Lord's Supper.

14

A Tours, Gien, garde gande seront yeux penetrans,
Descouvriront de loing la grand' sireine,
Elle & sa suitte au port seront entrans,
Combats poussez, puissance souveraine.

At Tours, Gienn, on guard shall be piercing eyes,
Who shall discover before long the great queen,
She and her suite shall enter into the port,
By the fight shall be thrust out the reigning power.

The Goddess of Reason, installed to replace supernatural religion, approaches the centers of Culture.

15

Un peu devant monarque trucide,	A little before a monarch is killed,
Castor, Pollux, en nef, astre crai- nite,	Castor, Pollux, and a Comet in the sky appears,
L'Arain public, par terre & mer vuide,	The public Brass, by land and sea shall be emptied,
Pise, Ast, Ferrare, Turin, terre in- terdicte.	Pisa, Asti, Ferra, Turin shall be forbidden countries.

A time of unrest is prophesied—great disturbances in Castor and Pollux, the constellations of the Twins or Gemini. Toward the Ship or Argonauts, a Comet will appear.

16

Naples, Palerme, Sicile, Syracuse,	Naples, Palermo, Sicily, Syracuse,
Nouveaux Tyrans, Fulgures, faex celestes,	New tyrants, Lightnings, Celestial Fires,
Force de Londres, Gand, Bruxelles & Suise	An Army from London, Ghent, Brussels,
Grand hecatombe, triomph, faire festes.	And Switzerland, a sacrifice, tri- umph and feasts.

The British army will invade Europe, and meanwhile Switzerland, untouched, will benefit thereby.

17

Le camp du temple de la vierge vestale,	The camp of the temple of the vestal virgin,
Non esloigne d'Ethene & monts Pyrenees;	Not far from Ethene and the Pyr- enees Mountains,
Le grand conduit est cache dans la male,	The great passage is driven in the wall,
North, getez, fleuves, & vigues mas- tinees.	Rivers overflow in the North and the vines spoiled.

At Tivoli, the site of the antique temple of the Vestal Virgin, a great passage cuts through, and there will be a great flood.

18

Nouvelle pluie subite, impetueuse
Empeschera subit deux excertites,
Pierre, ciel, feux, faire la mer pier-
    reuse
La mort de sept, terre & marin
    subites.

A new rain, sudden, impetuous,
Shall suddenly hinder two armies,
Stone, heaven, fire, shall make the
    sea strong,
The death of seven shall be sudden
    upon land and sea.

At the D-Day Invasion of the Normandy Coast, the rain of missiles fired from new type rocket guns was most intense, also concrete floating docks were sunk at the beaches to form breakwaters and rallying points for the attack.

19

Nouveaux venus, lieu basty sans
    defence
Occuper place par lors inhabitable,
Prez, maisons, champs villes
    prendre a plaissance,
Faime, peste, guerre, arpent long
    labourable.

Newcomers shall build a place
    without a fence,
And shall occupy a place that was
    not then habitable,
They shall at their pleasure take
    fields, houses and towns,
There shall be famine, plague,
    war, and a long arable field.

Continuing the preceding stanza, the allied invaders occupy the unin-habited fortified coast and advance successfully inward.

20

Freres & Soeurs en plusieurs lieux
    captifs,
Se trouveront passer pres du Mon-
    arque
Les contempler ses Deux yeux en-
    tentifs,
Des plaisant voir, meton, frond,
    nez les marques.

Brothers and sisters shall be slaves
    in various places,
And shall pass before the monarch,
Who shall look upon them with
    attentive eyes,
They shall go in heaviness, witness
    their chin, forehead and nose.

The brutal enslavement of entire populations by the Nazis is explicitly foreshadowed.

21

L'Ambassadeur envoye par Birmes,
A my-chemin d'incogneus repoussez,
De Sel renfort viendront quartre
triremes,
Cordes & chaines en Negrepont
troussez.

The ambassador that was sent in
the small ship,
In the middle of the way, shall be
repulsed by unknown men,
And from the salt, to his rescue
shall come four great ships,
Ropes and chains shall be carried
to the Black Bridge.

Rudolph Hess, personal aide to the German Fuehrer, flew solo to England to contact influential British leaders with his unofficial peace terms
which were rejected in a closed session of Parliament.

22

Le Camp Ascop d'Europe partira,
S'adioignant proche de l'isle sub-
mergee,
D'Arton classe phalange pliera
Nombril du monde plus grand voix
subrogee.

The Camp Ascop shall go from
Europe,
And shall come near the sub-
merged Island,
From Arton shall a phalange go
by sea and land
By the navel of the world, a greater
voice shall be subrogated.

Apparently a reference to the submerged continent of Atlantis, originally the Navel, which nourished all ancient human culture.

23

Palais oyseaux, par oyseau dechasse,
Bien tost apres le Prince parvenu,
Combien qu' hors fleuve ennemy
repousse.
Dehors saisi, trait d'oyseau sous-
tenu.

Palace birds, driven away by a bird,
Soon after that, the Prince is come
to his own,
Although the enemy be driven beyond the river,
He shall be seized without, by a
trick of the bird.

Parasitic hangers-on will be expelled from the government, by one who
is an Eagle, and a master of stratagem.

24

Bestes farouches de faim fleuves tranner,
Plus part du camp encontre Ister sera,
En cage de fer le grand sera traisner,
Quand rien enfant Germain observera.

Wild beasts for hunger shall swim over the rivers,
Most of the field shall be near the Ister,
Into an iron cage he shall cause the great one to be drawn,
When the child of Germany shall observe nothing.

The country about the Danube—Ister—shall be desolated and famine-stricken, as the great one of Germany shall be exhibited in an iron cage and German children shall be blind.

25

La garde estrange trahyra for teresse,
Espoir & ombre du plus haut mariage,
Garde deceue, fort prins dans la presse,
Loire, Saone, Rhone, Gar a mort outragez.

The garrison of strangers shall betray the fort,
Under the game of hope of a higher union.
The garrison shall be deceived, and the fort taken quickly
Loire, Saone, Rhone, Gardone, outraged by death.

Fifth columnists working for a united Fascistic world shall be active, while the rivers of France shall be desecrated.

26

Pour la faveur que la cite fera,
Au grand qui tost perdra champ de bataille
Puis le sang Pau, Thesin versera
De sang, feux, morts, noyez de coupe de taille.

Because of the favor, the city shall show
To the great one, who soon shall lose the battle,
The Thesin shall pour blood into the River Po,
Of fire, blood, drowned, dead by the edge.

Because of disputes, a town on the River Thesin, a river which empties into the Po, shall see a great slaughter.

27

Le divin verbe sera du ciel frappe
Qui ne pourra proceder plus avant,
Du reserant le secret estoupe
Qu'on marchera par dessus & de-
vant.

The divine voice shall be struck by
heaven
So that he cannot proceed any
further,
The secret of close-mouthed one
shall be closed,
That people shall tread upon and
before it.

A voice, of celestial quality which will be perfection itself, shall appear,
the secret of which will be inviolate.

28

Le penultiesme du surnom de
Prophete,
Prendra Diane pour son jour &
repos,
Loing vauera par frenitique teste,
Et delivrant vn grand peuple d'im-
posts.

The last but one, of the surname
of Prophet,
Shall take Diana for his day and
his rest,
He shall wander far by reason of
his raving head,
Delivering a great people from im-
positions.

This concerns a false Prophet, which is here called the last but one of
that Surname, who shall make Diana (that is Monday, dedicated to Diana)
his Sabbath day; and he shall wander about persuading many people to
pay no taxes.

29

L'Oriental sortira se son siege,
Passer les monts Appenins, voir la
Gaule,
Transpassera le ciel, les eaux &
neige,
En un chacun frappera de sa gaule.

The Oriental shall come out of his
seat,
Shall pass over the Apennines
Mountains and see France,
Shall go over the air, the waters and
the snow,
And shall strike everyone with his
staff.

An invasion by an Eastern people shall strike France, by way of Italy,
utilizing the air, the sea and snow.

30

Un qui les dieux d'Annibal infer-
naux
Fera renaistre, effrayeur des hu-
mains,
Oncq plus d'horreur, ne plus dire
journaux,
Qu'advint viendra par Babel aux
Romains.

One that shall cause the infernal
gods of Hannibal
To live again, the terror of mankind,
There never was more horror, not
to say ill days,
Did happen, or shall, to the Romans by Babel.

Horrors, worse than any unloosed by Hannibal, the then enemy of
civilization, shall be unloosed upon the modern world.

31

En Campania Cassilin fera tant
Qu'on ne verra que d'eau les
champs couverts
Devant, apres, la pluye de long
temps
Hors mis les arbres rien l'on temps.

In Campania, the Castilian shall
so behave himself,
That nothing shall be seen but the
fields covered,
Before and after, it shall not rain
for a long time,
Except the trees, no green shall be
seen.

In Campania, the Spaniard will strip the country of all wealth even
to the verdure of the fields.

32

Laict, sang, grenovilles escondre en
Dalmatie
Conflt donne, peste preste, de ba-
liene
Cry sera grand par toute Esclavo-
nie,
Lors naistra monstre pres & dedans
Ravenne.

Milk, blood, frogs shall rain in
Dalmatia,
A battle fought, the plague near
Basel,
A great cry shall be through all
Slovakia,
Then shall be born a monster, near
and within Ravenna.

Dalmatia shall be in unrest, and Basel (Switzerland) and Czechoslovakia shall be in fear of an Italian monster.

33

Dans le torrent qui descend de Ve-
ronne,
Par lors qu'au Pau guidera son en-
tree,
Un grand naufrage, & non moins
en Garonne,
Quand ceux de Gennes marcheront
leur contree.

In the torrent which descends from
Verona,
About the place where it enters
into the Po,
A great shipwreck, and no less in
Garonne,
When those of Genoa shall go into
their country.

When the Italians of Genoa invade France, they are foredoomed to
destruction and shipwreck.

34

L'ire insensee du combat furieux,
Fera a table par freres le fer luyre,
Les departir mort blesse curieux,
Le fier duelle viendra en France
nuyre.

The mad anger of the furious fight,
Shall cause by brothers the iron to
glisten at the table,
To part them, one mortally
wounded, curious,
The fierce duel shall do harm after
in France.

A quarrel between two allies shall be the cause of a misunderstanding
that will do France much harm.

35

Dans deux logis de nuict le feu
prendra,
Plusieurs dedans estouffez & rostis,
Pres de deux fleuves pour seur il
adviendra,
Sol, l'Arc & Caper, tous seront
amortis.

The fire shall take by night in two
houses,
Many shall be stifled and burnt by
it,
Near two rivers it shall for certain
happen
Sun, Arc, Caper, they shall all be
mortified.

In a town near two rivers, a momentous decision will be made, and
many shall suffer by it—all this to happen when the Sun is in the signs of
Arc (Sagittarius), and Caper (Capricorn).

36

Du grand prophete lettres seront prinses,	The letters of the great prophet shall be intercepted,
Entre les mains du tyran deviendront,	They shall fall into the hands of the tyrant,
Frauder son roy seront les entreprinses,	His undertakings shall be to deceive his king,
Mais ses rapines bien tost le troubleront.	But his extortions shall trouble him soon.

Before the great prophet shall triumph, his plans shall be betrayed by selfish, tyrannical interests.

37

De ce grand nombre que l'on envoyera	Of the great number which shall be sent,
Pour secourir dans le fort assiegez,	To relieve the besieged in the fort,
Peste & famine tous les deux devorera,	Plague and famine shall devour them all,
Hors mis septante qui seront profligez.	Except seventy that shall be beaten.

A warning that biological warfare and fearful destruction of both plant and animal life is imminent.

38

Des condamnez sera fait un grand nombre,	There shall be a great number of condemned men,
Quand les monarques seront conciliez;	When the monarchs shall be reconciled,
Mais l'vn d'eux viendra si mal encombre,	But one of them shall come to such a bad obstacle,
Que guerre ensemble ne seront raliez.	That their reconciliation shall not last long.

At the finish of a great war, the guilty ones will be condemned but one of the victors will be much dissatisfied.

39

Un an devant le conflit Italique,
Germain, Gaulois, Espagnols pour
le fort,
Cherra l'escole maison de republic,
Ou, hors mis peu, seront suffoquez
morts.

One year before the Italian conflict,
German, French, Spaniards for the
fort,
The schoolhouse of the republic
shall fall,
Where except few, they shall be
suffocated to death.

One year before Italy enters World War III, Paris will be overwhelmed by a terrific onslaught of atomic-powered rockets.

40

Un peu apres non point longue in-
tervalle,
Par mer & terre sera fait grand
tumulte,
Beaucoup plus grand sera pugne
navalle,
Feux, animaux, qui plus feront
d'insulte.

A little while after, without any
great difference of time,
By land and sea shall a great tumult be made,
The sea fight shall be much greater,
Fire and beasts, which shall make
great affront.

Shortly after the time mentioned in the previous stanza, tremendous naval and military activity shall ensue, and bombardment by incendiary bombs will cause havoc on land and sea.

41

La grand estoile par sept jours
bruslera,
Nue fera deux soliels apparior,
Le gros mastin toute nuict hurlera,
Quand grand pontife changera de
terroir.

The great star shall burn for the
space of seven days,
A cloud shall make two suns appear,
The big mastiff shall howl all night,
When a great Pope shall change
his country.

In 1939, Pope Pius XII was installed. There also began a period of terrible sights for the world, amid the howling of the great Dogs of War.

42

Coq, chiens, & chats, de sang seront repeus,
Et de la playe du tyrant trouve
mort,
Au lict d'un autre jambes & bras
rompus,
Qui n'avoit pwu mourir de cruelle
mort.

A cock, dogs and cats shall be fed
with blood,
And with the wound of the tyrant
found dead,
In the bed of another with legs
and arms broken,
Who could not die before by a
cruel death.

The French Nation (the Cock), and the rabble of Paris (cats and dogs),
were satiated with the blood of the guillotine and the beheading of
Robespierre, the tyrant of the Revolution. He had been ordered seized by
the Convention, and in the struggle was dangerously wounded, tied on
a strange bed and executed the next morning.

43

Durant l'estoille cheuelue apparente,
Les trois grand princes seront faits
ennemys,
Frappez du ciel paix terre trembu-
lente,
Pau, Tymbre, Undans, serpens sur
le bord mis.

During the time when the hairy
star is apparent,
The three great princes shall be
made enemies,
Struck from heaven, place quaking
earth,
Arne, Tiber, full of surges, serpents
cast upon the shore.

The reappearance of Halley's Comet, due in 1985, will again presage
profound changes in human destiny.

44

L'aigle poussee entour des pavil-
lons,
Par autres oyseaux d'entour sera
chassee,
Quand bruit des cymbres, tubes et
sonnaillons
Rendront le sens de la Dame insensee.

The eagle flying among the tents,
By other birds shall be driven away,
When the voice of cymbals, trum-
pets, and bells
Shall make sense to the lady who
was insane.

During the festivities of the marriage of Napoleon with Marie Louise
(sister of the Emperor of Austria), Josephine, his divorced wife, was insane
with jealousy.

45

Trop le ciel pleure l'Androgin pro-
cree
Pres de ciel sang human respandu,
Par mort trop tarde grand peuple
recree,
Tard & tost vient le secours at-
tendu.

Heaven bemoaneth too much the
Androgyn born,
Near heaven human blood shall
be spent,
By death too late a great people
shall be diverted,
Late and soon cometh the help
expected.

The church shall bewail the birth of a Hermaphrodite who will cause
great shedding of blood of the Holy People. He shall not be disposed of
until he has done much harm.

46

Apres grand troche humain, plus
grand s'appreste.
Le grand moteur les siecles renou-
velle,
Pluye, sang, laict, famine, feu, &
pest;
Au ciel veu, courant longue estin-
celle.

After a great human change, another greater is near at hand.
The great motor, reneweth the
ages,
Rain, blood, milk, famine, sword,
plague,
In the heavens shall be seen a running fire with long sparks.

After the great industrial age of steam and electricity, another stupendous revolution will be near. A new type of motive power will accel-
erate all human progress, but before this happens, there will be seen awesome aerial projectiles causing much suffering.

47

L'ennemy grand vieil, dueil meurt
de poison,
Les souverains par infinis subju-
guez.
Pierres plouvoir cachez soubs la
toyson,
Par mort articles en vain sont alle-
guez.

The great and old enemy grieveth,
dieth by poison,
An infinite number of sovereigns
conquered.
It shall rain stones, they shall hide
under rocks,
In vain shall death assert articles.

The old enemy of mankind, war, shall no longer exist, nor will poverty
and the allied ills. All this will happen after a period of human suffering.

48

La grand coppie qui passera les monts,	The great army shall pass over the mountains,
Saturne en l'arc tournant du poisson Mars,	Saturn, Aries, Mars turning to the fishes,
Venins chachez soubs testes de Saulmons,	Poisons hidden in the heads of Salmons,
Leurs chefs pendus a fil de polemars.	Their captain hanged with a string of the polemars.

An invasion over the mountains is indicated, with melancholy results, as this force will be driven into the sea and the captain slain.

49

Les conseillers du premier monopole,	The counselors of the first monopoly,
Les conquerans seduits par la Melite,	The conqueror being seduced by the Melite,
Rhodes, Bisance pour leur exposant pole	Rhodes, Bizance, for exposing their pole
Terra faudra le pour suivants de suite.	The ground shall fail the followers of the runways.

In the Latin tongue, Melites are classified as the inhabitants of the Island of Malta. The sense seems to be that Malta will successfully oppose its would-be conquerors who shall not be able to land planes on its runways.

50

Quand ceux d'Hinault, de Gand & de Bruxelles	When those of Hainault, of Gand and Brussels
Verront a Langres le siege devant mis,	Shall see the siege laid before Langres,
Derriere leurs flancs seront guerres cruelles,	Behind their sides shall be cruel wars,
La pluye antique, fera pis qu' ennemys.	The old wound shall be worse than enemies.

War shall devastate various cities of Holland, Belgium and Northern France.

51

Le sang du juste a Londres sera
faute,
Bruslez par foudres de vingt trois
les six,
La dame antique cherra de place
haute,
De mesme secte plusieurs seront
occis.

The blood of the just shall be dry
in London,
Burnt by the fire of three times
twenty and six,
The ancient dame shall fall from
her high place,
Of the same sect many shall be
killed.

The great Fire of London, 1666, three times twenty and six, with the
subsequent falling of the statue of the Virgin from St. Paul's Steeple, is
exactly predicted and occurred as forecast.

52

Dans plusieurs nuicts la terre tremblera,
Sur le printemps deux efforts feront
suitte,
Corinthe, Ephese aux deux mers
nagers,
Guerre s'esmeut par deux vailants
de luitte.

During many nights the earth shall
quake,
About the spring, two great earthquakes shall follow one another,
Corinth, Ephesus shall swim in the
twin seas,
War shall be moved by two great
wrestlers.

An era of earth-shaking events will occur in the region of Greece,
caused by the actions of two great powers.

53

La grand peste de cite maritime
Ne cessera que mort ne soit vengee;
Du juste sang par pris damne sans
crime,
De la grand' dame par fainte n'out-
rages.

The great plague of the maritime
city,
Shall not cease until the death be
revenged,
Of the just blood by price condemned without crime,
Of the great dame not feigned
abused.

The great plague of London, 1665, shall be inflicted on the populace,
as a revenge for the execution of Charles I.

54

Par gent estrange, & de Romains loingtaine,	By a strange people and a remote nation,
Leur grand cite apres eau fort troublee;	The great city near the water shall be much troubled,
Fille sans main trop different domaine,	The girl without great difference for an estate,
Prins, chef terreure n'auoit este riblee.	The chief frightened, at not having been warned.

The great city, near the sea, shall be much troubled by a strange nation, and by a surprise attack.

55

Dans le conflit le grand qui peu valloit,	In the fight the great one, who was but little worth,
A son dernier fera cas merveilleux;	At his last endeavor shall do a wonderful thing,
Pendant qu'Hadrie verra ce qu'il falloit,	While Adria shall see what was wanting,
Dans le banquet pongnale l'orgueilleux.	In the banquet he shall stab the proud one.

The arch criminal seeing that the fight is lost shall go down in ruin, and drag his Italian fellow-conspirator with him.

56

Que peste & glaive n'a s'en definer,	He whom neither plague nor sword could destroy,
Mort dans le pluies sommet du ciel frappe,	Shall die in the rain being stricken by thunder,
L'abbe mourra quand verra ruyner	The abbot shall die when he shall see ruined
Ceux au naufrage, l'escueil voulant grapper.	Those in the shipwreck, striving to catch hold of the rock.

Continuation of the preceding stanza; the arch criminal shall escape from the area of conflict, and those left behind in the wreck shall not be saved.

57

Avant conflit le grand mur tombera,	Before the battle, the great wall shall fall,
Le grand a mort, mort trop subite & plainte,	The great one to death, too sudden and bewailed,
Nef imparfaict la plus part nagera,	The boat being imperfect the most part shall swim,
Aupres du fleuve de sang la terre tainte.	Near the river the earth shall be dyed with blood.

The great West Wall will fall, and the Great One and his cohorts, deserting the sinking ship, shall suffer heavy losses.

58

Sans pied ne main, dent aygue & forte	Without foot or hand, sharp and strong teeth,
Par globe au fort de port & l'aisne nay,	By a globe, in the middle of the port, and the first born,
Pres du portail desloyal se transporte,	Near the gate shall be transported by a traitor,
Seline luyt, petit grand emmene.	The moon shineth, the little great one carried away.

A kidnapping at night, by an alien, of an infant belonging to a great one, shall take place.

59

Classe Gauloise par appuy de grand' garde,	The French Fleet by the help of the great guards,
Du grand Neptune, & ses tridens soldats,	Of great Neptune, and his tridented soldiers,
Rongee Provence pour soustenir grand' bande,	Shall gnaw Provence by keeping great company,
Plus Mars, Narbon, par javelots & dards.	Also, Mars shall plague Narbonne by javelots and darts.

The French Fleet, with the aid of the British Navy, shall invade France, at the same time a heavy bombardment shall be kept up.

60

La Foy Punique en orient rompue,
Grand, Jud, & Rosne, Loyre &
    Tag, changeront,
Quand du mulet la faim sera re-
    peve
Classe espargie sang & corps na-
    geront.

The Punic Faith broken in the
    east,
Great Jud, and Rhone, Loire and
    Tagus shall be changed,
When the mule's hunger shall be
    satisfied,
The fleet scattered, blood and
    bodies shall swim.

The false faith broken in the East shall unleash a series of changes,
while the rivers shall be choked with bodies and the fields shall remain
uncultivated.

61

Agen, Tamins, Gironde & la Ro-
    chelle,
O sang Troien mort au port de la
    flesche,
Derriere le fleuve au fort mise l'es-
    chelle,
Pointes, feu, grand meurtre sus la
    breche.

Agen, Tomains, Gironde and Ro-
    chelle,
O Trojan blood, death is at the
    harbor of the arrow,
Beyond the river, the ladder shall
    be raised against the fort,
Points, fire, great murder upon the
    breach.

Civil Wars in France, between various cities, are predicted.

62

Mabus puis tost, alors mourra
    viendra,
De gens & bestes une horrible def-
    faite,
Puis tout a coup la vengeance on
    verra,
Sang, main, soif, faim, quand
    courra la comette.

Mabus shall come, and soon after
    shall die,
Of people and beasts shall be a
    horrible destruction,
Then on a sudden the vengeance
    shall be seen,
Blood, hand, thirst, famine, when
    the comet shall run.

The coming of the comet shall occur in the period of reconstruction,
and there will be vengeance for wrongs inflicted on humanity by selfish
interests.

63

Gauloise, Ausone, bien peu sub-
jugera,
Pau, Marne, & Seine fera perme
l'vrie,
Qui le grand mur contre eux dressera,
Du moindre au mur le grand perdra
la vie.

The French fleet shall a little subdue Ausonne,
Pau, Marne, and Seine shall make
permanent the truth,
Which shall raise a great wall
against them,
From the less to the wall the great
one shall lose his life.

Bordeaux is called Ausonne by Nostradamus because Ausonius, a Latin poet, was born there. During World War II part of the French fleet was sunk in the harbor of Bordeaux, thereby rendering it unfit for use by the Germans (creating a wall against them).

64

Seicher de faim, de soir gent Gene-
voise,
Espoir prochain viendra au defail-
lir,
Sur point tremblant sera loy Gehe-
noise,
Classe au grand port ne se peut
accueillir.

Those of Geneva shall be dried up
with hunger and thirst.
A near hope shall come when they
shall be fainting,
The Hellish law shall be upon a
quaking point,
The navy shall not be able to come
into port.

At Geneva men shall almost succeed in outlawing war and dismantling all navies, but those of Geneva shall have no support.

65

Le parc enclin grand calamite,
Par l'Hesperie & Insubre fera,
Le feu en nef, peste & captivite,
Mercure en l'arc, Saturne fenera.

The park inclineth to great calamity,
Which shall be through Hesperia
and Insubria,
The fire in the ship, plague and
captivity,
Mercury in Aries, Saturn shall
wither.

Spain and the House of Savoy (Italy) are due for a great calamity when the sun is in Mercury and Aries.

66

Par grand dangers le captif
  eschappe,
Peu de temps grand la fortune
  changee,
Cans le palais le peuple este attrape,
Par bon augure la cite assiegee.

The prisoner escaped through great
  danger,
A little while after shall become
  great, his fortune being changed,
In the palace the people shall be
  caught,
And by a good sign the city shall
  be besieged.

A reiteration of the escape and temporary ascendency of an ill-fated leader.

67

La blonde au nez forche viendra
  commettre
Par le duelle & chassera dehors.
Les exilez dedans fera remettre,
Aux lieux marins commettant les
  plus forts.

The fair one shall fight with the
  forked nose
In duel, and expel him forth.
The exiles shall be re-established,
Putting the stronger of them in
  maritime places.

La Belle France—the Fair One—shall expel the intruder, regaining peace and a strong navy.

68

De l'aquilon les efforts seront
  grande,
Sur l'ocean sera la porte ouverte,
Le regne en l'isle sera reintegrande,
Tremblera Londres par voile des-
  couverte.

The endeavors of the north shall
  be great,
Upon the ocean the gate shall be
  open,
The kingdom in the island shall
  be re-established,
London shall quake, for fear of sails
  discovered.

A very remarkable prophecy. Charles II is re-established on the British throne; and the forays of the Dutch Fleet under Admiral Van Tromp against quaking London are predicted.

69

Le Roy Gaulois par la Celtique dextre
Voyant discorde de la Grand Monarchie,
Sur les trois parts fera fleurir son sceptre,
Contre la cappe de la grand Hierachie.

The French King, by the Celtic right hand,
Seeing the discord of the Great Monarchy,
Upon three parts of it, will make his scepter to flourish,
Against the cap of the great Hierarchy.

Henry II, King of France, seeing the discord in England under the Commonwealth, will aid in the restoration of Charles II.

70

Le dard du Ciel fera son estendue,
Morts en parlant grande execution,
La pierre en l'arbre la fiere gent rendue,
Bruit humain monstre, purge expiation.

The dart of heaven shall make his circuit,
Some die speaking, a great execution,
The stone in the tree, the fierce people humbled,
Human noise, a monster purged by expiation.

The blitz of London is herewith prophesied—blockbusters, scattering stones into trees, will cause instant death and terror, even to the mightiest.

71

Les exiles en Sicile viendront,
Pour deliverer de la gent faim estrange,
Au point du jour les Celtes luy faudront,
La vie demeure a raison Roy se range.

The banished persons shall come into Sicily,
To free the foreign nation from hunger,
In the dawning of the day the Celts shall fail them,
Their life shall be preserved, the King shall submit to reason.

The Jews, banished from Italy by the Fascists, shall return at the invasion of Sicily, under the leadership of a Jewish General. The King will rescind the oppressive laws and the Jews will rebuild the shattered industrial machine.

72

Armee Celtique en Italie vexee,
De toutes parts conflit & grande
  perte,
Romains fuis, o Gaule repousee,
Pres du Thesin, Rubicon pugne in-
  certe.

'The French Army shall be vexed
  in Italy,
On all sides fighting, and a great
  loss,
The Romans run away, and though
  France, repulsed
Near the Ticino, by Rubicon the
  fight shall be doubtful.

A French Army will be routed from Italy. Two great battles will be
fought, one by the river Ticino, and one by the Rubicon; but so great will
be the slaughter that the victory will be a doubtful one.

73

Au Lac Fucin de Benacle rivage,
Prins du Leman ou port de l'Ori-
  guion,
Nay de trois bras predict belliq'
  image,
Par trois couronnes au grand Endy-
  mion.

At the Fucin Lake of the Benacle
  shore,
Near the Leman at the port of
  Lorguion,
Born with three arms, a warlike
  image,
By three crowns to the great Endy-
  mion.

Nostradamus confessed his inability to interpret this obscure stanza.
In this later day it becomes clearer. Fascism had its birth near Lake Fucino,
in Central Italy—the three-armed image indicates the strife and war that
will follow.

74

De Sens, d'Autun viendront jus-
  ques au Rhosne
Pour passer outre vers les monts
  Pyrenees,
La gent sortir de la marque d'Au-
  conne,
Par terre & mer le suyvra a grands
  trainnees.

They shall come from Sens and
  Autun, as far as the Rhone,
To go further to the Pyrenees
  Mountains,
The nation shall come from the
  mark of Ancona,
By land and sea shall follow speed-
  ily after.

Sens and Autun, two typical French towns, obviously represent the
spirit of the Maquis during World War II. Harassed by the Nazis,
the Maquis were forced to scatter, sometimes fleeing to the shelter of the
Pyrenees Mountains. The import of the remainder of this quatrain indicates quite clearly the eventual re-birth of France as a united nation.

75

La voix ouye de l'insolit oiseau,
Sur le canon du respiral estage;
Si haut viendra de froment le bois-
seau,
Que l'homme d'homme sera Antro-
pophage.

The noise of the unwanted bird
having been heard,
Upon the canon of the highest
story,
The bushel of wheat shall rise so
high,
That Man shall be a man-eater.

A period of great famine and high prices shall prevail, at the appearance of the bird of prey.

76

Foudre en Bourgogne fera cas por-
tenteux,
Que par engin homme ne pourroit
faire,
De leur senat, Sacrifiste fait boy-
teux,
Fera scavoir aux ennemis l'affaire.

Lightning in Burgundy, with mar-
velous portents,
Which never could have been done
by art,
Of their senate, Sacriste being
lamed,
Shall make known the business to
the enemies.

The Sacriste, or clergy, shall betray the interests of the state to the
enemies at a time of stress.

77

Par arcs, feux, poix, & par feu repoussez,
Crys, hurlemens sur la minuict
ouys;
Dedans sont mis par les ramparts
cassez,
Par cunicule les traditeurs fuis.

Being repulsed with bows, fires
and pitch,
Cries and howlings shall be heard
about midnight;
They shall get in through the
broken walls,
The betrayers shall run away
through the sewers.

By treason, some shall let in the enemy within the fortress, the betrayers themselves shall escape (the "fifth column" in Madrid).

78

Le grand Neptune du profond de la mer,
De gent Punique & sang Gaulois mesle,
Les isles a sang, pour le tardif ramer,
Pluy luy nuira que l'occult mal cele.

The great Neptune, in the deep of the sea,
Having joined African and French blood,
The islands shall be put to the sword and the slow rowing
Shall do them more harm than the concealed evil.

Great Britain in a joint invasion with France shall capture the Islands, the invaders suffering less from sunken mines than from tardiness in landing.

79

La barbe crespe & noire par engin,
Subjuguera la gent cruelle & fiere;
Le grand Chyren ostera du longin,
Tous les captifs par Seline baniere.

The frizzled and black beard by fighting
Shall overcome the fierce and cruel nation;
The great Henry shall free from bonds,
All the captives made by Selim's banner.

In 1571, five years after the death of Nostradamus, the Battle of Lepanto was fought. Don Juan of Austria, called the "Frizzled and Black Beard," defeated the Turks. Henry of France also redeemed many of the Christian slaves.

80

Apres conflit du leffe l'eloquence,
Par peu de temps se tramme saint, repos,
Point on n'admet les grands a delivrance,
Des ennemis sont remis a propos.

After the battle, the eloquence of the wounded man,
Within a little while shall procure a holy rest,
The great ones shall not be delivered,
But shall be left to their enemies' will.

A truce shall be proclaimed through the intercession of the church, but the agreement to parole the leaders shall be violated.

81

Par feu du ciel la cite pres qu'-
  aduste,
Urna menace encor Deucalion,
Vexes Sardaigne par la Punique
  fuste,
Apres qu Libra lairra son Phaeton.

By fire from heaven the city shall
  be almost burnt,
The waters threaten another Deucalion,
Sardinia shall be vexed bv an African fleet,
After that Libra shall have left
  her Phaeton.

Deucalion, a figure in Greek mythology, was the only human left after
the great flood.

A city shall be so destroyed from the air as to be nearly lifeless, all
this to occur when the sign of Libra has reached its last half.

82

Par faim la proye sera loup pris-
  sonnier,
L'assaillant hors en extreme detresse;
Un nay ayant au devant le dernier,
Le grand n'eschappe au milieu de
  la presse.

By hunger, the prey shall make the
  wolf prisoner,
Assaulting him then in great distress;
The eldest having got before the
  last,
The great one doth not escape in
  the middle of the crowd.

The Wolf (Rome), being hungry, shall snatch at the prey offered to
it and become entrapped, while the greatest of all shall not escape the
vengeance of the mob.

83

Par le traffic du grand Lyon change,
Et la plus-part tourne en pristine
  ruine,
Proye aux soldats par pille ven-
  dange,
Par jura mont & Sueve bruine.

The great trade of the great Lion
  altered,
The most part turns into pristine
  ruin,
Shall become a prey to soldiers and
  reaped by wound
In Mount Jura, and Suabia great
  fogs.

The industrial supremacy of the British Lion shall be endangered. England shall become the scene of pillage and the home of wounded soldiers.
Mt. Jura and Suabia (Germany) shall have some relation to these events.

84

Entre Champagne, Sienne, Flora, Ostie
Six mois neuf jours ne pleuvera une goutte;
L'Estrange langue en terre Dalamtie,
Courira sus, gastant la terre toute.

Between Campania, Sienna, Pisa and Ostia,
For six months and nine days there shall be no rain,
The strange language in Dalmatian land,
Shall overrun, spoiling all the country.

Italy, suffering much from want, shall seek to despoil Dalmatia—Albania—by overrunning the country.

85

Vieux plains de barbe sous le statut severe,
A Lyon fait dessus l'Aigle Celtique,
Le petit grand trop outre persevere,
Bruit d'armes au ciel, mer rouge Lygustique.

The old plain beard, under the severe statue,
Made at Lyon upon the Celtic Eagle,
The little great too far perseveres,
Noise of arms in the sky, and the Ligurian sea made red.

The power of the German Air Force will for a time sustain the big and little Fuehrers (obviously Hitler and his satellites), and war will rage in the air and on the sea.

86

Naufrage a classe pres d'onde adriatique,
La terre esmeu sur l'air en terre mis;
Egypte tremble augment Mahommetique,
L'Heraut se rendre a crier est commis.

A fleet shall suffer a shipwreck near the Adriatic sea,
The earthquakes, a motion of air comes upon the land;
Egypt trembles for fear of the Mohammedan increase,
The Herald surrendering shall be commissioned to cry.

In the Mediterranean Seas a fleet will be wrecked, the earth will shake with the sound of terrible weapons, and the air will vibrate with a strange whirring. Mohammedan influence will increase to the detriment of the rulers of Egypt. The mouthpiece shall desert to the Victor and shall be commissioned under him.

87

Apres viendra des estremes con-trees,	After that, shall come out of the remote countries,
Prince Germain sur le throsne dore.	A German Prince upon a gilded throne.
En servitude & par eaux recontrees	The slavery and waters shall meet,
La dame serve, son temps plus n'a dore.	The lady shall serve, her time no more worshipped.

The accession of the Hanoverian Kings of England commencing with George I is here indicated.

88

Le circuit du grand fait ruyneux,	The circuit of the great deed ruined,
Au nom septiesme le cinqueiesme sera;	The seventh name shall be that of the fifth,
D'un, tiers plus grand estrange bel-liquex,	From a third person, one greater, a warlike man,
Mouton, Lutece, Aix garantira.	Aries shall preserve Paris nor Aix.

The reference here is to the French league against Henry III and Henry IV, which numbers being joined together, make seven.

89

Un jour seront amis les deux grands maistres,	One day the two great masters shall be friends,
Leur grand pouvoir se verra aug-mente,	Their great powers shall be increased,
La terre nefue sera en ses hauts estres,	The new land shall be in a flourishing condition,
Au sanguinaire, le nombre ra-compte.	The number shall be told to the Bloody Person.

The new land of the United Americas shall enjoy great prosperity, due to its co-operation with the great land of the East, the United States of Europe, much to the displeasure of a cruel and bloody man.

90

Par vie & mort change regne d'-
Hongrie,
La loy sera sera plus aspre que serv-
ice,
Leur grand cite d'Urlemens, plaints
& cris,
Castor and Pollux ennemis dans la
lice.

By life and death the kingdom
of Hungary shall be changed,
The law shall be more severe than
the service,
Their great city shall be full of
howling and crying.
Castor and Pollux shall be enemies
in the lists.

Strict laws shall hamper the liberties of Hungary much to the detriment of their chief city. Brothers shall be enemies in the field.

91

Soleil levant un grand feu on verra,
Bruit & clarte vers Aquilon ten-
dant;
Dedans le rond mort & cris on
orra,
Par glaive, feu, faim, mort les at-
tendans.

At the rising of the sun a great fire
shall be seen
Noise and light tending to the
north;
Within the round, death and cries
shall be heard,
Death by sword, fire, hunger
watching for them.

A great calamity shall occur, when the rising sun shall attack early in the morning from a northerly direction.

92

Feu, couleur d'or de ciel en terre
veu,
Frappe du haut n'ay, fait cas mer-
veilleux;
Grand meurtre humain, prinse du
grand veveu,
Morts d'expectacles, eschappe l'or-
gueilleux.

Fire the color of gold, from
heaven to earth shall be seen,
Stricken of the high born, a mar-
velous event.
Great murder of mankind, great
loss of infants,
Some dead looking, the proud one
shall escape.

Continuation of the preceding stanza; the prophecy of an outstanding event, the greatest destruction of human life by unknown forces.

93

Bien pres du Tymbre presse la Ly- bitine, Un peu devant grand inondation; Le chef du nef prins, mis en la sentine, Chasteau, palais en conflagration.	Near the Tiber, going towards Libia, A little before a great inundation, The master of the ship being taken shall be put into the well, And a castle and a palace shall be burnt.

An event to take place in Italy. The head of the Ship of State (Mussolini) will be degraded and the king (Victor Emmanuel) will be exiled.

94

Grand Pau, grand mal pour Gau- lois recevra, Vain terreur au maritin Lyon, Peuple infiny par la mer passera, Sans eschapper un quart d'vn mil- lion.	Great Po shall receive great harm from the French, A vain terror shall seize upon the maritime lion, Infinite people shall go beyond the sea, Which shall not escape even a quarter million.

Italian cities shall receive great harm from the French, resulting in an exodus of their inhabitants.

95

Les lieux peuplez seront inhabi- tables, Pour champs avoir grand division; Regnes livrez a prudens incap- ables, Entre les freres mort & dissention.	The populous places shall be de- serted, A great division to obtain fields, Kingdom given to prudent inca- pable When the great brothers shall die by dissension.

Civil War will cause the populace to leave congested places and seek rural pursuits.

96

Flambeau ardant au ciel sera veu,
Pres de la fin & principe du
    Rhone,
Famine, glaive, tarde le secours
    poreu,
La Perse tourne envahir Mace-
    doine.

A burning shall be seen by night in
    Heaven,
Near the end and beginning of the
    Rhone,
Famine, sword, too late help shall
    be provided,
Persia shall come against Mace-
    donia.

Incendiary attacks will strike along the Rhone River in France, at the same time that the war will continue in the East.

97

Romain Pontife garde de t'ap-
    pocher,
De la cite qui deux fleuves arrouse;
Ton sang viendras aupres de la
    cracher,
Toy & les tiens quand fleurira la
    rose.

Roman Pontiff take heed to come
    near,
To the city watered with two riv-
    ers,
Thou shall spit there thy blood,
Thou and thine when the rose
    shall bloom.

The Pope is forewarned to stay close to Rome under penalty of death.

98

Celuy du sang resperse le visage,
De la victime proche sacrifice,
Venant en Leo augure presage,
Mais estre a mort lors pour la fi-
    ancee.

He that shall have his face bloody,
With the blood of the victims near
    to be sacrificed,
The sun coming into Leo shall be
    an augury by presage,
That then he shall be put to death
    for his confidence.

In the summer, one who is great oppressor of humanity shall be cut down by death, before his bloody plans fully mature.

99

Terroir Romain qu'interpretatoit augure,	The Roman country in which the augur did interpret,
Par gens Gauloise par trop sera vexee,	Shall be too much vexed by the French nation,
Mais nation Celtique craindra l'-heure,	But the Celtic nation shall fear the hour,
Boreas, classe trop loing l'avoir poussee.	The North Wind had driven the navy in too far.

Rome, site of the ancient college of Augurs, shall be at cross swords with the nation of Celts (France).

100

Dedans le isles si horrible tumulte,	In the islands shall be such horrible tumults,
Rien on n'orra qu'une bellique brigue,	That nothing shall be heard by a warlike surprise,
Tant grand sera des prediteurs l'insulte,	So great shall be the assault of the robbers,
Qu'on se viendra ranger a la grand ligne.	That everyone shall shelter himself under the great line.

The London blitz, with all its horrid tumult due to the assault by the Nazis, is clearly foreshadowed even to the seeking of shelter by the populace in the London underground lines.

1

A pres combat & bataille navale,	After the fight and sea battle,
Le grand Neptun a son plus haut beffroy,	The great Neptune in his highest steeple,
Rouge adversaire de peur deviendra pasle	The red adversary shall wax pale with fear,
Mettant le grand Ocean en effroy.	Putting the great Ocean in a fright.

After a war ending in a frightful sea battle, Great Britain shall rise to the heights of Empire, but not until her adversary shall first make the sea a frightful place for her mariners.

2

Le divin verbe pourra a la substance,	The divine word shall give to the substance
Comprins ciel, terre, or occult au fait mystique,	Heaven and earth, and gold hid in the mystic fact,
Corps, ame, esprit ayant tout puissance	Body, soul, spirit, having all power,
Tant soubs ses pieds comme au siege Celique.	As well under his feet, as in the Heavenly Seat.

A hermetic stanza, expounding the secret of the philosopher's stone, whereby medieval alchemists sought for a catalyst to convert base metals into gold.

3

Mars & Mercure & l'argent joint ensemble	Mars, and Mercury and silver joined together,
Vers le midy extreme siccite,	Towards the south a great drought,
Au fond d'Asie on dit a terre tremble,	In the bottom of Asia shall be a great earthquake
Corinthe, Ephese lors en perplexite.	Corinthe and Ephesus shall then be in perplexity.

From India, the bottom of Asia, a great movement shall spread, much to the perplexity of Christianity—II Corinthians 1–8 and Ephesians 3–3, "How that by revelations was made known to me the mystery, as I wrote before, in a few words."

4

Quand seront proches le deffaut des lunaires,	When default of the luminaries shall be near,
De l'un a l'autre ne distant grandement,	Not being far distant one from another,
Froid, sicite, danger vers les frontieres,	Cold, drought, danger towards the frontiers,
Mesme ou l'oracle a prins commencement.	Even where the oracle had his beginning.

When two great lights shall be nearly eclipsed, privations will be increased, even where the oracle (Nostradamus) was born.

5

Pres loing defaut de deux grand luminaires,	Near the eclipse of the two great luminaries,
Qui surviendra entre Avril & Mars,	Which shall happen between April and March,
O quel cherte! mais deux grande debonnaires,	O what a dearth! But two great ones bountiful
Par terre & sea secourront toutes parts.	By land and sea shall succour them on all sides.

Verification of the preceding verse, naming the time of the event, and also the rehabilitation and relief of the stricken areas by two bountiful nations.

6

Dans temples clos le foudre y entrera,
Les citadins dedans leurs forts grevez,
Chevaux, boeufs, hommes, l'onde leur touchera,
Par faim, soif, soubs les plus foibles armez.

In closed temples the lightning shall fall,
The citizens shall be distressed in their strength,
Horses, oxen, men, the water shall touch the wall,
By hunger, thirst, down shall come the worst provided.

The temples of learning shall be destroyed, but the citizens will hold fast, even through much suffering and loss.

7

Les fugitifs feu du ciels aux les piques,
Conflit prochain des corbeaux s'estatans;
De terre on crie, aide secours celiques,
Quand pres des murs seront les combatans.

The fugitives, fire of heaven on the pikes,
A fight near at hand, the ravens croaking,
They cry from the land, Help, O heavenly powers,
When near the walls shall be the fighting men.

A prediction of the taking of the Bastille, when the inflamed populace of Paris, armed largely with pikes, assaulted the walls of the fortress.

8

Les Cimbres joints avec leurs voisins,
Depopuler viendront presque l'Espagne,
Gens amaffez Guienne & Limousins,
Seront en ligue & leur feront compagne.

The Welsh, joined with their neighbors,
Shall come to depopulate most of Spain,
People gathered from French towns,
Shall be in league with them, and keep them company.

Spain will be almost depopulated by the efforts of the British and French volunteers.

9

Bordeaux, Rouen, & la Rochelle joints,	Bordeaux, Rouen and Rochelle joined together,
Tiendront autour de la grand mer Oceane,	Will range about upon the great ocean,
Anglois, Bretons, & les Flamens conjoints,	English, Bretons and Belgians, joined together,
Les chasseront jusques aupres de Rouane.	Shall drive them away as far as Rouane.

The great fleet of France will be driven from the seas by the British and Flemish fleets.

10

De sang & faim plus grand calamite,	Of blood and famine, what a great calamity,
Sept fois s'appreste a la marine plage,	Seven times is ready to come upon the sea coast,
Monech de faim, lieu pris captivite,	Monaco by hunger, the place taken captivity,
Le grand mene, croc, enferree cage.	The great one carried away, and shut up in a cage.

Monte Carlo (Monaco) shall starve during a period of national calamity, when the place is captured and the greatest one in France shall be imprisoned.

11

Les armes battre au ciel longue saison,	Armies shall fight in the air a great while,
L'arbre au milieu de la cite tombe,	The tree shall fall in the middle of the city,
Vermine, rongue, glaive en face tyfon,	Vermin, scabs, sword, firebrand in the face,
Lors le Monarque d'Adrie succombe.	When the Monarch of Venice shall fall.

A flaming tree shall fall in the middle of the city, spreading death and firebrands; aerial combat shall be the order of the day and the Italians shall be defeated.

12

Par la tumeur de Heb., Po, Tag.,
Tibre de Rome,
Et par l'estang Leman & Aretin,
Les deux grands chefs & citez de
Garonne,
Prins, morts, noyez, partir, humain
butin.

By the swelling of Heb., Po, Tag.,
Tiber of Rome,
And by Lake Leman, and cities of
Garonne,
The two great leaders will be taken,
Dead, drowned, the human booty
shall be divided.

Heb. is the river Hebrus in Thrace, the river Po is in Italy, and Tag. is the Tagus river in Portugal. Throughout Europe there will be a great disturbance, but the chief instigators will eventually meet violent deaths.

13

Par foudre en l'arche or & argent
fondu,
Des deux captifs l'un l'autre, man-
gera,
De la cite le plus grand estendu,
Quand submergee la classe nagera.

In the ark, lightning, gold and
silver melted,
Of two prisoners, one shall eat up
the other,
The greatest of the city shall be
laid down,
When the navy that was drowned,
shall swim.

When the ships that were sunk are afloat again, the greatest of the enemy's cities will be destroyed by a thunderbolt, leaving them with valueless money.

14

Par le rameau du vaillant person-
nage,
De France infirme, par le pere infelice,
Honneurs, richesses, travail en son
vieil age,
Pour avoir creu le conseil d'homme
nice.

By the branch of the valiant personage,
Of weak France, by the unfortu-
nate father,
Honours, riches, labour in his old
age,
For having believed the counsel of
a nice man.

Louis Philippe (whose father, descended from the brother of Louis XIV, was executed during the revolution) conspired with General Dumouriez and was exiled from Paris on the discovery of their plot to overthrow the Republic in 1793. Returning as King in 1830, he later enjoyed great riches and honors.

15

Coeur, vigueur, gloire, le Regne changera,	Heart, vigour and glory shall change the Kingdom,
De tous points, contre ayant son adversaire,	In all points, having an adversary against it,
Lors France enfance par mort sujugera,	Then shall France overcome childhood by death,
Le grand Regent sera lors plus contraire.	The great Regent shall then be most contrary to it.

The courage, vigor and glory of France were reanimated by Napoleon. His greatest adversary was the Pope, "Regent of St. Peter's Temporal Rule."

16

Le Prince Angloise Mars a son coeur de ciel,	The English Prince Mars has his heart from Heaven,
Voudre pour suyure sa fortune prospere;	Will follow his prosperous fortune;
Des deux duels l'vn percera le fiel,	Of two duels, one shall pierce the gall,
Hay de luy, bien ayme de sa mere.	Being hated of him, and beloved of his mother.

A martial English Prince will follow the dictates of his heart rather than his fortune, and his escapades shall cause much bitterness, but he shall still be beloved by the Queen.

17

Mont Aventine brusler nuict sera veu,	Mount Aventine shall be seen to burn in the night,
Le Ciel obscur tout a un coup en Flandres;	The Heavens shall be darkened upon a sudden in Flanders,
Quand le Monarque chassera son neveu,	When the Monarch shall expel his nephew,
Lors Gens d'eglise commettront les esclandres.	Then churchmen shall commit scandals.

The burning of Mount Aventine, one of the seven hills of Rome, is probably one of the many symbolizations used by Nostradamus to indicate war.

18

Apres la pluye laict, assez longuette,
En plusieurs lieux de Reims le ciel touche,
O quel conflit de sang pres d'eux s'appreste!
Peres & Fils, Roys n'oseront approche.

After a long rain of milk,
In many places of Rheims the lightning shall fall,
O what a bloody fight is making ready for them,
Father and Son, both Kings, shall not dare to come near.

After a period of peace and plenty, France shall be involved in a bloody war.

19

En Luques sang & laict viendra pleuvoir,
Vn peu devant changement de preteur,
Grand peste & guerre, faim & soif fera voir,
Loing ou mourra leur Prince & grand recteur.

In Lucca it shall rain blood and milk,
A little before the change of the magistrate,
A great plague, war, hunger and thirst shall be seen,
Along where their Prince and great director shall die.

In Italy, there will be alternating periods of depression and prosperity, then a change of chief magistrate, who will bring a plague, followed by war and hunger. The leader will die near Lucca.

20

Par les contrees du grand fleuve Betique
Loing d'Ibere au royanne de Grenade,
Croix respoussees par gens Mahometiques,
Un de Cordobe trahyra la contrade.

Through the countries of the great River Betis,
Far off from Iberia, in the kingdom of Grenada,
Crosses beaten back by Mohammedan people,
One of Cordoba shall at last betray the country.

The River Betis (Latin name) is the River Guadalquivir in Spain, on whose banks is the city of Seville. There Christians shall be betrayed by a Spaniard of Cordova, who will bring in Moors to slaughter his own people.

21

Au Crustamin par Mer Adraitique,	Among the Crustacea, near the Adriatic Sea,
Apparoistra vn horrible poisson,	A horrid fish shall appear,
De face humain & de corps aqua-tique,	Having a man's face and a fish's body,
Qui se prendra dehors de l'hame-con.	Which shall be taken without a hook.

The Manatee, an herbivorous aquatic mammal, inhabiting the African and Amazonian Coasts, often wanders far from his haunts. It was frequently mistaken for a human being, which its upper half resembles.

22

Six jours l'assaut devant citte donne,	Six days shall the assault be in front of the city,
Livres sera forte & aspre bataille,	A great and fierce battle shall be fought,
Trois la rendront & a eux par-donne,	Three shall surrender it, and be pardoned,
Le reste a feu & a sang tranche taille.	The rest shall be put to fire and sword, cut and slashed.

An episode in the perpetual wars that plague mankind, until the millennium, which Nostradamus mentions in a later prophecy.

23

Si, France, passe outre me Ligus-tique,	If France goeth beyond the Ligustic Sea,
Tu te verra en isles & mers enclos,	Thou shalt see thyself enclosed with islands and seas,
Mahomet contraire plus mer ad-riatique,	Mahomet, against thee besides the Adriatic Sea,
Chevaux & d'asnes tu rongeras les os.	Of horses and asses thou shalt gnaw the bones.

A warning to France not to advance beyond Corsica, or she will be attacked on all sides, blockaded and will suffer want of food.

24

De l'entreprinse grande confusion,	From the undertaking great con-
Perte de gens, tresor innumerables;	fusion,
Ty ny dois faire encores tension,	Loss of people and innumerable
France, a mon dire fais que sois	treasure,
recordable.	Thou ought not yet to tend that
	way,
	France! Endeavor to remember my
	saying.

A continuation of the preceding stanza, and of the same general tenor.

25

Qui au royanne Navarrois par-	He that shall obtain the kingdom
viendra,	of Navarre,
Quande le Sicile & Naples seront	When Sicily and Naples shall be
joints,	joined,
Bigorre & Landes par Foix lors on	Bigorre and Landes they by Foix
tiendra,	shall be held,
D'un qui d'espagne sera par trop	Of one who shall too much be
conjoints.	joined to Spain.

At a time when Italy is united, one who is deeply involved with Spain shall also obtain his way in France.

26

Des Roys & princes dresseront si-	Some kings and princes shall set
mulachres,	up idols,
Augures cruez, esclevez aruspices;	Divinations and hollow raised di-
Corne victime doree, & d'azur d'-	vinators,
nacre,	Victim with gilded horns, set with
Interpretez seront les estipices.	azure and mother of pearl,
	The looking into the entrails shall
	be interpreted.

Some Kings and Princes shall set up idols of Nationalism, supported by a prostituted clergy. Their victims will be glorified and from their remains, seers shall find much to interpret.

27

Prince Lybinique puissant en Occident,	A Libian Prince being powerful in the West,
Francois d'Arabe viendra tant enflammer;	The French shall love so much the Arabian language,
Scavans aux lettres sera condescendent,	That he, being a learned man, shall condescend
La langue Arabe en Francois translater.	To have the Arabian tongue translated into French.

An African potentate, being honored by the French, shall return the honor by translating his orders into the French tongue.

28

De terre foible & pauvre parentelle,	One weak in lands and of poor kindred,
Par bout & paix parviendra dans l'Empire,	By thrusting and peace shall attain to Empire,
Long temps regner une jeune femelle,	Long time, shall reign a young woman,
Qu'onc q'en regne n'en furvint un si pire.	Such as in a reign was never worse.

Madame Du Barry, mistress of Louis XV, is expressly indicated—from a poor milliner, she rose to be the power behind the throne of France.

29

Les deux neveaux en divers lieux nourris,	The two nephews brought up in divers places,
Navale pugne, terre peirres tombees.	A sea fight, fathers fallen to the earth.
Viendront si haut esleve enguerris,	They shall come highly educated and expert in arms,
Venger l'injure ennemys succombez.	To avenge the injury, their enemies shall fall down under them.

Two people of the same blood, from opposite sides of the ocean, shall unite and crush their common enemy.

30

Celuy qu'en luitte & fer au fait bellique,	He who in wrestling and martial deeds,
Aura porte plus grand que luy le prix,	Had carried the prize before his better,
De nuit au lit six luy feront la pique,	By night six shall abuse him in his bed,
Nud sans harnois subit sera surprins.	Being naked and without harness he shall suddenly be surprised.

The Earl of Montgomery, who accidentally killed Henry II of France, in a sporting bout, was afterward beheaded for being one of the Protestant Party.

31

Aux champs de Mede, d'Arabe & d'armenie	In the fields of Media, Arabia and Armenia,
Deux grands copies trois fois s'assembleront,	Two great armies shall meet thrice,
Pres du rivage d'Araxes la mesnie,	Near the shore of Araxes, the people,
Du grand Soliman en terre tomberont.	Of great Solyman shall fall down.

In the Near East, two great armies will clash, the net result of which will be that the Jews will suffer thereby.

32

Le grand sepulchre du peuple Aquitanique,	The great grave of the Aquatanic people
S'approchera aupres se la Toscane,	Shall approach to Tuscany,
Quand Mars sera pres du coing Germanique,	When Mars shall be in the German corner,
Et au terroir de la gent Mantuane.	And in the territory of the Mantuan people.

When war shall be in Italian territory sponsored by the Germans, then the British shall suffer much loss of life in Tuscany.

33

En la cite ou le loup entrera,
Bien pres de la les ennemis seront;
Copie estrange grand pays gastera,
Aux monts & Alpes les amis passeront.

In the city wherein the wolf shall go,
Near the place the enemies shall be,
An army of strangers shall spoil a great country,
The friends shall go over the mountains of the Alps.

The city of the Italian Wolf shall be besieged and almost overcome by a great army of strangers until assistance shall be rendered by those on the other side of the Alps.

34

Quand le deffaut du soleil lors sera,
Sur le plain jour le monstre sera veu;
Tout autrement on l'interpretera,
Cherte n'a garde, nul n'y aura pourveu.

When the eclipse of the sun shall be,
At noon day, the monster shall be seen,
It shall be interpreted other ways,
Then for a dearth, because nobody hath provided for it.

When the eclipse of Liberty shall be at its zenith, a monstrous movement shall arise, disguised as freedom; running its course it will cause great havoc.

35

Du plus profond de l'Occident d'-Europe,
De pauvres gens un jeune enfant naistra,
Qui par sa langue seduira grande trouppe,
Son bruit au regne d'orient plus croistra.

Out of the deepest part of the west of Europe,
From poor people a young child shall be born,
Who with his tongue shall seduce many people,
His fame shall increase in the Eastern Kingdom.

Adolf Hitler, born in Austria of poor parents, with his knowledge of mob psychology and powers of speech, was successful in seducing many people, even in the Eastern Empire of Japan.

36

Ensevely non mort apoplectique,
Sera trouve avoir les mains man-
    gees,
Quand la cite damnera l'heretique
Qu'avoit leurs loix ce leur sembloit
    changees.

One burned, not dead, but apo-
    plectical,
Shall be found to have eaten up
    his hands,
When the city shall damn the
    heretical man,
Who as they thought had changed
    their laws.

The escape of Hitler from embattled Berlin is here foreshadowed.

37

Avant l'assaut l'oraison prononcee,
Milan prins d'Aigle par embusches
    deceus,
Muraille antique par cannons en-
    foncee.
Par feu & sang a mercy peu receus.

Before the assault, the prayer shall
    be said,
A kite shall be taken by the eagle,
    being deceived by an ambuscade.
The ancient wall shall be beaten
    down with cannons,
By fire and blood, a few shall have
    quarter.

A play on words, Milan being both the name of an Italian city and
a bird.

38

La gent Gaulois & nation estrange,
Outre les monts, prins & profligez;
Au moys contraire & proche de ve-
    dange,
Par les Seigneurs en accord redigez.

The French people and another
    nation,
Being over the mountains, shall die
    and be taken,
In a month contrary to them, and
    near the vintage,
By the Lords agreed together.

Sometime in the month of September, the French and their Allies,
attempting to invade a foreign shore, shall be decisively beaten.

39

Les sept en trois mis en concorde,	The seven shall agree together within three months,
Pour subjuguer les Alpes Ape-ninnes,	To conquer the Apennine Alps,
Mais le tempeste & ligure courade,	But the tempest and the cowardly Genoese,
Les profligent en subiets ruynes.	Shall sink them into sudden ruin.

Seven persons shall take three months to make an agreement to conquer the Italians, but the invasion shall be held up by bad weather.

40

Le grand theatre se viendra redres-ser,	The great theatre shall be raised up again,
Le dez jette & les rets ia tendus,	The die being cast and the net spread,
Trop le premier en glaz viendra lasser,	The first too much in tolling shall weary,
Par arcs prostraits de long temps ia fendus.	Beaten down by bows, who long before were split.

An ironic commentary on the varying fates of nations, wherein the vanquished rises to fight and becomes the victor, then in turn is vanquished. And thus there can be no true victory by the sword.

41

Bossu sera esleu par le conseil,	Crook-back shall be chosen by council,
Plus hydeux monstre en terre n'-aperceu;	A more hideous monster I never saw upon earth,
Le coup volant prelat crevera l'oeil,	The flying blow shall put out one of his eyes,
Le traistre au Roy pour fidelle re-ceu.	The traitor to the King shall be admitted as faithful.

A hunchback will be elected to a position of power, but will turn out to be a traitor to the King.

42

L'enfant naistra a deux dents en la gorge,	A child shall be born with two teeth in his mouth,
Pierre en Tuscie par pluye tomberont;	It shall rain stones in Tuscany.
Peu d'ane apres ne sera bled ne orge,	A few years after there shall be neither wheat nor barley,
Pour faouller ceux qui de faim failleront.	To feed those that shall faint for hunger.

A world famine will occur after the birth of a prodigy and the falling of bombs in Tuscany.

43

Gens d'alentour de Tarn, Loth, & Garonne,	People that live about the Tar, Lot and Garonne,
Gardez les monts Apennines passer,	Take heed to go over the Apennine Mountains,
Vostre tombeau pres de Rome & d'Anconne	Your grave is near Rome, and Ancona,
Le noir poil crespe fera trophee dresser.	The black-haired ones shall set up a trophy.

The people of France, near the Tar, Lot and Garonne Rivers, are warned not to go into Italy, the home of the Black Shirts. The "trophy" refers to the dishonored corpse of the former duce—Mussolini.

44

Quand l'animal a l'homme domestique,	When the beast familiar to mankind,
Apres grand peine & saute viendra parler;	After great labour, and leaping shall come to speak,
Le foudre a vierge sera si malefique,	The lightning shall be so hurtful to a virgin,
De terre prinse & suspendue en l'air.	That she shall be taken from the earth and suspended in the air.

The dogs of war will be unleashed and shall come to "speak." An explosion in a church shall blow a Virgin skyward, and initiate a period of great uncertainty.

45

Les cinq estrangers entrez dedans le temple	The five strangers having come into the church,
Leur sang viendra la terre prophaner;	The blood shall profane the ground,
Aux Thoulouseins sera bien dure exemple	It shall be a hard example to those of Toulouse,
D'un qui viendra les loix exterminer.	Concerning one that came to break their laws.

In Toulouse, five alien officials will be assassinated in a church, profaning the ground according to clerical opinion. The assassins shall be penalized heavily for it.

46

Le Ciel (de Plancus la cite) nous presage	The Heaven foretelleth concerning the city of Plancus,
Par clairs insignes & par estoilles fixes,	By clear signs and fixed stars,
Que de son change subit s'approche l'aage,	That the time of her sudden change is near at hand,
Ne pour son bien ne pour les malefices.	Neither because of her goodness nor wickedness.

The city of Plancus is Lyons, as Plancus was its founder. She is due for a sudden change in fortune.

47

Le vieux monarque dechasse de son regne,	The old monarch being expelled out of his reign,
Aux Orients son secours ira querre,	Shall go into the East to get assistance
Pour peur de croix ployers son enseigne,	For fear of the crosses he shall fold up his colours,
En Mitilens ira par port & par terre.	He shall go into Mitylene by sea and land.

The old King of Norway, Haakon, shall go to Russia for assistance to help expel those of the crooked crosses.

48

Sept cens captifs attachez rude- ment,	Seven hundred prisoners shall be tied together,
Pour la moitie meurdrir, donne le fort;	To murder half of them, the lot being cast,
La proche espoir si promptement,	The next hope shall come quickly,
Mais non si tost qu 'vne quinzi- esme mort.	And not so quickly, but fifteen shall be dead before.

An example of Nazi brutality to both civilians and combatants in World War II.

49

Regne Gaulois tu seras bien change,	French Kingdom, thou shalt be much changed,
En lieu estrange l'Empire translate,	The Empire is translated in an- other place,
En autres loix & moeurs seras range,	Thou shalt be put to other manners and laws,
Rouen & Chartres te fera bien du pire.	Rouen and Chartres shall do the worst they can to thee.

A prediction of the change of form of Government in France from Monarchy to Republic.

50

La Republic de la grande Cite	The Republic of the great City,
A grand rigueur ne voudra consen- tir;	With great harshness shall not con- sent,
Roy sortir hors par trompette cite,	That the king should go out being summoned by the city's trum- pet,
L'eschelle au mur la cite repentir.	The ladder shall be put to the wall and the city repent.

The government of Paris, with great harshness, summons and arrests the King and the Bastille is stormed.

51

Paris conjure un grand meurtre commettre
Blois le fera sortir en plain effect;
Ceux d'Orleans voudront leur chef remmettre,
Angiers, Troye, Langres leur foront grand forfait.

Paris conspireth to commit a great murder,
Blois shall cause it to come to pass,
Those of Orleans will set up their head again,
Angiers, Troyes, Langres will do them harm.

In Paris the Reign of Terror commences, and spreads to all France. The house of Orleans again will ascend the Throne, in the person of Louis Philippe.

52

En la campagne sera si longue pluye,
Et en l'Apoville si grande siccite,
Coq verra l'Aigle mal acomplie,
Par lyon mise sera en extremite.

In the country shall be so long a rain,
And in Apulia so great a drought,
The cock shall see the eagle with his wing injured,
And by him the lion brought to extremity.

The Gallic Cock shall see the American Eagle and the British Lion in great peril, during a long war.

53

Quand le plus grand emportera le pris,
De Nuremberg, D'usburg, & ceux de Basle,
Par Agripine chef Frankfort repris,
Traverseront par Flamens jusque'en Gale.

When the great one shall carry the prize,
Of Nuremberg, Augsburg and Basle,
By Agrippina the Chief of Frankfort shall be taken,
They shall go through Flanders as far as France.

When the Commander in Chief shall have captured other German cities, after the blasting of Cologne (ancient name, Agrippina), the German Commander shall be captured and imprisoned in France.

54

L'un des plus grands fuyra aux
    Espagnes,
Qu'en longue playe apres viendra
    feigner,
Passant copies par les hautes mon-
    tainges,
Devastant tout & puis en paix reg-
    ner.

One of the greatest shall run away
    into Spain,
That shall cause a wound to bleed
    long,
Leading armies over high moun-
    tains,
Destroying all, and afterwards shall
    reign.

General Franco and his destruction of the Spanish People's Republic are
indicated here.

55

En l'an qu'un ceil en France reg-
    nera,
La court sera en vn bien fascheux
    trouble,
Le grand de Bloys son amy tuera,
Le regne mis en mal & doubte dou-
    ble.

In the year that one eye shall reign
    in France,
The court shall be in the very same
    trouble,
The great one of Blois shall kill his
    friend,
The kingdom shall be in an evil
    way, and double doubt.

A King blind in one eye shall rule a court that is just as shortsighted.

56

Mantauban, Nismes, Avignon, &
    Besiers,
Peste, tonnerre, & gresle a fin de
    Mars,
De Paris pont Lyon mur, Montpel-
    lier,
Depuis six cens et sept vingt, trois
    parts.

Montauban, Nismes, Avignon and
    Besier.
Plague, lightning and hail at the
    end of March,
The Bridge of Paris, the Wall of
    Lyons, and Montpellier shall
    fall
From six hundred and seven score
    three parts.

Widespread destruction shall befall France in March, in 12,143 parts.

57

Sept fois changer verrez gent Britannique,	Seven times you shall see the English to change,
Taints en sang en deux cents nonante an;	Dyed in blood, in two hundred and ninety years,
France, non, point par appuy Germanique,	Not France, by the German support,
Aries double son Pole Bastarnan.	Aries doubles his Bastarnan Pole.

England will see many changes, and all will occur under bloody circumstances. France, with the support of Germany and under the benevolent influence of Aries, will remain stable.

58

Aupres du Rhin des Montagnes Noriques,	Near the Rhine out of the Norick Mountains,
Naistra un grand de gens trop tard venu,	Shall be born a great one, though come too late.
Qui deffendra Saurome & Pannoniques,	Who shall defend the Poles and Hungarians,
Qu'on ne scaura qu'il sera devenu.	So that it shall not be known what is become of him.

Nostradamus remarks on the above that, "This is plain." It obviously refers to an event and character in his time now lost in the maze of history.

59

Barbare Empire par le iters usurpe,	A Barbarian Empire shall be usurped by a third person,
La plus part de son sang mettre a mort,	Who shall put to death the greater part of his kindred,
Par mort senile, par luy, le quart frappe,	By death of old age, the fourth shall be stricken by him,
Par peur que sang par la sang en soit mort.	For fear that blood should not die by blood.

Henry Pu Yi was installed by Japan in 1934 as Ruler of Manchukuo, usurped from China, and Nostradamus foresees that his dynasty will fail.

60

Par toute Asie grande proscription,
Mesme en Mysie, Lysie, & Pam-
    phylie;
Sang versera par dissolution,
D'un jeunne noir remply de felon-
    nie.

Through all Asia shall be a great
    proscription,
The same as in Mysia, Lydia, and
    Pamphilia,
Blood shall be spilled by the de-
    bauchness
Of a dark young man, full of trea-
    son.

An Asiatic shall force the hordes of Asia into armies of conquest.

61

La grand bande & secte crucigere
Se dressera en Mesopotamie,
Du proche fleuve compagnie legere,
Que telle loy tiendra pour ennemis.

The great band and sect wearing
    a cross,
Shall rise up out of Mesopotamia,
Near the river shall be a light
    company,
Which shall hold that law for the
    enemy.

A great organization, with some kind of cross as its emblem, shall emerge in a land between two rivers. Near one of those rivers, some traitors shall give the enemy assistance.

62

Proche del Duero par mer Cyrene
    close,
Viendra percer les grands Monts
    Pyrenees,
La main plus courte & sa percee
    close,
A Carcassonne conduira ses me-
    nees.

Near the Duro, closed by the Cy-
    renian Sea,
Shall come to pierce the Pyrenees
    Mountains,
The shorter hand and his pierced
    criticism,
Shall in Carcassone lead his plot.

Near the Duro River, which rises in Spain near the Pyrenees Mountains, the one with a short hand shall lay a plot that will eventually embroil the strongest fort of France, Carcassone.

63

Romain pouvoir sera du tout a bas,	The Roman power shall be quite put down,
Son grand voisin imiter ses vestiges;	His great neighbor shall follow his steps,
Occultes haines civiles & debats	Secret and civil hatreds and quarrels,
Retarderont aux bouffons leurs follies.	Shall stop the buffoon's folly.

The collapse of power under Mussolini, the Roman buffoon, was quickly followed by the downfall of his neighbor, Hitler.

64

Le chef de Perse remplira grands Olchades,	The head of Persia shall fill great merchant ships,
Classe trireme contre gent Mahometique,	A fleet of warships against the Mohammedan folk,
De Parthe & Mede, & pilliers les Cyclades,	From Parthia and Media they shall come to plunder the Cyclades,
Repos long temps au grand port Ionique.	A long rest shall be on the Ionic port.

A great potentate shall send a fleet of warships supported by a well-supplied group of commercial vessels against a Moslem League, and commerce in the Mediterranean shall be stagnant.

65

Quand le sepulcre du grand Romain trouve	When the sepulcher of the great Roman shall be found,
Le jour apres sera esleu pontife,	The next day after a Pope shall be elected,
Du senat gueres il ne sera prouve	Who shall not be much approved by the Senate,
Empoisonne son sang au sacre scyphe.	Poisoned, his blood in the sacred chalice.

On the election of a Pope, great turmoil will arise due to disapproval by the Senate, and he will be assassinated.

66

Le grand Baillif d'Orleans mis a
mort,
Sera par un de sang vindicatif;
Demort merite ne mourra ne par
fort,
Des pieds & mains mal le faisoit
captif.

The great Bailiff of Orleans, shall
be put to death,
By one of revengeful and vindictive
blood,
He shall not die of a deserved death
nor by chance,
But the disease of being tied hand
and foot. hath made him prisoner.

The grim Rabelaisian humor of the age is well displayed here. A great
personage of France will meet an untimely death at the hands of a vindictive enemy.

67

Une nouvelle secte de Philosophes,
Mesprisant mort, or, honneurs &
richesses,
Des monts Germains seront fort
limitrophes,
A les ensuyure auront appuy &
presses.

A new sect of Philosophers shall
rise,
Despising death, gold, honors and
riches,
They shall be near the mountains
of Germany,
They shall have abundance of others to support and follow them.

In Central Germany, near the Alps, a fanatical group shall arise and
they will find much support and many followers throughout the world.

68

Peuple sans chef d'Espagne & d'-
Italie,
Morts profligez dedans la Cherre-
nosse,
Leur duict trahy par legere folie,
Le sang nager par tout a la traverse.

A people of Spain and Italy with-
out a head
Shall die, being overcome in the
Crimea,
Their saying shall be betrayed by
their folly,
The blood shall swim all over at
random.

The Blue Division, Fascist Spain's contribution to Hitler's invasion of
Russia in World War II, was entirely exterminated on this front.

69

Grand exercite conduit par jou-
venceau,
Se viendra rendra aux mains des
ennemis;
Mais le vieillard nay au demy pour-
ceau.
Fera Chalon & Mascon estre amis.

A great army led by a young man,
Shall yield itself in the hand of
enemies,
But the old man born at the sign
of the Half Hog,
Shall cause Chalon and Mascon to
be friends.

Great French Armies shall be betrayed to the enemy by an inexperi-
enced leader, but the old man shall reunite all.

70

Le grand Bretagne comprinse d'Angleterre,
Viendra par eaux si fort a inondre,
La ligue neufue d'Ausonne fera
guerre,
Que contre eux il se viendront
bander.

Great Britain including all of England,
Shall suffer so great an inundation
of waters,
The new league of Italy shall make
wars,
So that they shall stand against
them.

Great Britain will be endangered by floods; and at the same time a
New League, under Italian leadership, will threaten her shores.

71

Ceux dans les Isles de long temps
assiegez,
Prendront vigueur force contre ennemis,
Ceux par behors morts de faim
profligez,
En plus grand faim que jamais
seront mis.

Those in the Islands that have long
been besieged,
Shall take vigour and force against
the enemies,
Those without shall die for hunger,
being overcome,
They shall be put in greater famine
than they were before.

The Dutch, being besieged, shall break the dikes to flood the country,
confronting the enemy with great danger and hunger.

72

Le bon vieillard tout ensevely,
Pres du grand fleuve par faux soup-
    con,
Le nouveau vieux de richesse en-
    nobly,
Prins a chemin tout l'or de la ran-
    con.

The good old man shall be buried
    alive,
Near the great river by a false sus-
    picion,
The new old one made noble by
    his riches,
The gold of his ransom shall be
    taken in the way.

A good ruler, grown old in service to his country, shall be deposed by
a new one, who will gain his ends through bribery.

73

Quand dans le regne parviendra le
    boiteux,
Competiteur aura proche bastard,
Luy & le regne viendront si fort
    rogneux
Qu'ains qu'il guerisse son fait sera
    bien tard.

When the lame man shall attain
    to the kingdom,
He shall have a bastard for his near
    competitor,
He and his kingdom shall be so
    scabby,
That before he be cured it will be
    late.

An event that must have taken place in the days of Nostradamus, and
which has now lost its meaning.

74

Naples, Florence, Fayence, &
    Imole,
Seront en termes·de telles fascherie,
Que pour complaire aux malheu-
    reux de Nole
Plaint d'avoir fait a son chef mo-
    querie.

Naples, Florence, Fayenza and
    Imola,
Shall be put into so much distress,
For being complacent to the un-
    happy one of Nola,
Who was complained of for having
    mocked his superior.

Italian factional disputes shall flourish because of the lack of unity
among the people.

75

Pau, Veronne, Vincence, Sara-
gousse,
De Glaives atteints terriors de sang
humides;
Peste si grande viendra a la grande
gousse,
Proches securs & bien loings les
remedes.

Pau, Verona, Vicenza, Saragossa,
Hit by the Sword, the country shall
be moist with blood,
So great a plague and so vehement
shall come
That though help be near, the
remedy shall be far off.

Italian cities, suffering from plague and famine, shall not be able to
avail themselves of assistance, due to lack of organization.

76

En Germanie naistront diverses
fectes,
S'approchant fort de l'heureux pa-
ganisme,
Le coeur captif, & petites receptes
Feront retour a payer le vray disme.

In Germany shall divers sects arise,
Coming very near to happy paganism,
The heart captivated and small re-
ceivings,
Shall open the gate to pay the true
tithe.

A prophetic description of the rise of the pagan doctrine of National
Socialism.

77

Le tiers climat sous Aries comprins,
L'ans mil sept cens vingt & sept en
Octobre,
Le Roy de Perse par ceux d'Egypte
prins,
Conflit, mort, perte, a la croix
grand opprobre.

The third climate comprehended
under Aries,
In the year 2025, the 27th of October,
The King of Persia shall be taken
by those of Egypt,
Battle, death, loss, a great shame
to the Christians.

In the year 2025, under a special chronology enumerated by Nostradamus, strange events are to take place in the Orient much to the shame
of Christians.

78

Le chef d'Escosse, avec six d'Ale-
magne,
Par gens de mer Orientaux captifs,
Traverseront le Calpre & Espagne,
Present en Perse au nouveau Roy
craintif.

The chief of Scotland with the six
of Germany,
Shall be taken prisoners by the sea-
men of the east,
They shall go through the Calpre
and Spain,
And shall be made a present in
Persia to the new fearful king.

A new King of the East shall arise and conquer many lands, and a
British leader and six Germans shall be brought to him as hostages, by
way of Calpre (the Straits of Gibraltar).

79

Le grand criard sans honte auda-
cieux,
Sera esle gouverneur de l'armee.
La hardiesse de son contentieux,
Le pont rompu, Cite de peur pa-
smee.

The great squawker proud without
shame,
Shall be erected governor of the
army,
The stoutness of his competitor,
The bridge being broken, the city
shall faint for fear.

A great demagogue, without shame or conscience, shall obtain control
of the army, much to the citizens' helpless fear.

80

Erins, Antibe villes autour de Nice,
Seront vastees fort, par mer & par
terre,
Les sauterelles terre & mer vent
propice,
Prins, morts, trossez, pillez sans loy
de guerre.

Ervins, Antibes, and the towns
about Nice,
Shall be destroyed by land and sea,
The grasshoppers shall have the
land, the sea and wind favorable.
They shall be taken, killed, thrust
up, plundered, without law of
war.

The tremendous air fleets used in the invasions of France are clearl··
indicated.

81

L'ordre fatal sempiternel per chaine,	The fatal and eternal order by chain,
Viendra tourner par ordre consequent;	Shall come to turn by consequent order,
Du port Phocen sera rompue la chaine,	Of Port Phocen the chain shall be broken,
La cite prinse l'ennemy quant & quant.	The city taken, and the enemy presently after.

Phocen is the ancient name for Marseilles. Her harbor chain shall be pierced by the enemy and the port captured.

82

Du regne Anglois l'indigne dechasser,	From the English Kingdom the unworthy driven away,
Le conseiller, par ite mis a feu;	The councillor through the anger shall be burnt,
Ses adherants iront si bas trasser,	His partners shall creep so low,
Que le bastard sera demy receu.	That the bastard shall be half received.

Rudolf Hess, as peace messenger to the Cliveden Set, was repudiated both by his master and also by his British partners, after the chief councillor of Britain, Winston Churchill, burnt with anger on the notification of his errand.

83

Les longs cheveux de la Gaule Celtique,	The long hairs of the Celtic Gaul, Joined with foreign nations,
Accompagnez d'estranges nations,	Shall put in prison the Aquatanic agent,
Mettront captif la gent Aquatanique,	To make him yield to their intentions.
Pour succomber a leurs intentions.	

The intellectuals of Northern France, with the support of foreign agents, shall stamp out and imprison their opponents that favor the opposite view.

84

La grand cite sera bien desoles,
Des habitans un seul ny demourra,
Mur, sexe, temple, & vierge violee,
Par fer, feu, peste, canon, peuple
   mourra.

The great city shall be made very
   desolate,
Not one of the inhabitants shall be
   left in it,
Wall, sex, church and virgin ravished,
By sword, fire, plague, cannon,
   people shall die.

This incident occurred many times during the last World War but is
especially applicable to Lidice.

85

La Cite prinse par tromperie &
   fraude,
Par le moyen d'un beau jeune at-
   trappe,
L'assaut donne, Raubine pres de
   Laude,
Luy & tours morts pour avoir bien
   trompe.

The City shall be taken by cheat
   and deceit,
By means of a fair young one
   caught in it,
Assault shall be given Raubins near
   Lande,
He and all shall die for having de-
   ceived.

Through the treachery of a light-complexioned person, a City will be
pillaged by German robbers (Raubins) but he himself and his fellow
conspirators shall not escape.

86

Un chef d'Ausonne aux Espagnes
   ira,
Par mer fera arrest dedans Marseille,
Avant sa mort un long temps lan-
   guira,
Apres sa mort l'on verra grand
   merveille.

A chief man of Ausonne shall go
   into Spain,
By sea, he shall stay at Marseilles,
He shall languish a great while before his death,
After his death great wonders shall
   be seen.

Nostradamus makes constant reference to happenings connected with
Ausonne (the city of Bordeaux), and for the most part they are veiled
in obscurity.

87

Classe Gauloise n'approches de
   Corsegne,
Moine de Sardaigne tu t'en repen-
   tiras,
Trestous mourrez frustres de l'Aide
   grogne,
Sang nagera captif ne me Croiras.

French Fleet, do not come near
   unto Corsica,
Much less to Sardinia, thou shalt
   repent it.
All of you shall die frustrate of the
   help of the great ships,
Blood shall swim, being captive
   thou shalt not believe me.

The French are warned to steer clear of Corsica, the birthplace of
Napoleon.

88

De Barcelone par mer si grande
   armee,
Toute Marseille de frayeur trem-
   blera,
Isles saisies, de mer aide fermes,
Ton traditeur en terre nagera.

From Barcelona, shall come by sea,
   so great an army,
That Marseilles shall quake for
   fear,
The Islands shall be seized, help by
   sea shut up
Thy traitor shall swim to land.

The victory of a force coming from Barcelona is predicted.

89

En ce temps la sera frustre Cypres,
De son secours de ceux de Mer Ae-
   gee,
Vieux trucidez, mais par Mesles &
   Lipre,
Seduict leur Roy, Royne plus out-
   ragee.

At the time Cyprus shall be frus-
   trated,
Of its help, those of the Aegean
   Sea,
Old ones shall be killed, but by
   Mesles and Lipre,
Their King shall be seduced, and
   the Queen more wronged.

The Island of Cyprus will be besieged, the Greeks will not be able
to come to their assistance; at the same time the King and Queen will
be in exile.

90

Le grand Satyre & Tygre d'Hycar-
nie,
Don presente a ceux de l'Ocean,
Un chef de classe iastra de Car-
manie,
Que prendra terre au Tyrran Phocean.

The great Satyr and Tiger of Hir-
cania,
Shall be a gift presented to those
of the Ocean,
An admiral of a fleet shall come
out of Carmania,
Who shall land in the Thyrren
Phocean.

Hercynia, in ancient geography, is the mountain region of Germany. The Tiger will be taken prisoner and turned over to a maritime people. Carmania (now called Kerman) is in Persia, and the Thyrren Phocean is Marseilles.

91

L'arbre qu'estoit nar si long temps
seche,
Dans une nuict viendra a reverdir;
Son Roy malade, prince pied
estache,
Craint d'ennemis fera voiles
bondir.

The tree that has been long dead
and withered,
In one night shall grow green again,
His king shall be sick, the prince
shall have his foot tied,
Being feared by his enemies, he
shall make his sail rebound.

A metaphorical description of a renaissance of human understanding to take place in the future.

92

Le monde proche du dernier pe-
riode,
Saturne encor tard sera de retour;
Translat empier devers nation
Brodde,
L'oeil arrache a Narbon par autour.

The world being near its last period,
Saturn shall come yet late to his
return,
The empire shall be changed into
black nations,
Narbonne shall have her eye picked
out by a hawk.

Along toward the end of the world, the dark nations shall reign supreme.

93

Dans Avignon tout le chef de l'Empire,	In Avignon all the chief of the Empire
Fera appreste, pour paris desole;	Shall stay, by reason of Paris being desolate,
Tricast tiendra l'Annibalique ire,	Tricast shall stop the Hanniballic anger,
Lion par change sera mal console.	The Lion by change shall be ill-comforted.

Avignon, once the seat of the Papal government (1307–76), shall again have power, after Paris is desolate by reason of an African (Hanniballic) anger, and much to the disappointment of the British Lion.

94

De cinq cens ans plus compte l'on tiendra,	For five hundred years no account shall be made
Celuy qu'estoit l'ornament de son temps,	Of him who was the ornament of his time.
Puis a un coup grande clarte donra,	Then of a sudden he shall give so great a light,
Que par es siecle les rendra tres contens.	That for that age he shall make them to be most contented.

Sir Francis Bacon (1561–1620), scientist, philosopher, statesman, and alleged author of the Shakespearean plays, shall be disclosed in a new light.

95

La Loy Moricque on verra deffaillir,	We shall see the Moorish Law to decline,
Apres une autre beaucoup plus seductive,	After which another more seducing shall arise,
Boristhenes premier viendra faillir.	Boris Thenes shall be the first that shall fall,
Par dons & langues une plus attractive.	By gifts and tongue that law shall be most seducing.

After religious intolerance falls, a new ideology shall seduce mankind; the first ones to be attracted to this revolutionary concept shall be the Russians.

96

Chef de Fossan aura gorge couppes,
Par le ducteur du Limier & L'-
  curier,
Le fait patre par ceux du mont
  Tarpee,
Saturns en Leo treziesme Fevrier.

The chief of Fossan shall have his
  throat cut.
By the leader of Hunt and Grey-
  hound,
The act committed by those of the
  Tarpian Rock,
Saturn being in Leo, the Thir-
  teenth of February.

The chief man of Northern Italy shall be hunted down by those of
Rome and shall die an infamous death.

97

Nouvelle loy terre neuve occuper,
Vers la Syrie, Judee & Palestine,
Le grand Empire Barbare corruer,
Avant que Phebe son siecle deter-
  mine.

A new law shall occupy a new
  country,
Towards Syria, Judea and Palestine,
The great Barbarian Empire shall
  fall down,
Before Phoebe makes an end of
  her course.

The Arab Confederacy shall fall of its own weight and a new Judea
and Palestine shall occupy the place of Syria.

98

Deux Royals Freres si fort guer-
  royeront,
Qu'entre 'eux sera la guerre si mortelle,
Qu'un chacun places fortes occuperont,
De regne & vie sera leur grand que-
  relle.

Two Royal Brothers shall war so
  much one against the other,
That the war between them shall
  be mortal,
Each of them shall seize upon
  strong places,
Their quarrel shall be concerning
  kingdom and life.

An incident to occur before the World Organization of Nations out-
laws wars for personal aggrandizement.

99

Aux champs herbeux d'Alein & du Varneigne,
Du Mont Lebron proche de la Durance,
Camp des deux parts conflit sera si aigre.
Mesopotamie deffaillira en la France.

In the meadow fields of Alein and Varneigre,
Of the brown mountains near the Durance,
Armies on both sides, the fight shall be so sharp,
That Mesopotamia shall be wanting in France.

France is to be the battleground for contending armies in a decisive engagement involving heavy losses.

100

Entre Gaulois le dernier honore,
D'homme ennemy sera victorieux,
Force & terrior en moment explore,
D'un coup de trait quand mourra l'envieux.

He that least honored among the French,
Shall be conqueror of the man that was his enemy,
Strength and terror shall in a moment be tried,
When the envious shall be killed with an arrow.

The underprivileged classes of France shall emerge victors after overthrowing a conspirator who will continue to be their greatest enemy.

1

Cela du reste de sang non espande,	There shall be a remnant of blood unspilt,
Venise quiert secours esntre donne,	Venice shall seek for succour,
Apres avoir bien long temps attendu,	After having long waited for it,
Cite livree au premier cornet sonne,	The city delivered at the first sound of the trumpet.

This concerns the Siege of Candia which lasted for twenty years. The Venetians fought a losing battle with the Turks, expecting, but never receiving, help from the Christian Princes, until eventually the city was compelled to surrender.

2

Par mort la France prendra voyage a faire,	By reason of a death, France shall undertake a journey,
Classe par mer, marcher monts Pyrenees.	They shall have a fleet at sea, and march towards the Pyrenees,
Espagne en trouble, marcher gent militaire,	Spain shall be in trouble by an army,
Des plus grand; dames en France emmences.	Some of the greatest ladies in France carried away.

Conditions in France and Spain during a revolutionary period are forecast in this verse.

3

D'Arras & Bourges de Brodes grands enseignes.
Unplus grand nombre de Gascons battre a pied,
Ceus long du Rhosne saigneront les Espagnes,
Proche du mont ou Sagonte s'assied.

From Arras and Bourges many colours of Dark men shall come.
A great number of Gascons shall go on foot,
Those along the Rhone shall let Spain blood,
Near the mountain where Saguntus is seated.

Saguntus, a city in Spain destroyed by the Romans, is here used symbolically. Men of the dark Mediterranean races shall roam widespread over Spain, to her detriment.

4

L'impotent prince fasche, plainte & querelles,
De raps & pilles par coqs & par Lybiques,
Grand est par terre, par mer infinies voilles,
Seule Italie sera chassant Celtiques.

The impotent prince angry complains and quarrels,
Concerning rapes and plunderings done by the cocks and Libiques.
Great trouble by land, by sea infinite sails.
Italy alone shall drive away the French.

French and African forces joined together shall sack and pillage a helpless country, while Italy alone will be able to defend her shores.

5

Croix paix soubs un, accomply divin verbe,
Espaigne & Gaule seront unis ensemble,
Grand clad proche, & combat tresacerbe,
Coeur si hardy ne sera qui ne tremble.

The cross shall have peace, under an accomplished divine word,
Spain and France shall be united together,
A great battle near hand and a most sharp fight,
No heart so stout but shall tremble.

After a terrific struggle Spain and France shall be united in a form of government satisfactory to Christians.

6

D'habits nouveaux apres fait la treuve,
Malice tramme & machination;
Premier mourra qui en sera la preuve,
Couleur Venise insidiation.

After the new clothes shall be found out,
There shall be malice, plotting and machination,
He shall die the first, that shall make trial of it.
Under cover of Venice, shall be a conspiracy.

A new form of government, by conspirators cast out by the Italians, shall destroy the innovators.

7

Le mineur fils du grand & hay prince,
De lepre aura a vingt ans grande tache;
De dueil sa mere mourra bien trist & mince,
Et it mourra la ou tombe chef lasche.

The younger of the great and hated prince,
Being twenty years old shall have a great touch of leprosy,
His mother shall die of grief, very sad and lean,
And he shall die of the disease loose flesh.

The King of Rome, Napoleon II, son of Napoleon and the ill-fated Marie Louise, died in 1832 after a wasting sickness lasting a year, at the age of twenty.

8

La grand cite d'assaut pront & repentin,
Surprins de nuict, gardes interrompus,
Les excubies & veilles saint Quintin,
Trucidez gardes & les portails rompus.

The great city shall be taken by a sudden assault,
Being surprised by night, the watch being beaten,
The court of guard and watch of St. Quentin,
Shall be killed, and the gate broken.

The battle of St. Quentin was one of the decisive fights in World War I. The Germans almost broke the Allied lines at this point in a surprise attack.

9

Le chef du camp au milieu de la presse,
D'un coup de flesche blesse aux cuisses.
Lors que Geneve en larmes & en detresse
Sera trahy par Lozan & Souysses.

The chief of the camp in the middle of the crowd,
Shall be wounded with an arrow through both his thighs,
When Geneva being in tears and distress,
Shall be betrayed by Lausanne and the Swiss.

The Treaty of Lausanne completely sabotaged the work of the League of Nations.

10

Le jeune Prince accuse feucement,
Mettra en trouble le camp & en querelles;
Meurtry le chef pour le sous Levement,
Scepter appraiser, puis guerur escrouelles.

The young prince being falsely accused,
Shall put the camp in trouble and in quarrels.
The chief shall be murdered by the tumult,
The scepter shall be appeased and later cure the king's evil.

A young prince shall be falsely accused of treason. After being found innocent, he shall take his rightful place as the head of the State, and his accuser shall be slain by the people.

11

Celuy qu'aura couvert de la grand cappe,
Sera induit a quelque cas patrer;
Le douze rouges viendront souiller la nape,
Soubs meurtre, meurtre se viendra perpetrer.

He that shall be covered with a great cloak
Shall be induced to commit some great act,
The twelve red ones shall soil the table cloth,
Under murder, murder shall be committed.

Evidently a phase of the activities of the Roman Catholic Church—the Twelve Red Ones, being Cardinals, and the Great Cloak, the Pope.

12

Le camp plus grand de route mis
  en suit,
Geures plus outre ne sera pour-
  chasse;
Ost recampe & region reduicte
Puis hors de Gaule du tout sera
  chasse.

The greatest camp being in disorder shall be routed,
And shall be pursued not much
  after,
The army shall encamp again, and
  the troops set in order,
Then afterwards, they shall be
  wholly driven out of France.

The invasions of France by the Germans are here predicted. Nostradamus forecasts the eventual, and complete, victory of France.

13

De plus grand perte nouvelles rap-
  portees,
Le rapport fait le camp s'eslong-
  nera,
Bendes unies encontre revoltes,
Double phalange, grand abandonnera.

News being brought of a great loss,
The report divulged, the camp
  shall be astonished,
Troops being united and revolted,
The falange shall forsake the great
  one.

The revolt of the Spanish Army and Falangists against Franco's dicta-
torial power is predicted.

14

La mort subiette du premier per-
  sonnage,
Aura change & mis un autre au
  regne,
Tost, tard venu a si haut & bas age,
Que terre & mer faudra qu'on le
  craingne.

The sudden death of the chief
  man,
Shall cause a change, and put another in the reign soon,
Late come to so high a degree in
  a low age,
So that by land and sea he must
  be feared.

A regency shall be proclaimed when a young person is raised to the
throne, and the clique in control shall misrule for a considerable period.

15

D'ou pensera faire venir famine,	Whence one thought to make
De la viendra le rassassiement;	famine to come,
L'oeil de la mer par avare canine,	Thence shall come the fullness,
Pour de l'un l'autre donra huille	The eye of the sea through a dog-
froment.	gish covetousness,
	Shall give to both, oil and wheat.

The low lands of Holland and the Zuider Zee were flooded by the Germans, but Nostradamus assures us that they will again be fertile.

16

La cite franche de liberte fait serue,	The free city from a free one shall
Des profligez & resueurs fait azyle;	become slave,
Le Roy change a eux non si pro-	And of the banished and dreamers
terue,	shall be a retreat,
De cent seront devenus plus de	The King changed in mind shall
mille.	not be so unfavorable to them,
	Of one hundred, they shall become
	more than a thousand.

The Free City of Danzig, enslaved by the Nazis, was nevertheless highly favored by them, even to the point of expansion.

17

Changer a Beaune, Nuis, Chalons,	There shall be a change at Beaune,
Dijon,	Nuis, Chalons, Dijon,
Le Duc voulant amender la barree,	The Duke going about to raise
Marchant pres fleuve, poisson bec	taxes,
de Plongeon,	The Merchant near the river shall
Verra la queue port sera serree.	see the tail
	Of a fish, having the bill of a loon,
	the door shall be shut.

A submarine shall be seen by a merchant, in a river near the above-mentioned French towns.

18

Des plus lettrez dessus les faits ce-lestes,	The most learned in the celestial sciences,
Seront par princes ignorans reprou-vez,	Shall be found fault with by ignorant princes,
Punis d'edit, chassez comme ce-lestes,	Punished by a proclamation, chased away as wicked,
Et mis a mort la ou seront trouvez.	And put to death where they shall be found.

The warnings of learned scientists shall be scoffed at by ignorant persons in power, even to the point of persecution.

Nostradamus explicitly charges mankind to heed the warnings of science and take atomic power under international control.

19

Devant Rouan d'insubres mis le siege,	Before Rouen, a siege shall be laid by the Italians,
Par terre & mer enfermez les pas-sages,	By sea and land the passages shall be shut up.
D'Haynaut, & Flandres de Gand & ceux de liege,	Those of Hianaut, Flanders, Ghent and Liege,
Par dons levees raviront les rivages.	With them troops shall plunder the sea shore.

An incident in the many wars among the European nations is here forecast.

20

Paix ubertre long temps Dieu louera,	Peace and plenty shall be not long praised,
Par tout son regne desert la fleur de lis	All the time of his reign the Fleur de Lys shall be deserted,
Corps morts d'eau, terre la l'on apportera,	Bodies shall die by water, earth shall be bought,
Aperant vain heur d'estre la ense-velis.	Hoping vainly to be there buried.

This predicts a great famine and flood in France, here signified by the Fleur de Lys.

21

Le changement sera fort difficile,
Cite province au change gain sera,
Coeur haut, prudent mis, chasse
   luy habile,
Mer, terre, peuple, son estat chang-
   era.

The change shall be very hard,
The city and country shall gain by
   the change,
A high prudent heart shall be put
   in, the unworthy expelled,
Sea, land, people, its state shall
   change.

This is the forecast of a revolution that will bring great and good changes to all.

22

La grand copie que sera dechassee,
Dans un moment fera besoin au
   Roy,
La foy promise de loing sera faus-
   see,
Nud se verra en piteux desarroy.

The great army that shall be rejected,
In a moment shall be wanted by
   the King,
The faith promised afar off shall
   be broken,
So that he shall be left naked in a
   pitiful case.

A continuation of the preceding stanza, this tells of the disintegration of the royal army and their desertion from the King to the cause of revolution.

23

La Legion dans la Marine classe,
Calcine, Magne, souphre & poix
   bruslera,
Le long repos de l'asseuree place,
Port Selyn chercher feu les con-
   sumera.

The Legion in the Maritime Fleet,
Calcining greatly, shall burn brim-
   stone and pitch,
After a long rest in the secure
   place,
They shall seek Port Selyn, but
   fire shall consume them.

A terrific assault by a great fleet equipped with weapons employing potent chemical agents, shall attack a country which has long enjoyed peace and security. They shall attack the great Port of LES N. Y. but will be repulsed by weapons even more terrible.

24

Ouy sous terre saincts d'ame voix
  fainte,
Humains flamme pour divin voir
  luire,
Fera des seuls de leur sang terre
  tainte,
Et les saints temples pour les im-
  pure destruire.

Underground, shall be heard the
  feigned voice of a holy dame,
A human flame to see a divine one
Shall cause the ground to be dyed
  with their own blood,
And the holy temples to be destroyed by the wicked.

Under the guise of a so-called reform movement, humanity shall suffer
much and the holy temples shall be destroyed.

25

Corps sublimes sans fin a l'oeil visi-
  bles,
Obnubiler viendra par ses raisons,
Corps, front comprins, sense, chef
  & invisibles,
Dimineant les sacrees oraisons.

The celestial bodies that are always
  visible to the eye,
Shall be darkened for these reasons,
The body with the forehead, sense
  and head invisible,
Diminishing the sacred prayers.

The occult knowledge of "prophets" shall flourish during this period,
keeping alive the hope of the world.

26

Lou grand cyssame le levera d'al-
  belhos,
Que non sauran don, te signen ven
  guddos,
Denech l'embousq, sou gach sous
  las treilhos,
Cuitad trahido per cinq lengos non
  nudos.

The great swarm of bees shall rise,
And it shall not be known whence
  they come,
Towards the ambush, the jay shall
  be under a trellis,
A city shall be betrayed by five
  tongues not naked.

When a swarm of bees alight from an unknown source, then shall be
seen a Jay under the trellis and the city shall be betrayed by five different
nations.

27

Salon, Mansol, Tarascon de Sex l'arc,
Ou est debout encor la pyramide;
Viendront livrer le prince d'Denemark,
Rachapt honny au temple d'Artemide.

Salon, Mansol, Tarascon of six arches
Where is still standing the pyramids,
Shall come to deliver the Prince of Denmark,
A shameful ransom shall be paid into the temple of Artemis.

Provincial towns are named here and the arches mentioned are the ruins of ancient triumphal monuments erected by the Romans. Artemis is another name for Diana.

28

Lors que Venus du Sol sera couvert;
Soubs l'esplendeur sera forme occulte;
Mercure au feu les aura descouvert,
Par bruit bellique sera mis a l'insulte,

When Venus shall be covered by the Sun,
Under the splendor it shall be an occult form,
Mercury in the fire shall discover them,
And by a warlike rumor shall be provoked.

An allegorical stanza, wherein is expressed a hidden formula, having to do with the preparation of the elixir to make the hermetic Philosophers' Stone. The same occult directions are given also in the three stanzas following.

29

Le Sol cache eclipse par Mercure,
Ne sera mis que pour le ciel second;
De Vulcan Hermes sera faite pasture,
Sol sera veu pur rutilant & blond.

The Sun shall be hid and eclipsed by Mercury,
And shall not be set but for the second heaven,
Hermes shall be made a prey to Vulcan,
And after that the Sun shall be seen pure, shining and yellow.

The Sun refers to gold, the second heaven means a furnace. "Hermes a prey to Vulcan" indicates the elixir to be put upon the fire in a furnace.

30

Plus unze fois Lune Sol ne voudre,
Tous augmentez & baissez de de-
gree;
Et si bas mis que peu d'or le secret,
Qu'apres faim, peste, decouvert le
secret.

The Moon will not have the Sun
above eleven times.
Then both shall be increased and
lessened in degree,
And put so low, that a little gold
shall be sewed up,
So that hunger and plague, the
secret shall be discovered.

Alchemical formulae and processes are clearly expressed for the adept,
but are most confusing for the uninitiated.

31

Le lune au plain de nuict sur le
haut mont
Le nouveau sophe d'vn seul cerveau
l'a veu,
Par ses disciples estre immortel se-
mond,
Yeux au midy, en sens mains corps
au feu.

The moon at full by night upon
the high mount,
The new Sophe with only one
brain has seen it,
Invited by his disciples to become
immortal,
His eyes to the south, his hands
and body to the fire.

The Sophe, or wise man, has mastered the secret. Invited to reveal
the secret to the world, by his disciples, he refuses, and does not become
immortal.

32

Es lieux & temps chair au poisson
dorna lieu.
La loy commune sera faite au con-
traire,
Vieux tiendra fort, puis este du
milieu,
Le Panta, Choina Philon, mis fort
arriere.

In places and times, flesh shall give
way to flesh,
The common law shall be made
against it;
The old man shall stand fast, then
being taken away,
Then all things common among
friends, shall be set aside.

Panta, Choina Philon are Greek words expressed best in English as
"All things are common among friends."

33

Jupiter joint plus Venus qu'a la
    Lune,
Apparoissant   de   plentitude
    blanche;
Venus cachee sous la blancheur
    Neptune,
De Mars frappee par la grande
    branche.

Jupiter being more joined to Venus
    than to the Moon,
Appearing in a full whiteness,
Venus being hid under the white-
    ness of Neptune,
Stricken by Mars through the en-
    graved branch.

Those in power shall give more time to the pleasures of Venus than to other activities, until the sudden onslaught of a war.

34

Le grand mene captif d'estrange
    terre,
D'or enchaine au Roy Chyren of-
    fert;
Qui dans Ausonne, Milan perdra la
    guerre,
Et tout son ost mis a feu & a fer.

The great one brought prisoner
    from a far country,
And chained with gold, shall be
    presented to Henry, the ruler,
Being then at Ausonne, Milan shall
    lose the war,
And all its host put to fire and
    sword.

Nostradamus interprets this literally, thus: When a great one from a far country shall be brought prisoner chained with gold, and presented to a King called Henry (for Chyren by transposition of letters is Henryc) who then shall be at Bordeaux (Ausonne), Milan shall lose a great army.

35

Le feu estaint les vierges trahyront,
La plus grand part de la bande vou-
    velle;
Poudre a fer, lance les seule Roy
    garderont,
Etrusque & Corse de nuict gorge
    allumelle.

The fire being put out, the virgins
    shall betray,
The greatest part of the new troup,
Gunpowder, lance, shall keep only
    the King,
In Etruria and Corsica by night,
    throats shall be cut.

An insurrection in Italy (Etruria) is predicted, which shall take place at night and be betrayed by Virgins.

36

Les jeux nouveaux en Gaule redres-
sez,
Apres victoire de l'Insubre cam-
pagne,
Monts d'Esperie, les grands liez
troussez,
De peur trembler la Romaine &
Espagne.

The new plays shall be set up again
in France,
After the victory obtained in Piedmont,
Mountains of Spain, the great ones
tied and carried away,
Romania and Spain shall quake for
fear.

France again will be triumphant after a victory over the Italians.
Over the mountains of Spain the great ones will be carried away, and
Romania and Spain shall be in terror.

37

Gaulois par sauts, monts viendra
penetrer.   ·
Occupera le grand lieu de l'Insubre;
Au plus profond son ost fera entrer,
Gennes, Monech pousseront classe
rubre.

The French by leaping shall go
over the mountains,
And shall seize the great mount of
the Savoyard,
He shall cause his army to go to
the furthermost,
Genoa, and Monaco shall set out
their red fleet.

This prophecy concerns Henry IV, King of France, who went over
the Alps and conquered the dukedom of Savoy.

38

Pendant que Duc, Roy, Roynes
occupera,
Chef Bizantin captif en Samoth-
race;
Avant l'assaut l'vn l'autre mangera,
Rebours ferre suyura de sang la
trace.

While the Duke shall keep the
King and Queen busy,
A great man of Constantinople
shall be prisoner in Greece;
Before the assault one shall eat up
the other,
Rebours armored shall trace one
by the blood.

A great tumult and riot will occur before the city is captured by the
heavily armored enemy.

39

Les Rodiens demanderont secours,	The Rhodians shall ask for aid,
Par le neglet de ses hoirs delaisses,	Being forsaken by the neglect of her heirs,
L'empire Arabe revalera son cours,	The Arabian Empire shall slack his course,
Par Hesperies la cause radressee.	By means of Spain the care shall be mended.

Nostradamus looks into time, and see the Turks assuming a minor role in history. In 1555, when the *Centuries* were first issued, Turkey was in a position to challenge the Christian nations for a position of world supremacy.

40

Les forteresses des assiegez ferrez,	The strong places of the besieged shall be pressed.
Par poudre a feu profondes en abysme;	By gunpowder they shall be plunged into a pit,
Les proditeurs seront tous vifs serrez,	The traitors shall be shut up alive,
Onc aux Sacristes n'advint si piteux scisme.	Never did happen so pitiful a schism to the *Sacristes*.

By *Sacristes*, the author means that part of the Roman Catholic Church that is in charge of the books and property. There seems to be a warning implicit in this quatrain—probably slanted against those whom Nostradamus considered heretics.

41

Gynique sexe captive hostage,	Gynical sexe being captive by hostage,
Viendra de nuict custodes devevoir;	Shall come by night to deceive her keepers,
Le chef du camp deceu par son lignage,	The chief of the camp being deceived by her language,
Liarra le genre, fera piteux avoir.	Shall keep her folks, a thing pitiful to behold.

Gynical sexe is taken from a Greek word meaning woman. A woman shall captivate the chief of her captors, and cause him to betray his trust.

42

Geneve & Langres par ceux de
Chartre & Dole
Et par Grenoble captif au Montli-
mar,
Seysset, Losanne par fraudulente
dole,
Les trahyront par or soixante marc.

Geneva and Langres by those of
Chartres and Dole,
And by one of Grenoble captive at
Montlimar,
Seisset, Lausanne by a fraudulent
deceit,
Shall betray them for thirty pounds
weight of gold.

The sense is plain, and this apparently refers to struggles among various
towns in France.

43

Seront ouys au ceil les armes battre,
Celuy an mesme les divins ennemis,
Voudront Loix Sainctes injuste-
ment debatre,
Par foudre & guerre bien croyants
a mort mis.

There shall be heard in the air the
noise of weapons,
And in that same year, the divines
shall be enemies,
They shall unjustly put down the
Holy Laws,
And by thunder and the war, true
believers shall die.

A religious war shall break out, during which many true believers will
suffer greatly.

44

Deux gros de Mende de Rhodes &
Millaud,
Cahors, Limoges, Castre malo sep-
mano,
De nuech l'intrado, de Bordeaux
an cailhau,
Par Perigort au toc de la Campano.

Two great ones of Mendes, of
Rhodes and Millaud,
Cahors, Limoges, Castres, an evil
week,
By might the entry shall be from
Bordeaux one cailhau,
Through Perigort at the ringing of
the bell.

Towns near the home of Nostradamus are spoken of here, and a rising
against tax collectors is indicated.

45

Par conflit Roy Regne abandonnera,	By a battle the King shall forsake his kingdom,
Le plus grand chef faillira au besoing,	The great commander shall fail in time of need,
Morts profligez, peu en rechappera,	They shall be killed and routed, few shall escape,
Tous destranchez, un en sera tesmoin.	They shall be cut off, one only shall be left for a witness.

The Battle of Waterloo is prognosticated. His defeat in this battle, due to the failure of Marshal De Grouchy, caused Napoleon to lose his Empire.

46

Bien deffendu le fait par excellence,	The fact shall be defended excellently well,
Garde toy Tours de ta proche ruyne;	Tours beware of thy approaching ruin,
Londres & Nantes par Rheims fera deffence	London and Nantes by Rheims shall stand upon their defence,
Ne passez outre au temps de la bruyne.	Do not go further in foggy weather.

Tours, a city in France, is warned of a fog, and told to beware of her approaching ruin.

47

Le noir farouche quand aura essaye,	The wild black one, after he shall have tried,
Sa main sanguine par feu, fer arcs, tendus,	His bloody hand by fire, sword, bended bows,
Trestout le peuple sera tant effraye,	All the people shall be so frightened,
Voir les plus grands par col & pieds pendus.	To see the greatest hanged by neck and feet.

Astonishingly accurate prophecy of the fate of Mussolini, Leader of the Black Shirts. After his death, he was hung by his feet for the mob to spit upon.

48

Plannure, Ausonne fertille, spacieuse,	The plain about Bordeaux fruitful and spacious,
Produira tahons si tant de sauterelles,	Shall produce so many hornets and so many grasshoppers,
Clarte solaire viendra nubileuse,	That the light of the sun shall be darkened,
Ronger le tout, grand peste venir d'elles.	They shall fly so low, a great plague shall come from them.

The prediction here is of the D-Day invasion of France by the Allies in World War II; at that time the sky was darkened by the tremendous concentration of Air Power.

49

Devant le peuple sang sera respandu,	Before the people, blood shall be spilt,
Que du haut ciel ne viendra eslongner;	Who shall not come far from high heaven,
Mais d'un long temps ne sera entendu,	But it shall not be heard of for a great while,
L'esprit d'un seul le viendra tesmoigner.	The spirit of one shall come to witness it.

A worthy person shall be murdered openly. His blood shall cry to heaven, but shall not be heard for a time, but at last it shall be discovered.

50

Libra verra regner les Hesperies,	Libra shall see Spain to reign,
De Ciel & Terra tenir la monarchie,	And have the monarchy of Heaven and Earth,
D'Asie forces nul ne verra peries,	Nobody shall see the forces of Asia to perish,
Que sept ne tiennent par rang la Hierarchie.	Till seven have kept the Hierarchy successively.

A Spaniard shall attain to the office of Pope, Monarch of Heaven and Earth, and after seven of the Spanish faction have reigned successively then the Asiatic forces will be overcome.

51

Un Duc cupide son ennemy en-
suyvre,
Dans entrera empeschant la pha-
lange,
Hastez a pied si pres viendront
poursuyvre,
Que la journee conflit pres de
Gange.

A Duke being earnest in the pursuit of his enemy,
Shall come in, hindering the falange,
Hastened on foot shall follow them
so close,
That the day of the battle shall be
near Ganges.

In India, near the Ganges, there will be a battle, involving a falange (squadron of soldiers) and a Duke.

52

En cite obsessee aux murs hommes
& femmes,
Ennemys hors le chef prest a soy
rendre,
Vent sera fort encontre les gens-d'-
armes,
Chassez seront par chaux, poussiere
& cendre.

In a besieged city, men and women
being upon the walls,
The enemy without, the governor
ready to surrender,
The wind shall be strong against
the soldiers
They shall be driven away by lime,
dust and cinders.

A besieged city shall be saved from captivity by means of a powerful chemical apparently borne by a strong wind, which will drive away the besiegers.

53

Les fugitifs & bannis revoquez,
Peres & fils grand garnissant les
haut poits;
Le cruel pere & les siens suffoquez,
Son fils plus pire submerge dans le
puis.

The fugitive and banished men being rescued,
Fathers and sons garnishing the
high walls,
The cruel father and his retinue
shall be suffocated,
His son, being worse, shall be
drowned in the well.

The reappearance of evil men, banished because of their part in the making of war, once again shall usher in a period of destruction.

54

Du nom qui onc ne fut au Roy
   Gaulois,
Jamais ne fut un foudre si crain-
   tif,
Tremblant l'Italie l'Espagne & les
   Anglois,
De femme estrangers grandement
   attentif.

Of a name that a French King
   never was,
There was never a lightning so
   much feared,
Italy shall tremble, Spain and the
   English
He shall be much taken with
   women strangers.

This concerns Napoleon Bonaparte, even to his many amours.

55

Quand la Corneille sur tour de
   brique jointe,
Durant sept heures ne fera que
   crier,
Mort presagee de sang statue
   tainte,
Tyran meurtry, aux Dieux peuple
   prier.

When the Crow on a tower made
   of brick
For seven hours shall do nothing
   but cry,
Death shall be foretold and the
   statue dyed with blood,
Tyrant shall be murdered and the
   people pray to the Gods.

The extraordinary spectacle of a continuous alarm, by a crow, for seven hours from a brick tower will be a sign that some infamous tyrant will meet his end, and the populace shall show fear.

56

Apres victoire de raibeuse langue,
L'esprit tempte en tranquil & repos;
Victeur sanguin par conflit fait
   harangue,
Rostir la langue, & la chair & les
   os.

After victory over a raging tongue,
The mind that was tempted shall
   be in tranquility and rest,
The bloody emperor by battle shall
   make a speech,
And roast the tongue, the flesh and
   the bones.

Vengeance shall be taken by a conqueror over his critics who had spoken against him.

57

Ignare envie du grand Roy sup-
portee,
Tiendra propos deffendre les escrits;
Sa femme non femme par un autre
tentee,
Plus double deux ne feront ne cris.

Ignorant envy being supported by
the great King
Shall talk of prohibiting the writings,
His wife no wife, being tempted
by another,
Shall no more than they two prevail by crying.

Envious persons, in favor with the King, shall attempt to suppress
learning. But the King's mistress shall persuade him to the contrary, and
shall prevail.

58

Soleil ardant dans le gosier coller,
De sang humain arroser terre
Etrusque;
Chef seille d'eau mener son fils
filer,
Captive dame conduite en terre
Turque.

Burning sun shall pour into the
throat,
This human blood shall wet the
Etruscan ground,
The chief pail of water shall lead
his son to spin,
A captive lady shall be carried into
the Turkish country.

Molten gold shall be poured into a throat and human blood shall
flow. Because of this, a great water carrier shall make his son effem-
inate, and a captive lady shall be exiled.

59

Deux assiegez en ardante fureur,
De soif estaints pour deux plaines
tasses,
Le fort limen & vn viellard resueur,
Aux Genois de Nizza monstrera
trasse.

Two besieged, being in a burning
heat,
Shall die for thirst, want of two
cups full,
The fort being filed, an old doting
man,
Shall show to the Genoese the way
to Nice.

Nice shall be taken by the Italians through the help of an old dotard.

60

Les sept enfans en hostage laissez,
Le tiers viendra son enfant trucider;
Deux par son fils seront d'estoc per-
cez,
Gennes, Florence, lors viendra en-
conder.

The seven children being left in
hostage,
The third shall come to kill his
child,
Two by their sons shall be run
through,
Genoa and Florence shall second
them.

Evidently this indicates an event which occurred during the time of
Nostradamus, and according to him should be understood by all.

61

Le vieux mocque, & prive de sa
place,
Par l'estranger qui le subornera;
Mains de son fils mangees devant
sa face
Les freres a Chartres, Orleans,
Rouen trahyra.

The old man shall be baffled and
deprived of his place,
By the stranger that shall have instigated him,
But his sons shall be eaten before
his face,
The brother at Chartres, Orleans
shall betray Rouen.

General Henri Petain, dictator of Vichy France, under Nazi supervision,
was deposed by General De Gaulle. During the time Petain was in power
the captured French were used by the Germans as slave laborers.

62

Un coronel machine ambition,
Se saisira de la plus grande armee;
Contree son prince fainte inven-
tion,
Et descouvert sera sous sa ramee.

A colonel intrigues a plot by his
ambition,
He shall seize upon the best part
of the army,
Against the prince he shall have a
feigned invention.
And shall be discovered under the
harbour of the vine.

An accurate picture of the rise of Oliver Cromwell to the height of
power in England.

63

L'armee Celtique contre les Montagnars,	The Celtic army shall go against the Highlanders,
Qui seront sceus & prins a la pipee;	Who shall stand upon their guard, and being taken with trickery,
Paysans irez pouseront tost faugnars,	The peasant being angry, shall roll down the stones,
Precipitez tous au fil de l'espee.	They shall be all put to the edge of the sword.

The heroic peasant rebellion of the Austrian Tyrol, under Andreas Hofer, against the French Republican Army, is here prophesied by our author.

64

Le deffaillant en habit de bougeois,	The guilty, in a citizen's habit,
Viendra le Roy tempter de son offense,	Shall come to tempt the King concerning his offense,
Quinze soldats la plus part ostagois,	Fifteen soldiers the most part hostages,
Vie derniere & chef de sa chevance.	Last shall be his life and the best part of his estate.

The King shall be taunted by the citizens, and a guard of fifteen soldiers shall be put over him.

65

Au deserteur de la grand forteresse,	To the deserter of the great fortress,
Apres qu'aura son lieu abandonne;	After having forsaken his place,
Son adversaire fera si grand provesse,	His adversary shall do great feats,
L'Empereur tost mort sera condamne.	That the Emperor shall soon be condemned to death.

Treachery shall play a prominent part in the destruction of a future emperor who will be condemned to a living death.

66

Soubs couleur fainte de sept'testes rasees,
Seront semez divers explorateurs;
Puys & fontaines de poison arrousees,
Au fort de Gennes humaine devorateurs.

Under the feigned colour of seven shaven heads,
Shall divers spies be framed,
Wells and fountains shall be sprinkled with poison,
In the fort of Genoa shall be human devourers.

Seven priests or monks shall poison the well of public opinion, and in Genoa shall be those that live on human flesh.

67

L'an que Saturne & Mars eagaux combust,
L'air fort seiche, longue trajection;
Par feux secrets, d'ardeur grand lieu adust
Peu pluye, vent, chaud, guerres, incursions.

In the year that Saturn and Mars shall be fiery,
The air shall be very dry, in many countries,
By secret fires, many places shall be burnt with heat,
There shall be scarcity of rain, hot winds, wars, wounds.

A prognostication that Saturn (Commerce) and Mars (War) shall have a Roman Holiday.

68

En l'an bien proche eslongue de Venus,
Les deux plus grands de L'Asie & d'Affrique;
De Rhin, & Hyster, qu'on dira sont venus.
Cris, pleurs a Malte & coste a Lycustique.

In the year that is to come soon, and not far from Venus,
The two greatest ones of Asia and Africa,
Shall be said to come from the Rhine and Ister,
Crying and tears shall be at Malta and on the Italian Shore.

From the shores of the Rhine and Danube shall come those who will bring woe on Malta and also to the Italian shores.

69

La cite grande les exilez tiendront,
Les citadins morts meurtris & chassez;
Ceux d'Aquilee a Parmee promettront,
Monstrer l'entree par les lieux non trassez.

The banished shall keep the great city,
The citizens being dead, murdered and expelled,
Those of Aquelia shall promise to Parma,
To show the entrance by unknown paths.

Aquelia and Parma are Italian cities and, according to Nostradamus, they will be involved in inter-city warfare.

70

Bien contigue des grands monts Pyrenees,
Un contre l'Aigle grand copie addresser;
Ouvertes vaines, forces exterminees,
Que jusque a Pau, le chef viendra chasser.

Near the great Pyrenees Mountains,
One shall raise a great army against the Eagle,
Veins shall be opened, forces driven out,
So that the chief shall be driven as far as the Po.

Near the Spanish border one shall raise an army against an Emperor, whose emblem is the Eagle, but to no avail, as the chief of the army will flee and his forces will be scattered.

71

En lieu d'espouse les filles trucidees,
Meurtre a grand faute ne sera superstile;
Dedans le puys vestuies inondees,
L'espouse estaint par hauste d'Aconite.

Instead of the bride, the maid shall be killed,
The murder shall be a great fault, none shall be surviving,
In the well they shall be drowned with their clothes,
The bride shall be disposed of by high Aconite.

This tells of the tragic aftermath of a marriage, in which the bridesmaids shall be drowned in their wedding finery and the bride poisoned by Aconite.

72

Les Artomiques par Agen & Lectoure,
A saint Felix feront leur parlement,
Ceux de Basas viendront a la mal-
heure,
Saisir Condon & Marsan promptement.

The Artomiques, through Agen
and Lectoure,
Shall keep their parliament at Saint
Felix,
These of Bazan shall come in an
unhappy hour,
To seize Condon and Marsan
speedily.

By Artomiques, our author means the Protestants, who take the Com-
munion with leavened bread, called in Greek, Artos. The towns mentioned
are all in Gascony.

73

Le nepveu grand par forces prou-
vera,
Le peche fait du coeur pusillanime;
Ferrare & Ast le Duc esprouvera,
Par lors qu'au soir fera la panto-
mime.

The great nephew by force shall
provoke,
The sin committed by a pusillan-
imous heart,
Ferrari and Asti shall make a trial
of the Duke,
When the pantomime shall be in
the evening.

While the performance of a comedy is being enacted, a cowardly person,
provoked by his nephew, shall go on a rampage.

74

Du lac Leman & ceux de Bran-
nonices,
Tous assemblez contre ceux d'Aquitaine,
Germains beaucoup encor plus
souisses,
Seront defaicts avec ceux d'Humaine.

From Lake Geneva and to Verona,
They shall be gathered against
those of England,
Great many Germans and many
more mercenaries,
Shall be routed together with
many people.

The Germans and their allies shall be decisively beaten by the English-
speaking allies during a great campaign in Italy.

75

Prest a combattre fera defection,
Chef adversaire obtiendra la vic-
toire,
L'arriere garde fera defension,
Les deffaillans mort au blanc terri-
toire.

One being ready to fight shall faint,
The chief of the adverse party shall
obtain the victory,
The rear guard shall fight it out,
Those that fall away shall die in the
white country.

In a time of stress, the leader of one side, profiting by his opponent's weakness, shall grasp power, and the northern nations shall be worsted in the struggle.

76

Les Nictobriges par ceux de Peri-
gort,
Seront vexez tenant jusques au
Rhosne,
L'associe de Gascons & Bigorre,
Trahir le temple, le prestre estant
au prosne,

The Nictobriges by those of Pe-
rigort,
Shall be vexed as far as the Rhone,
The associate of the Gascons and
Bigorre,
Shall betray the church while the
priest is in his pulpit.

Nictobriges, in Greek, signifies a people of a dark and moist country. —Perigort and Bigorre are towns in France.

77

Selyn monarque, L'Italie pacific-
que,
Regnes unis Roy Chrestien du
monde;
Mourant voudra coucher en terre
belsique,
Apres pyrates avoir chasse de l'-
onde.

Selyn being monarch, Italy shall be
in peace,
Kingdoms shall be united, a Christian King of the world,
Dying, shall desire to be buried
in Europe.
After he shall have driven the pirates from the sea.

During a time of peace, all the world will be united under a great and noble king who will be a Christian.

78

La grand armee de la pugnee civille,
Pour de nuict Parme a l'estrange
  trouvee
Septante neuf meurtris dedans la
  ville,
Les estrangers passez tous a l'espee.

The great army belonging to the
  civil war,
Having found by night Parma possessed by strangers,
Shall kill seventy-nine in the town
And put all the strangers to the
  sword.

Great civil wars are promised for Parma and other Italian cities.

79

Sang Royal fuis, Monheurt, Mas
  Aiguillon,
Remplis seront de Bourdelois les
  Landes,
Navarre, Bigorre, pointes & eguil-
  lons,
Profonds de faim, vorer de liege,
  glandes.

Royal Blood run away from Monheurt, Marsan, Aiguillon,
The Landes shall be full of Bourdelois,
Navarre, Bigorre, shall have points
  and pricks,
Being deep in hunger, they shall
  devour the cork and acorns.

Bourdelois refers to the people of Bordeaux. Landes is a desert region
in France near the towns of Navarre and Bigorre. As in quatrain 76,
there seems to be no deeper significance beyond Nostradamus' concern
with these French towns and their current troubles.

80

Pres du grand fleuve grand fosse
  terre egeste
En quinze part sera l'eau divisee,
La cite prinse, feu, sang cris, conflit mestre,
Et la plus part concerne au colli-
  see.

Near the great river, a great pit,
  earth dug out,
In fifteen parts, the water shall be
  divided,
The city taken, fire, sword, blood,
  cries, fighting,
The greatest part concerns the Col-
  osseum.

In Rome there shall be a great tumult and fighting, concerning in most
part a revival of ancient ideas.

81

Pont on fera promptement de na-
celles,
Passer l'armee du grand prince Bel-
gique;
Dans profondrees & non loing de
Bruxelles,
Outre passez, destrenchex sept a
picque.

A bridge of boats shall suddenly
be made,
To pass over the army of the great
Belgian Prince.
In deep places, and not far from
Brussels,
Being gone over, there shall be
seven cut with a pike.

A prophecy of the Siege of Antwerp by the Spanish under the Prince
of Parma, who eventually erected a pontoon bridge over the River Schelde
and captured the city.

82

Amas s'approche venant d'Escla-
vonie,
L'Olestant vieux cite ruynera;
Fort desclee vera sa Romaine,
Puis la grand flamme estaindre ne
scaura.

A great troop gathered shall come
from Russia,
The old Olestant shall ruin a city,
He shall see his Romania very
desolate,
And after that, shall not be able
to quench that great flame.

A Russian advance to the West shall be slowed up by an attack by an
Olestant (Duke). But he will thus meet his ruin and his country will be
made desolate.

83

Combat nocturne le vaillant capitaine,
Vaincu fuyra, peu de gens profli-
gee;
Son peuple esmeu, sedition non
vaine,
Son propre fils le tiendra assiege.

In a fight by night, the valiant captain
Being vanquished shall run away,
overcome by few.
His people being moved, shall
make no small mutiny,
His own son shall besiege him.

An event in Nostradamus' time which he felt needed no explanation.

84

Un grand d'Auxerre mourra bien
  miserable,
Chasse de ceux qui soubs luy ont
  este,
Serre de chaisnes, apres d'un rude
  cable,
En l'an que Mars, Venus, Sol mis
  en este.

A great man of Auxerre shall die
  very miserably,
Being expelled by those who have
  been under him,
Bound with chains, and after that,
  with a strong cable,
In the year that Mars, Venus, and
  Sol shall be in conjunction.

Auxerre is a city in France about fifty miles from Paris. And this stanza merely concerns the unhappy fate of one of its chief men—many, many years ago.

85

Le charbon blanc du noir sera
  chasse,
Prisonnier fait mene au tumbereau,
More chameau sus pied estrelassez,
Lors le puisne fillera l'aubereau.

The white coal shall be expelled
  by the black one,
He shall be made prisoner carried
  in a dung cart,
His feet twisted on a black camel,
Then the youngest, shall suffer the
  Falcon to have more freedom.

A white prince shall be overcome by a black one, and carried to his execution in a dung cart. According to Nostradamus, this is both "allegorical and metaphorical, and the judgment must be left to the reader."

86

L'an que Saturne en eau sera con-
  joinct,
Avec Sol, le Roy fort & puissant,
A Rheims & Aix sera receu &
  oingt,
Apres conquestes meurtrura innocens.

In the year that Saturn in Aquarius
  shall be in conjunction
With Sol, the King being strong
  and powerful,
Shall be received and anointed at
  Rheims and Aix,
After conquest he shall murder in-
  nocent persons.

Rheims, a city in France, and Aix, a city in Germany, shall both be the scene of the coronation of a common ruler. Afterwards his actions shall be ominous.

87

Un fils du Roy tent de langues aprins,
A son sisne au regne different,
Son pere beau au plus beau fisz comprins,
Fera perir principe adherent.

A son of a King having learned divers languages
Shall fall out with his elder brother for the kingdom,
His father-in-law being more concerned with his elder son,
Shall cause the principal adherent to perish.

A King having two sons, the elder shall succeed him. The younger, being well educated, shall rebel against the King, his father, but shall be slain by his own father-in-law.

88

Le grand Anthoine du moindre fait sordide,
De Phytriase a son dernier ronge,
Un qui de plomb voudra estre cupide,
Passant le Port d'Esleu sera plonge.

The great Anthony by name, but, in effect sordid,
By lice, shall at last be eaten up,
One that shall be covetous of lead,
Passing the Port Esleu shall fall into the water.

One who pretends to greatness shall at last realize his failure. He shall commit suicide by drowning himself.

89

Trente de Londres secret conjureront,
Contre leur Roy, sur le pont l'entreprinse,
Les satalites la mort degousteront,
Un Roy esleu blonde, natif de Frize.

Thirty of London shall secretly conspire,
Against the King, upon the bridge the plot shall be made,
These satellites shall taste of death,
A King shall be elected, fair, and born in the low countries.

The Guy Fawkes gunpowder plot against the British Throne is clearly outlined here.

90

Les deux copie aux murs ne pourront joindre,	The two armies shall not be able to join by the walls,
Dans cest instant trembler Milan Ticin,	At the instant Milan and Ticin shall tremble
Faim, soif, doutance si fort les viendra poindre,	Hunger, thirst, and fear shall so seize upon them
Chair, pain, ne vivres, n'auront un seul bouncin.	They shall not have a bit of meat, bread nor victuals.

A description of conditions in Italy during a war is here given, referring specifically to the city of Milan.

91

Au Duc Gaulois constranet battre au duelle,	A French Duke compelled to fight a duel,
La nef Mole Monech n'approchera,	The ship of Mole shall not approach Monaco,
Tort accuse prison perpetuelle,	Wrongfully accused, shall be perpetually imprisoned,
Son fils regner auant mort taschera	His son shall endeavor to reign before his death.

"The Man in the Iron Mask," whose name was never known, was a French prisoner who died on November 19, 1703. His identity has been the source of much romantic speculation. Here Nostradamus gives us a clue.

92

Teste trenchee du vaillant Capitaine,	The head cut off of the valiant Captain,
Sera jette devant son adversaire,	Shall be thrown down before his adversary,
Son corps pendu de sa classe a l'antenne,	His body hanged from the ship's antenna,
Confus furia par rames a vent contraire.	Confused, they shall fly with oars against the wind.

This quatrain caused confusion in the mind of Nostradamus. To us, there is an obvious reference to radio in it—but the event itself remains obscure.

93

Un serpent veu proche du lit Royal,	A serpent shall be seen near the Royal bed,
Sera par dame, nuict chiens n'ab-bayeront;	By a lady of the night, the dogs shall not bark,
Lors naistre en France un Prince tant Royal	Then shall be born in France a Prince so much royal,
Du ciel venu tous les Princes ver-ront.	Come from heaven all the Princes shall see it.

All the princes of the world will acknowledge a French Prince as the greatest of them all. The serpent is an allusion to his greatness, as when Alexander was born, a serpent was seen near his mother's bed.

94

Deux grands freres seront chassez d'Espaigne,	Two great brothers shall be driven from Spain,
Laisne vaineu soubs les monts Py-renees;	The elder of them shall be over-come under the Pyrenean Moun-tains,
Rougir mer, Rosne sang Leman d'-Alemagne,	Bloody sea, Rhone, bloody Geneva of Germany,
Narbon, Blyterres, d'Agath, con-taminees.	Narbonne, the Land of Agath con-taminated.

The two great brothers in crime, Nazism and Fascism, will be driven from Spain, but not before a great struggle takes place near the border of France.

95

Le regne a deux laisse bien peu tiendront,	The reign left to two they shall not keep it long,
Trois ans sept mois passez feront la guerre;	Three years and seven months be-ing past,
Les deux vestales contre rebeller-ont,	The vestals shall rebel against them,
Victor puis nay en Armorique terre.	The youngest shall be the con-queror of the Armorick country.

This signifies a Kingdom that shall be left to two, who shall keep it but a short while. Their title will be challenged by two Nuns.

96

La soeur aisnee de l'Isle Britannique,
Quinze ans devant le frere aura
  naissance,
Par son promis moyennant verri-
  fique,
Succedera au regne de Balance.

The eldest sister of the Britannic
  Island
Shall be born fifteen years before
  her brother,
By what is promised her and by
  help of truth,
She shall succeed in the Kingdom
  of Libra.

The eldest sister of Britain, the U. S. A., was born in 1776. Fifteen
years later, 1791, the Republic of France (brother) came into being.

97

L'an que Mercure, Mars, Venus
  retrograde,
Du grand Monarque la ligne ne
  faillir,
Esleu du peuple lusitant pres de
  Pactole,
Que'n paix & regne viendra fort
  envillir.

When Mercury, Mars and Venus
  shall retrograde,
The line of the great Monarch shall
  be wanting,
He shall be elected by the Portu-
  guese near Pactole,
And shall reign in peace a good
  while.

This signifies the change of state in Portugal, when they threw off
the yoke of Spain, and chose their own King.

98

Les Albanois passeront dedans
  Rome,
Moyennant Langres dimiples affu-
  blez,
Marquis & Duc ne pardonner a
  homme,
Feu, sang morbile, point d'eau,
  faillir les bleds.

The Albanians shall pass through
  Rome,
By means of Langres covered with
  half helmets,
Marquis and Duke shall spare no
  man,
Fire, blood, smallpox, water shall
  fail us, also corn.

The Albanians shall conquer a large territory and take Rome, and
desolation shall follow in their wake.

99

L'aisne vailland de la fille du Roy,
Repoussera si avant les Celtique,
Qu'il mettra foudres, combien en
tell arroy,
Peu, & loing puis profondes Hes-
perique.

The valiant eldest son of the
daughter of the King,
Shall beat back so far, those of
Flanders,
That he shall employ lightnings,
how many in such order,
Little and far, after shall go deep
in Spain.

An able leader of noble birth shall show great skill in employing the
forces of nature in conquering Flanders and Spain.

100

De feu celeste au Royal edifice,
Quand la lumiere du Mars deffail-
lira,
Sept mois grand' Guerre, mort
gent de malefice,
Rouen Eureux, au Roy ne faillira.

Fire shall fall from the skies on
the King's palace
When Mar's light shall be eclipsed,
Great war shall be for seven
months, people shall die by
witchcraft,
Rouen and Eureux shall not fail
the King.

A seven months' war, of tremendous destructive force such as the
world has never seen before, shall terrify mankind.

CENTURY V

1

Avant venus du ruyne Celtique,	Before the coming of the ruin of the Celts,
Dedans le temple deux parlemente-ront,	Two shall discourse together in the church,
Poignart coeur, d'un monte au coursier & pique,	Dagger in the heart of one, on horseback and spurring,
Sans faire bruit le grand enterre-ront.	Without noise they shall bury the great one.

The Irish, or Celts, shall be eventually ruined but, before this happens, two shall talk together in a church; one of these will be stabbed and the other will flee.

2

Sept conjurez au banquet feront luyre,	Seven conspirators at a banquet shall make their iron glisten
Contre les trois le fer hors de na-vire,	Against three, out of a ship,
L'un les deux classes au grand fera conduire,	One shall carry the two fleets to the great one,
Quand par le mail denier au front luy tire.	When in the promenade, the last one shall shoot him in the forehead.

At a banquet a conspiracy of seven shall succeed against three. A naval officer shall deliver two fleets to a great one, and for his treachery shall be shot in the forehead.

3

Le successeur de la Duche viendra,	The successor to the Dukedom shall come
Beaucoup plus outre que la mer de Toscanne,	Far beyond the Tuscan sea,
Gauloise branche la Florence tiendra,	A French branch shall hold Florence,
Dans son giron d'accord nautique Rane.	In its lap, to which the Sea Frog shall agree.

Il Duce, after his fall, shall be succeeded by a non-Italian. Florence will be under French influence.

4

Le gros mastin de cite dechasse,	The great mastiff being driven from the city,
Sera fasche de l'estrange alliance,	Shall be angry at the strange alliance,
Apres aux champs avoir le chef chasse,	After he shall have hunted the hart in the fields,
Le loup & l'ours se donneront defiance.	The wolf and the bear shall defy one another.

England shall be angry at a strange alliance, whereby the helpless are hunted down. The Italian Wolf and the Russian Bear shall defy one another.

5

Sous ombre saincte d'oster de servitude,	Under the feigned shadow of freeing people from slavery,
Peuple & cite l'usurpera luy-mesmes,	He shall usurp the people and city for himself,
Pire fera par faux de jeune pute,	He shall do worse by the deceit of a young whore,
Libre au champ lisant le faux proesme.	For he shall be betrayed in the field reading a false proem.

This prognosticates the "final" days and actions of Hitler, his false marriage to the actress Eva Braun, and his spurious will at his supposed death.

6

Au Roy l'augure sur le chef la
  main mettre,
Viendra prier pour la paix Italique,
A la main gauche viendra changer
  le sceptre,
De Roy viendra Empereur pacifique.

The augur shall come to put his
  hand on the King's head,
And pray for the peace of Italy,
In the left hand he shall change
  the scepter,
From a King he shall become a
  pacific Emperor.

The Latin word augur may mean one who foretells events, or may also
be taken for a clergyman. Here the significance is, that a priest shall put
his hand upon a King's head (Napoleon) and, praying for the peace of Italy,
shall place a scepter in his hand, and install him as Emperor.

7

Du triumvir seront trouvez les os,
Cerchant profond tresor enigma-
  tique,
Ceux d'alentour ne seront en repos,
De concaver marbre & plomb me-
  talique.

The bones of the triumvirate shall
  be found out,
When they shall seek for a deep
  and enigmatical treasure,
Those there about shall not be in
  rest,
This concavity shall be of marble
  and metallic lead.

This delves into Roman history, and tells of the plot of Octavius Caesar,
Marcus Antonius and Lepidus to make themselves masters of the Roman
Empire and to divide the spoils among the three of them.

8

Sera laisse le feu mort vif cache,
Dedans les globes horribles espou-
  ventable
De nuict a classe cite en poudre
  lache,
La cite a feu, l'ennemy favorable.

The fire shall be left burning, the
  dead shall be hid,
Within the globes terrible and
  fearful,
By night the fleet shall shoot
  against the city,
The city shall be on fire, the enemy
  shall be favorable to it.

Terrible new weapons launched from ships shall create fearful destruction and cause unquenchable fires; and so complete will be the havoc, it
will be impossible to count the dead.

9

Jusques au fond la grand arq de malve
Par chef captif l'amy anticipe,
Naistra de dame front face chevelue,
Lors par astuce Duc a mort attrapppe.

At the bottom of the great evil arch,
By a chief that is a captive, the friend shall be anticipated,
One shall be born of a lady with hairy face and forehead,
Then by craft shall a duke be put to death.

These words are too veiled in obscurity for either Nostradamus or myself to render a clear interpretation.

10

Un chef Celtique dans le conflit blesse,
Aupres de cave vouant siens mort abbatre,
De sang & playes & d'ennemis presse,
Et securs par incogneuz de quatre.

A Celtic leader wounded in battle,
Near a cellar, seeing death about to overthrow his people,
Being much oppressed with blood, wounds and enemies,
Is succoured by four unknown.

An event that needs no interpretation as it is self-explanatory.

11

Mer par solaires seure ne passera,
Ceux de Venus tiendront toute l'Affrique;
Leur regne plus Sol, Saturne n'occupera,
Et changera la mort Asiatique.

Sea by solars, she shall pass safely,
Those of Venus shall hold all Africa,
Saturn shall hold their kingdom no longer,
And shall change the Asiatic port.

Those of Venus, born to the sea, are the English; as a maritime nation they shall hold great colonial possessions.

12

Aupres de Lac Leman sera conduite,
Par garse estrange cite voulant
  trahir,
Avant sen meurtre a Aspurg la
  grand suitte,
Et ceux du Rhin la viendront envahir.

Near Lake Geneva shall be a plot,
By a strange whore to betray a city,
Before she be killed, her great reti-
  nue will come to Augsburg,
And those of the Rhine shall come
  to invade her.

The corrupting influence of Fascism had its inception in northern Italy,
close to Lake Geneva. Before it ran its mad course it also ruined the
Germans.

13

Par grand fureur le Roy Roman
  Belgique,
Vexer voudra par phalange barbare,
Fureur grincent chassera gent Ly-
  bique,
Depuis Pannons jusques Hercules
  la Bare.

By great fury, the Roman-Belgic
  Kingdom,
Shall come to vex, by their bar-
  barian falange,
Gnashing fury shall pursue the
  Savage people,
From Hungary as far as the Straits
  of Gibraltar.

A coalition of nations shall vex Europe sorely with its barbarian tactics;
the climax of its misdeeds is clearly indicated.

14

Saturne & Mars en Leo Espagne
  captive,
Par chef Libique au conflit attrape;
Proche de Malte, heredde Prinse
  vive,
Et Romain sceptre sera par coq
  frappe.

Saturn and Mars being in Leo,
  Spain shall be captive,
By an African general taken in
  battle,
Near Malta, a hereditary Prince
  shall be taken alive,
And the Roman sceptre shall be
  struck by the cock.

Under the joint influence of Saturn (commerce) and Mars (war)
Spain shall suffer great defeat. France (the cock) shall contribute to her
downfall.

15

En navigant captif prins grand
  pontife;
Grands apprestez saillir les clercs
  tumultuez,
Second esleu absent son bien de-
  bise,
Son favory bastard a mort tue.

In sailing a pope shall be taken
  captive,
After which, shall be a great uproar
  amongst the clergy,
A second absent elected, consumed
  his goods,
His favorite bastard shall be killed.

A controversy shall arise in the Catholic Church, caused by the election of a Pope who is in disfavor with the clergy.

16

A son haut prix la lerme Sabee,
D'humains chair pour mort en cendre mettre,
A l'isle Pharos par croisars pertur-
  bee,
Alors qu'a Rhodes paroistra dure
  espectre.

The Sabean tear shall be no more
  at its high price,
To turn human flesh by death into
  ashes,
The island Pharos shall be troubled
  by croisars,
When at Rhodes shall a hard
  phantom appear.

Sabean tear, a term used to describe frankincense, was a vegetable product extensively used in embalming. Pharos, an island opposite Alexandria, shall be troubled by Christians (croisars) when a vision appears in Rhodes.

17

De nuict passant le Roy pres d'une
  Andronne
Celuy de Cypres & principal
  guerre,
Le Roy failly la main fuit long du
  Rhosne,
Les conjurez l'iront a mort mettre.

The King going by night near an
  Andronne,
He of Cyprus and chief of war,
The King having missed the hand,
  along by the Rhone,
The conspirators shall put him to
  death there.

A noted military figure shall conspire against France, but in southern France he shall meet his just fate.

18

De dueil mourra l'infelix proflige,
Celebrera son vitrix l'heccatombe;
Pristine loy, franc edit redige,
Le mur & Prince au septieme jour
tombe.

The unhappy one, being overcome,
shall die of grief,
His victrix shall celebrate the hecatomb,
The former law and free edict shall
be brought again,
The wall and seventh Prince shall
go to the grave.

Victrix is a Latin word, the feminine gender of the word victor; Hecatomb was a Grecian sacrifice whereby 100 oxen were killed.

19

Le grand Royal d'or, d'airain aug-
mente,
Rompu la pache, par ieune ouverte
guerre,
Peuple afflige par unchef lamente,
De sang barbare sera couvert de
terre.

The great golden Royal, being increased with copper,
The agreement being broken by a
young man, there shall be open
war,
People afflicted by the loss of a
chief lamented,
The ground shall be covered with
barbarous blood.

An alliance between a rich nation with one of little wealth shall result
in an open warfare, in which the chief will lose his life.

20

De la les Alpes grande armee pas-
sera,
Un peu devant naistra monstre va-
pin;
Prodigieux & subit tournera,
Le grand Toscan a son lie plus pro-
pin.

Beyond the Alps shall a great army
go,
And a little while before shall be
born a vapin monster,
Prodigious and suddenly the great
Tuscan,
Shall return to his own nearest
place.

Napoleon shall cross the Alps with a great army.

21

Par les trespas du Monarque Latin,
Ceux qu'il aura par regne secourus;
Le feu livra divuse le butin,
La mort publique au hardis incorus.

By the death of the Latin Monarch,
Those that he shall have succoured in his reign,
The fire shall shine, the booty shall be divided,
The bold comers in, shall be put to public death.

A people shall be pillaged after the death of a monarch of Latin origin. However, the persecutors will eventually be publicly executed.

22

Avant qu'a Rome grand aye rendu l'ame,
Effrayeur grand a l'armee estrangere;
Par escadrons l'embusche pres de Parme,
Puis des deux rouges ensemble feront chere.

Before a great man renders up his soul at Rome,
The army of strangers shall put into a great fright,
By squadrons the ambush shall be near Parma,
After that, the two red ones shall make good cheer together.

The invaders of Italy shall be put into a great fright and driven out of the country; after that, two red ones (cardinals) will be highly satisfied.

23

Les deux contents seront unis ensemble,
Quand la pluspart a Mars sera conjonct,
Le grand d'affrique en effrayeur & tremble,
Duumvirat par la classe des joints.

The two contested shall be united together,
When the most part shall be joined to Mars,
The great one of Africa shall be in fear and terror,
Duumvirat shall by the pursuit be disjointed.

Two nations, previously at war with each other, shall ally themselves against a great one, of Africa. But this alliance (duumvirat) shall not last long.

24

Le *Kegne* & *Roy soubs Venus*
  esleve,
Saturne aura sur jupiter empire,
Be loy & *regne par le Soleil leve,*
Par Saturnius endurera le pire.

The Kingdom and King being
  joined under Venus,
Saturn shall have power over Jupiter,
The law and reign raised by the
  Sun,
Shall be put to the worse by the
  Saturnians.

The frivolous court of Louis XV, led by Madame Du Barry, made a
farce of law and order, by their Saturnine revels.

25

Le *prince Arabs, Mars, Sol, Venus,*
  Lyon,
Regne d'Eglise par mer succom-
  bera,
Devers la Perse bien pres d'un mil-
  lion,
Bisance, Egypte, Ver. Serp. in-
  vadera.

The Arab Prince, Mars, Sol, Venus,
  Leo,
The Kingdoms of the Church
  shall be overcome by the sea,
Towards Persia very near a million,
Turkey, Egypt, Ver. Serp. shall
  invade.

Christian ideals will be overcome by Oriental ideology (Ver. Serp.
meaning true serpents).

26

La *gent esclave par un heur martiel,*
Viendra en haut degre tant esleve,
Changeront prince, naistra un pro-
  vincial,
Passer la mer, copie aux monte leve.

The Slavic Nation shall by martial
  luck,
Be raised to so high a degree,
That they shall change their Prince
  and elect one among themselves,
They shall cross the sea with an
  army raised in the mountains.

Russians, by a military revolution, shall change their form of government and they will grow to be a great power and invade many countries.

27

Par feu & armes non loing de la Mer Negro,	By fire and sword not far from the Black Sea,
Viendra de Perse occuper Trebisonde;	They shall come from Persia to seize upon Trebisonde,
Trembler Pharos Methelin, Sol alegro,	Pharos and Methelin shall quake, Sun be merry,
De sang Arabe d'Adrie covert l'onde.	The sea of Adria shall be covered with Oriental blood.

A Russian invasion, coming through Iran, shall seize Mediterranean ports. In the Adriatic Sea they shall be driven back with great losses.

28

Le bras pendu & la jambe liee,	The arm hanging and the leg bound,
Visage pasle, au sein poignard cache;	With a pale face, a dagger in the bosom,
Trois qui seront jurez de la meslee,	Three shall be sworn to the fray,
Au grand de Gennes sera le Fer lasche.	To the great one of Genoa the Iron shall be darted.

Three wounded men shall conspire to stab the great one of Genoa.

29

La liberte ne sera recouvres,	Liberty shall not be recovered,
L'occupera noir, fier, vilain inique;	It shall be occupied by a black, fierce and wicked villain,
Quand la matiere du pont sera ouvree,	When the work of the Danube bridge shall be ended,
D'Hister, Venise faschee la republique.	The Italian commonwealth shall be angry.

The black-shirted villain shall destroy Italian liberty. When the wreck of the German alliance is complete, then Italy will really show her anger.

30

Tout a l'entour de la grande cite,
Seront soldats logez par champs &
villes,
Donner l'assaut Paris, Rome incite,
Sur le pont lors sera faite grand
pille.

Round about the great city,
Soldiers shall be in fields and towns,
Paris shall give the assault, Rome
shall be incited,
Then upon the bridge shall be
great plunderings.

The capture and sacking of Rome by the French Duke of Bourbon is here described.

31

Par terre Attique chef de la sapi-
ence,
Qui de present est la Rose du
Monde;
Pont ruyne & sa grand preemi-
nence,
Sera subdite & naufrage de undes.

In the country of Attica which is
the head of wisdom
And now is the Rose of the World,
A bridge shall be in ruins with its
great preeminence,
It shall be subdued and made a
wreck by the waves.

The country of Attica, or Greece, famed for its wisdom, shall be corrupted by the usages of mankind.

32

Ou tout bon est, tout bien Soleil
& Lune,
Est abondent, sa ruyne s'approche,
Du ciel s'advance vaner ta fortune,
En mesme estat que la septiesme
roch.

Where all well is, are good Sun
and Moon,
Is existent, its ruin approaches
near,
The heaven is making haste to
change thy fortune,
Into the same state as the seventh
rock.

This dark stanza seems to predict the bad times that shall exist during a civil war between the Catholics and Protestants.

33

Des principaux de cite rebellee,
Qui tiendront fort pour liberte r'avoir,
Detrencher masses infelice meslee,
Cris hurlemens a Nante; piteux voir.

Of the principal men in a rebelled city,
Who shall stand out to recover their liberty,
The males shall be cut in pieces, O unhappy quarrels!
Cries and howlings, it shall be pity to see at Nantes.

Nantes in France, shall be the seat of a rebellion against the rest of France. Tremendous massacres of the natives shall follow.

34

Du plus profond de l'occident Anglois,
Ou est le chef de l'isle Britannique;
Entrera classe dans Garonne par Blois,
Par vin & sel, feux cachez aux barriques.

From the most westerly part of England,
Where the chief of the British Island is,
A fleet shall come into the Garonne by Blois,
By wine and salt, fire shall be hidden in barrels.

A British Fleet shall plant mines (barrels) in French waters.

35

Par cite franche de la grand Mer Seline,
Qui porte encore a l'estomach la pierre;
Angloise classe viendra sous la bruine,
Un rameau prendre du grand ouverte guerre.

By a free city of the Mediterranean Sea,
Which carries yet the stone in the stomach,
An English Fleet shall come under a fog,
To take a branch of great open war.

The Free City of Venice in the Mediterranean, shall be invaded by an English Fleet under cover of a fog.

36

De soeur le frere par simulte fain-
    tise,
Viendra mesler rosee en mineral;
Sur la placente donne a vieille tar-
    dive,
Meurt le goustant sera simple &
    rural.

The brother of the sister, by
    feigned simulation,
Shall mix dew with mineral;
The aftermath being given to a
    slow old woman,
She died tasting, the deed shall
    be simple, and rural.

A brother shall poison his sister during childbirth.

37

Trois sens seront d'un vouloir &
    accord,
Qui pour venir au bout de leur
    attainte,
Vingt mois apres tous & records,
Leur Roy trahir simulant haine,
    fainte.

Three hundred shall be of one
    mind and agreement,
That they may attain their ends.
Twenty months after by all of
    them and their partners,
Their King shall be betrayed by
    simulating a feigned hatred.

The Legislative Assembly after a period of deliberation finally ordered King Louis XVI to stand trial for treason.

38

Ce grand monarque qu'an mort
    succedera,
Donnera vie illicite & lubrique;
Par nonchalance a tous concedera,
Qu'a la parfin faudra la loy Salique.

The great monarch that shall suc-
    ceed to the great one,
Shall lead a life unlawful and
    lecherous,
By carelessness he shall give to all,
So that in conclusion, the Salic
    law shall fail.

The Salic law, most famous for its chapter on succession to private property, which declares that daughters cannot inherit land, is here referred to in an incident which seems to indicate the degeneracy of the males of a royal line, which eventually led to the enthroning of a woman.

39

Du vray rameau des fleurs de lys issu,	Issued out of the true branch of the city,
Mis & loge heritier d'Hetrurie;	He shall be set for heir of Etruria;
Son sang antique de longue main tissu,	His ancient blood weaned by a long while,
Fera Florence florir en l'Armoirie.	Shall cause Florence to flourish in the coats of arms.

A reference to the Medici family and their alliance with the Crown of France—Catherine de Medici, wife of Henry II, was Queen of France when Nostradamus lived.

40

Le sang Royal sera si tresmesle,	The Royal blood shall be so much mixed,
Contrainct seront Gaulois de l'-Hesperie;	The French shall be constrained by the Spaniards,
On attendra que terme soit coule,	They shall stay till the term is past,
Et que memoire de la voix soit perie.	And the remembrance of the voice is over.

This merely signifies the alliance between France and Spain by reason of royal intermarriages.

41

Nay sous les umbres & journee nocturne,	Being born in the shadows and nocturnal time,
Sera en regne & bonte souveraine,	He shall be a sovereign in kingdom and bounty,
Fera renaistre son sang de l'antique urne,	He shall cause his blood to be born again from the antique urn,
Renouvellant siecle d'or pour l'ai-rain.	Renewing a golden age instead of a brass one.

A great king, born in a time of darkness, shall reign with a bountiful sceptre and lead the land to a golden age.

42

Mars esleve en son plus haut bef-
froy,
Fera retraire les Allobrox de France,
La gent Lombarde fera si grand
effroy,
A ceux de l'aigle compris sous la
Balance.

Mars being raised in its highest
watch tower,
Shall cause the Allobrox to retreat
from France,
The people of Lombardy shall be
in so great fear
Of those of the eagle, comprehended under Libra.

The Allobrox are those of Savoy, or Italians; retreating from France,
they shall cause great havoc.

43

La grand ruyne des sacrees ne
s'eslongne,
Provence, Naples, Sicile, Seez &
Ponce,
En Germanie, au Rhin & la Co-
logne,
Vexez a mort par tous ceux de Mo-
gonce.

The great ruin of the sacred things
is not far off.
Provence, Naples, Sicily, Sez and
Ponce,
In Germany towards the Rhine
and Cologne,
They shall be vexed to death by
those of Moguntia.

Great damage to sacred monuments of art and religion is predicted.
There will be religious troubles in the regions mentioned.

44

Par mer le rouge sera prins des pyrates,
La paix sera par son moyen trou-
blee;
L'ire & l'aure commettra par sainct
acte,
Au grand pontife sera l'armee dou-
blee.

By sea the red one shall be taken
by pirates,
The peace by that means shall be
troubled,
He shall commit anger by a feigned
act,
The high priest shall have a double army.

A cardinal, taken prisoner by pirates, shall cause a crisis between two
nations and, in order to protect the Pope a double army will be granted
to guard him.

45

Le grand Empire sera tost desole,
Et translate pres d'Arduenne silve;
Les deux bastards pres l'aisne de-
colle,
Et regnera Aeneodarb, nes de
milve.

The great Empire shall soon be
made desolate,
And shall be transplanted near the
Forest of Arden,
The two bastards shall have their
heads cut off by the eldest son,
And he that shall reign shall have
a reddish beard and a hawk's
nose.

The great Empire of Germany shall be broken up and its lands,
especially near the borders of France, will be divided and ruled by many
strangers.

46

Par chappeaux rouges querelles &
nouveaux scismes,
Quand on aura esleu le Sabinois,
On produira contre luy grands
sophismes,
Et sera Rome lesee par Albanois.

By red hats, quarrels and new
schisms,
When the Sabine shall be elected,
Great sophisms shall be produced
against him,
And Rome shall be damaged by the
Albanians.

The cardinals of Rome shall raise great quarrels and schisms when a
man of Sabine (a region near Rome) is chosen Pope. Rome will further
be endangered by the war-like advances of the Albanians.

47

Le grand Arabe marchera bien
avant,
Trahy sera par les Bisantinoise,
L'antique Rhodes luy viendra au
devant,
Et plus grand mal par austre Pannonois.

The great Arab shall proceed a
great way,
He shall be betrayed by the Turks,
Ancient Rhodes shall come to
meet him,
Great evil by a south wind from
Hungary.

The Arab confederacy shall be betrayed by Turkey to the Hungarians.

48

Apres la grande affliction du scep-
    tre,
Deux ennemis par eux seront de-
    faits,
Classe d'Affrique aux Pannonois
    viedra naistre,
Par mer & terre seront horribles
    faits.

After the great afflictions of the
    sceptre,
Two enemies shall be overcome by
    themselves,
A fleet of Africa shall go toward
    the Hungarians,
By sea and land shall be horrid
    facts.

This has relation to the preceding stanza; due to a falling out between
two enemies, the Hungarians will be the gainers.

49

Nul de l'Espagne, mais de l'antique
    France,
Ne sera esleu pour le tremblant na-
    celle;
A l'ennemy sera faicte fiance,
Qui dans son regne sera peste cru-
    elle.

None out of Spain, but of the an-
    cient France,
Shall be elected to govern the tot-
    tering ship.
The enemy shall be trusted,
Who to his kingdom shall be a
    cruel plague.

A Frenchman shall be chosen Pope, and he shall try to save the (ship of)
state of the Church.

50

L'an d'eux les freres du lys seront
    en aage,
L'un d'eux tiendra la grande Ro-
    manis,
Trembler les monts, ouvert Latin
    passage,
Pache marcher contre fort d'Ar-
    menie.

In the year that the brothers of the
    lilies shall be of age,
One of them shall hold the great
    Romany,
The mountains shall tremble, the
    Latin passage shall be opened,
A Pascha shall march against the
    fort of Armenia.

One of France's generals will occupy Rome after crossing the Alps
with a mighty army. At the same time an Oriental ally will assist the
French by marching in from the Near East.

51

La gent de Dace, D'Angleterre & Polonne,	The people of Romania, England, and Poland,
Et de Bohesme seront nouvelle ligue;	And of Bohemia shall make a new league,
Pour passer outre d'Hercules la Colonne,	To go beyond the Pillars of Hercules,
Barcyns, Thyrrens dresser cruelle brigue.	Barcins and Thyrrens shall make a cruel plot.

Romania, England, Poland and Czecho-slovakia shall attempt a united invasion beyond Gibraltar, but will meet with great resistance.

52

Un Roy sera qui donrra l'opposite,	A King shall be, who shall be of the opposite,
Les exilez eslevez sur le Regne,	To the banished persons raised upon the Kingdom,
De sang nager la gent caste hypolite,	The chaste Hippolite nation shall swim in blood,
Et florira long temps soubs telle enseigne.	And shall flourish a great while under such a design.

Hippolytus, a son of Theseus and the Amazon Queen Antiope, lost his life when Poseidon, the Sea God, caused a sea monster to appear, who so frightened his horses that they overturned the chariot and Hippolytus was thrown out and killed.

53

La loy de Sol, & Venus contendans,	The law of the Sun and Venus contending,
Apparopriant l'esprit de prophetie,	Appropriating the spirit of prophecy,
Ne l'un ne l'autre ne seront entendans,	Neither one nor the other shall be heard,
Par Sol tiendra la loy du grand Messie.	By Sol the law of the great Messiah shall subsist.

The forces of light and darkness, struggling for domination over the spirit of man, shall both be superseded by the new law of the great Saviour.

54

Du pont Euxine & la grand Tar-
    taric,
Un Roy sera qui viendra voir la
    Gaule,
Transpercera Alane & l'Armenie,
Et dans Bisance lairra sanglante
    Gaule.

From the Black Sea and great Tar-
    taria,
A King shall come to see France,
He shall go through Alanea and
    Armenia,
And shall leave a bloody rod in
    Constantinople.

An Asiatic power shall come to France, by way of Armenia and Turkey.
Constantinople will be governed by one of his tools.

55

De la felice Arabie contrade,
Naistra puissant de loy Mahome-
    tique,
Vexer l'Espagne, conquester la
    Grenade,
Et plus par mer a la gent Lygus-
    tique.

Out of the country of greater
    Arabia,
Shall be born a strong master of
    Mohammedan law,
Who shall vex Spain and conquer
    Grenada,
And by sea shall come to the
    Italian nation.

From a country of Mohammedan law (Morocco), shall come one who
is a strong master of their law—the sword—who will cause grief to Spain
and conquer her. He shall be friendly to the Italians.

56

Par le trespas du tres vieillard
    pontife,
Sera esleu Romain de bon aage;
Qu'il sera dit que le siege debiffe,
Et long tiendra & de picquant
    courage.

By the death of the very old high
    priest,
Shall be elected a Roman of good
    age,
Of whom it shall be said, that he
    dishonors the seat,
And shall live long, and be of fierce
    courage.

Always deeply concerned with matters of the Church, Nostradamus
here discusses one of the many schisms then current among the clergy.

57

Istra du mont Gaulsier & Aven-
tine,
Qui par le trou advertira l'armee;
Entre deux rocs sera prins le butin,
De Sext. Mansol faillir la renom-
mee.

One shall go out of the mountains
Gaulsier and Aventine,
Who through a hole shall give
notice to the army,
Between two rocks shall be taken
the prize,
And the glory of the Sun shall lose
its renown.

The mountains of Gaulsier and Aventine, two of the seven hills of
Rome, are here used symbolically by Nostradamus. The reference seems
to be to one of the old struggles involving both the army and the church,
in which a treacherous person within the church allows the army to take
over some of its wealth.

58

De l'Aqueduct d'Uticense, Gardoing,
Par la forest & mont inaccessible,
Emmy du pont sera tasche ou po-
ing,
Le chef Nemans qui tant sera terrible.

From the Aqueduct of Uticense
and Gardoing,
Through the forest and inaccessible mountains.
In the middle of the bridge shall
be tied by the wrist,
The chief Nemans, that shall be so
terrible.

An incident in a future war, in France, is here obscurely described. The
various places mentioned are probably points of attack.

59

Au chef Anglois a Nimes trop sejour,
Dever l'Espagne au secours Aeno-
barbe,
Plusieurs mourront par Mars ouvert ce jour,
Quand en Artois faillir estoille en
barbe.

The chief English shall stay too
long at Nismes,
A red-haired man shall go to the
help of Spain,
Many shall die by open war that
day,
When in Artois the star shall fail
in the beard.

A play on words, this appears to have no deep significance, and the
only clear reference concerns a bearded comet, or cometa barbatus as it
is known in Latin.

60

Par teste rase viendra bien mal
  eslire,
Plus que sa charge ne porte passera;
Si grand fureur & rage fera dire,
Qu'a feu & sang tout sexe tran-
  chera.

By a shaven head shall be made
  an ill choice.
That shall go beyond his commis-
  sion,
He shall proceed with so great fury
  and rage,
That he shall put forth both sexes
  to fire and sword.

Six years after the death of Nostradamus, on St. Bartholomew's Day,
August 24, 1572, a massacre of the Huguenots began in Paris. Spurred on
by the high clergy of the Catholic Church, it spread to many provinces
of France, and before it was checked many, many thousands of people
were killed.

61

L'enfant du grand n'estant a sa
  naissance,
Subjuera les hauts monts Apen-
  nins,
Fera trembler tous ceux de la bal-
  ance,
Et des Monts Feurs jusques a Mont
  Cenis.

The child of the great one that was
  not at his birth,
Shall subdue the high Apennine
  Mountains,
Shall make all those under Libra
  to quake,
From Mount Feurs, as far as
  Mount Cenis.

A person, of illegitimate but noble birth, shall attain great heights as
a military figure and shall cause havoc in both France and Italy by reason
of his conquests.

62

Sur les rochers sang on verra pleuvoir,
Sol Orient, Saturn Occidental,
Pres Orgon guerre, a Rome grand
  mal voir,
Nefs parfondrees & prins le Tri-
  dental.

It shall rain blood upon the rocks,
The sun being in the east, and Saturn in the west,
War shall be near Orgon and a
  great evil at Rome,
Ships shall be cast away, and the
  trident be taken.

This quatrain carries on Nostradamus' repeated warnings of a future
war between the Orient and Occident, and the horrible consequences
thereof.

63

De vaine emprinse l'honneur in- deue plainte,	Honor brings a complaint against a vain undertaking,
Gallots errants, par Latins froid, faim vagues;	Galleys shall wander through the Latin seas, cold, hunger, wars,
Non loing du Tybre de sang terre tainte,	Not far from Tiber, the earth shall be dyed with blood,
Et sur humaine seront diverses plagues.	And upon mankind shall be vari- ous plagues.

Tiber is the river on which Rome is situated; and the rest of the verse indicates incidents which shall come to pass.

64

Les assemblez par repos du grand nombre,	The assembly by the rest of the great number
Par terre & mer, conseil contre- mande;	By land and sea shall recall their council.
Pres de l'Autonne, Gennes, Nue de l'ombre,	Near Autonne, Gennes, Cloud of the shadow,
Par champs & villes le chef con- trebande.	In fields and towns, the chief shall be one against another.

Here we have a prognostication of the dissensions among the heads of nations gathered ostensibly for a council of peace.

65

Subit venu l'effrayeur sera grande,	One coming upon a sudden shall cause a great fear,
Des principaux de l'affaire cachez,	To the principals that were hidden and concerned in the business,
Et dame en braise plus ne sera veus,	And the fiery lady shall be seen no more,
Et peu a peu seront les grands fachez.	And little by little the great ones shall be angry.

Consternation shall seize the betrayers of the people when they perceive the growing strength of the masses and their insistence upon a voice in their destiny.

66

Soubs les antiques edifices estaux,
Non eslonguez d'aqueduct ruyne,
De Sol & Luna mont les luysants
  metaux,
Ardante lampe Trajen d'or burine.

Under the ancient edifices of the
  vestals,
Not far from a ruined aqueduct,
Are the bright metals of sun and
  moon,
A burning lamp of Trajan, of en-
  graved gold.

Near a ruined aqueduct will be found ancient articles of gold and silver,
including a Roman lamp of gold, inscribed with Trajan's name.

67

Quand chef Perousse n'osera sa
  tunique,
Sens au couvert tout nud s'expolier,
Seront print sept faict aristocra-
  tique,
Le pere & fils morts par points au
  collier.

When the chief of Perouse shall
  not dare without a tunic,
To expose himself naked in the
  dark,
Seven shall be taken for setting up
  an aristocracy,
The father and son shall die by
  pricks in the collar.

Perugia is a city in Italy, which will be the seat of an unsuccessful attempt at setting up a revolution.

68

Dans le Danube & du Rhin viendra
  boire,
Le grand Chameau, ne s'en repen-
  tira;
Trembler du Rhosne & plus fort
  ceux de Loire,
Et pres des Alpes Coq les ruynera.

In the Danube and Rhine shall
  come to drink,
The great camel and shall not repent,
The Rhone shall tremble and more
  those of Loire,
And near the Alps the Cock shall
  ruin him.

A Turkish invasion shall reach Germany as far as the Rhine and
Danube. France shall be in danger for a while, but shall finally triumph
in a battle near the Alps.

69

Plus ne sera le grand en faux sommeil,
L'inquietude viendra prendre repos;
Dresser phalange d'or, azur & vermeil,
Subjuger Affrique la ronger jusque aux os.

The great one shall be no more in a false sleep,
The restlessness shall take rest,
He shall raise an army of gold and azure
He shall conquer Africa and gnaw it to the bone.

A great nation shall awake from its false sense of security and isolationism, and raise an immense amount of gold and a great navy. With its new-found strength it will invade the African shore.

70

Les regions suvjettes a la Balance,
Feront trembler les monts par grande guerre;
Captif tout sexe deu & toute Bisance,
Qu'on criera a l'aube terre a terre.

The regions under the sign of Libra,
Shall make the mountains quake with great war,
Slaves of all sexes, with all Constantinople,
So that in the dawn, they shall cry from land to land.

The European nations shall embark on a universal war, with the complete destruction of Constantinople promised.

71

Par la fureur d'un qui attendra l'eau,
Par la grand rage tout l'exercite esmeu,
Charge de nobles a dix-septe batteaux,
Au long du Rhosne tard messager venu.

By the fury of one looking forward to the water,
By his great rage the whole army shall be troubled,
There shall be seventeen boats full of noblemen,
Along the Rhone the messenger shall come too late.

The fury and rage of an invader driving his legions toward English shores, shall result in a great destruction of navies.

72

Pour le plaisir d'edict voluptueux,
On meslera la poison dans la loy,
Venus sera en cours si vertueux,
Qu obsuquera du Soleil tout aloy.

By the pleasure of a voluptuous
  edict,
The poison shall be mixed with the
  law,
Venus shall be in so great request,
That it shall darken all the alloy
  of the sun.

A voluptuous pleasure-loving era shall be made possible by corrupt laws.
Sin will prevail, and piety shall be obscured.

73

Persecutee de Dieu sera l'Eglise,
Et les saints temples seront expo-
  liez;
L'enfant la mere mettra nud en
  chemise,
Seront Arabes aux Polons railez.

The church of God shall be persecuted,
And the holy temples shall be
  spoiled,
The child shall turn out his mother
  nude in her shirt,
Arabians shall agree with Polo-
  nians.

The Catholic Church shall be persecuted and its temples despoiled.
Anti-Semitism shall be rampant among the Arabs and Poles.

74

De sang Troy en naistra coeur Ger-
  manique,
Qui de viendra en si haute puissance,
Hors chassera gent estrange Arabique,
Tournant l'Eglise en pristine pre-
  eminence.

Of Trojan blood shall be born a
  German heart,
Who shall attain to so high a
  power,
That he shall drive away the East-
  ern people,
Restoring the church to pristine
  pre-eminence.

A German of great courage shall attain great eminence by destroying
the influence of Oriental power and re-establishing the Church.

75

Montera haut sur le bien plus a dextre,
Demourra assis sur la pierre carree;
Vers le midy pose a sa fenestre,
Baston tortu en main bouchee serree.

Mounting high on the good, more to the right,
He shall remain sitting upon the square stone,
Towards the South, being set on the left hand,
A crooked stick in his hand and his mouth shut.

This predicts and describes the hectic sessions of the National Assembly during the French Revolution, where the parties of the left and the right contended for the power.

76

En lieu libere tendra son pavillon,
Et ne voudra en citez prendre place;
Aix, Carpen, l'Isle, Volce, Mont Cavaillon
Par tout les lieux abolira la trasse.

He shall pitch his tent in the open air,
Refusing to lodge in the city,
Aix, Carpentres, Lille, Volce, Mont Cavaillon,
In those places, he shall abolish his trace.

All the places mentioned in this stanza are in Provence. The event referred to has no current interest.

77

Tous les degrez d'honneur Ecclesiastique,
Seront changez en Dial Quirinal;
En Martial Quirinal flaminique,
Puis un Roy de France le rendra Vulcanal.

All the degrees of Ecclesiastical honor
Shall be changed into a Quirinal Dial,
Into Martial Quirinal, Flaminus,
After that, a King of France shall make it Vulcanal.

This is another discussion of clerical affairs in the Catholic Church in Nostradamus' time.

78

Les deux unis ne tiendront longue- ment.	The two united shall not hold long,
Et dans treze ans au Barbare Sat- trappe;	Within thirteen years to the Bar- barian Satrap,
Aux deux costez feront tel perde- ment,	They shall cause such loss on both sides,
Qu'un benira la barque & sa cappe.	That one shall bless the boat and its covering.

Adolf Hitler and Von Hindenburg first became associated (historically) in 1920, the year that the Nazi Party was founded. Thirteen years later, just prior to Hindenburg's death, Hitler assumed full power, resulting in the ultimate ruin and destruction of the German State.

79

Le sacree pompe veindra baisse les aisles	The sacred pomp shall bow down her wings,
Par la venue du grand Legislateur;	At the coming of the great law giver,
Humble haussera, vexera les re- belles,	He shall raise the humble and vex the rebellious,
Naistra sur terre aucun semulateur.	No emulator of his shall be born.

The advent of Abraham Lincoln is plainly prophesied here.

80

L'Ogmion grand Bisance approch- era,	The Ogmion shall come near great Constantinople,
Chasses sera la Barbarique Ligue,	And shall expel the Barbarian League,
Des deux loix l'une l'unique lasch- era,	Of the two laws, the wicked one shall yield,
Barbare & France en perpetuelle brigue.	The Barbarian, and the French shall be in perpetual friction.

A King of France shall go to Constantinople, and shall break the Barbarian League; that is, Christian principles shall triumph over the Mohammedan law.

81

L'Oyseau Royal sur la cite Solaire,
Sept mois devant fera nocturne augure,
Mur d'Orient cherra tonnerre esclaire,
Sept jours aux portes les ennemis a l'heure,

The Royal Bird upon the city of the Sun,
Seven months together shall make a nocturnal augury,
The Eastern wall shall fall, the lightning shall shine,
Then the enemies shall be at the gate for seven days.

The Royal Bird (eagle) shall fly for many months over an Eastern city. When it unlooses its most deadly weapon (which shines with the brilliance of lightning) the Eastern wall will crumble.

82

Au conclud pache hors de la forteresse,
Ne sortira celuy en desespoir mis,
Quand ceux d'Arbois, de Langres, contre Bresse,
Auront monts Dolle bouscade d'ennemis.

On the conclusion of the pact made, out of the fortress,
Shall not come he that was in despair,
When those of Arbois, of Langres, against Brescia,
Shall put in Dolle an ambuschade of foes.

During a war a truce will be declared, but the commander of the besieged city shall refuse its terms.

83

Ceux qui auront entrepris subvertir,
Nompareil regne puissant & invincible,
Feront par fraude, nuicts trois advertis
Quand le plus grand a table lire Bible.

Those that shall have undertaken to subvert,
The kingdom that has no equal in power and victories,
Shall cause by fraud, notice to be given for three nights together
When the greatest shall be reading a Bible at the table.

A subversive movement within a great nation shall have its inception on a Sunday night.

84

Naistra du gouphre & cite emme-
suree,
Nay de parens obscurs & tene-
breux;
Quand la puissance du grand Roy
reveres,
Voudre destruire par Rouen &
Eureux.

One shall be born out of the gulf
and immeasurable city,
Born of parents obscure and dark,
Who, by means of Rouen and Eureux,
Will go about to destroy the power
of the great King.

A person of obscure and dark parentage is predestined to destroy the
power of a great King.

85

Par les Sueves & lieux circonvoi-
sins,
Seront en guerre pour cause des
neuus.
Gamp marins locustes & cousing,
Du Leman fautes seront bien des-
nuees.

Through Switzerland and the
neighboring places,
By reason of the clouds shall fall
to war.
The lobsters, locusts, and gnats,
The fault of Geneva shall appear
very naked,

The failure of the League of Nations and the advent of war are
prophesied.

86

Par les deux testes & trois bras se-
parez,
La cite grande par eau sera vexes,
Des grandes d'entr'aux par exil
esgarez,
Par teste Perse, Bisance fort
pressee.

Divided in two heads and parted
in three arms,
The great city shall be troubled
with waters,
Some great ones among them scattered by banishment,
By a Persian head, Turkey shall be
much oppressed.

Paris will be threatened by an inundation, and the great ones will be
forced to flee; during the same period there will be much unrest in the East.

87

L'an que Saturne sera hors de serv-
age,
Au franc terroir sera d'eau inonde;
De sang Troyen sera son mariage,
Et sera seur d'Espagnol circonder.

In the year that Saturn out of servi-
tude,
In the free country shall be
drowned by water,
With Trojan blood his marriage
shall be,
And he surely shall be surrounded
by Spaniards.

The term "Trojan blood" refers to the French Nation. The meaning
to be gathered from this stanza seems to be that, at the time of a great
flood in France, a notable marriage will be made which will endanger
French and Spanish relations.

88

Sur le sablon par un hydeux deluge,
Des autres mers trouve monstre
marin;
Proche du lieu sera fait un refuge,
Tenant Savone esclave de Turin.

Upon the sand through a hideous
deluge
Of other seas, shall be found a sea
monster,
Near to that place shall be made
a sanctuary,
Which shall make Savoy a slave to
Turin.

Warfare between two Italian political factions is here predicted.

89

Dedans Hongrie par Boheme, Na-
varre,
Et par bannieres feintes seditious;
Par fleurs de lys pays portant la
barre,
Contre Orleans fera esmotions.

In Hungaria, through Bohemia and
Navarre,
And by banners feigned seditious,
By Fleur de Lys, peace that carries
the bar,
Against Orleans shall make com-
motions.

The first two lines of this quatrain foretold the religious troubles that
were to happen in Hungaria, Bohemia and Navarre. The last two tell of
the Prince of Condé, whose coat of arms bears the flower and the bar, who
seized Orleans for the Protestant party.

90

Dans les Cyclades, en Corinthe, &
  Larisse,
Dedans Sparte tout le Peloponese;
Si grand famine, peste, par faux
  connisse,
Neuf mois tiendra & tout le cher-
  rouesse.

In the Cyclades, in Corinth and
  Larissa,
In Sparta, and all the Pelopon-
  nesus,
Shall be so great a famine and
  plague
To last nine months in the south-
  ern peninsula.

All the Greek regions mentioned shall be afflicted with famine and
plague.

91

Au grand marche qu'on dit des
  mesongers,
De tout torrent & champ Athe-
  nien,
Seront surprins par les chevaux
  legers,
Par Albanois, Mars, Leo, Sat, au
  versien.

In the great market called of the
  liars,
Which is all torrent and Athenian field,
They shall be surprised by the light
  horses,
Of the Albanese, Mars in Leo, Saturn in Aquarius.

Athens shall be overrun by the Nordics, here called Albanese by Nostradamus, after albus, Latin for white or blond.

92

Apres le siege tenu dix sept ans,
Cinq changeront en tel revolu
  terme,
Puis sera l'un esleu de mesme
  temps,
Qui des Romains ne sera trop con-
  forme.

After the seat possessed seventeen
  years,
Five shall change in such a space
  of time,
After that, one shall be elected at
  the same time,
Who shall not be very conformable
  to the Romans.

A Pope shall hold office for seventeen years. After that, within the
space of seventeen years, five others shall be elected; and finally, a Pope
shall be chosen who will not be approved by the Roman Clergy.

93

Sous le terroir de rond globe lu-
naire,
Lors que sera dominateur Mercure,
L'isle d'Escosse sera un luminaire,
Qui les Anglois mettra a deconfi-
ture.

Under the territory of the round
lunary globe,
When Mercury shall be lord of the
ascendant,
The Island of Scotland shall make
a luminary,
That shall put the English to a
revolution.

Out of Scotland shall come a great light that will bring about a revolution in England.

94

Translatera en la grand Germanie,
Brabant & Flandres, Gand, Bruges,
& Bologne;
La treue sainte le grand duc d'Ar-
menie.
Assaillira Vienne & la Cologne.

He shall translate into the Great
Germany,
Brabant, Flanders, Gand, Bruges
and Bullen,
The truce feigned, the great Duke
of Armenia,
Shall assault Vienna and Cologne.

Germany will attempt to assimilate Belgium and Holland, while a
feigned truce with the great Eastern Power will be broken, and the end
will be the destruction of Germany itself.

95

Nautique rame invitera les umbres
Du grand Empire, lors viendra con-
citer;
La mer Egee des lignes les en-
combres,
Empeschant l'onde Tyrrene de
floter.

The nautical branch shall invite
the shadows,
Of the great Empire, then it shall
come to stir,
The Aegean Sea, with lines of en-
cumbers,
Hindering the Tyrrenian Sea to
roll.

The navy of a great Empire shall take the lead in a rebellion centering
in the Mediterranean.

96

Sur le milieu du grand monde la rose,	In the middle of the great world shall be the rose,
Pour nouveaux faits sang public espandu,	For new deeds, blood shall be publicly spilt,
A dire vray on aura bouche close,	To say the truth, every one shall close his mouth,
Lors au besoin viendra tard l'attendu.	Then at the time will be the one long looked for.

Nostradamus predicts the coming of a great world leader and, by a simple play on words as expressed in the first line, we have his name: rose and world (welt, in German) combine to make Roosevelt.

97

Le nay difforme par horreur suffoque,	The deformed shall through horror be suffocated,
Dans la cite du grand Roy habitable,	In the habitable city of the great King.
L'edit severe des captifs rovoque,	The severe edict against the banished shall be revoked,
Gresle & tonnerre Condon inestimable.	Hail and thunder shall do inestimable harm at Condon.

Condon is a city in old France, the rest is obvious.

98

A quarante-huit degre climatterique,	At the climacterical degree of eight and forty,
Afin de Cancer si grande secheresse,	At the end of Cancer, shall be such a drought,
Poisson en mer, fleuve, lac cuit hectique,	That fish in the sea, river, and lake shall be boiled hectic,
Bearn, Bigorre par feu ciel en detresse.	Bearn and Bigorre by heavenly fire shall be in distress.

Nostradamus here foretells of a period of great heat and drought, mostly in provinces in France.

99

Milan, Ferrare, Turin & Aquillee,
Capne, Brundis vexez par gent Cel-
tique,
Par le Lyon a Phalange aquilee,
Quand Rome aura le chef vieux
Britannique.

Milan, Ferrara, Turin and Aquilia,
Capne, Brundis, shall be vexed by
the French,
By the Lion and Troop of Aquelia,
When Rome shall have as chief,
old Britannia.

England shall conquer Italy assisted by the French Army, and the military Governor of Rome shall be an Englishman.

100

Le boute-feu par son feu attrape,
De feu du ciel par Tarcas & Co-
minge,
Foix, Aux, Mazeres, haut vieillard
eschappe,
Par ceux de Hasse, des Saxons &
Turinge.

The arsonist shall be overtaken by
his own fire,
Heavenly fire shall fall at Tartas
and Cominge,
Foix, Auch, Mazere, a tall old man
shall escape,
By means of those of Hesse, Saxony, and Thuringia.

The ones who set the world on fire, shall be overtaken by stern justice. The Germans shall aid in the escape of one of the guilty ones.

1

Au tour des Monts Pyrenees grand amas, De gent estrange, secourir Roy nouveau; Pres de Garonne du grand temple du Mas, Un Romain chef le craindra dedans l'eau.	About the Pyrenean Mountains there shall be a great gathering Of strange nations to succour a new King, Near Garonne and the great temple of the Maas, A Roman captain shall fear him in the water.

Assistance by a group of nations shall raise a new ruler to power near the Pyrenees Mountains. A Roman leader shall fear this new threat.

2

En l'an cinq cens octante plus & moins, On attend le siecle bien estrange; En l'an sept cens & trois (cieus en testmoins) Que plusieurs regnes un a cinq feront change.	In the year five hundred eighty more or less, There shall be a strange age, In the year seven hundred and three (witness heaven) Many kingdoms, one to five shall be changed.

Nostradamus commences his count of time from A. D. 325, the date of the Council of Nicaea. In the above stanza, by using the figure 325 as a key, we find that (1)589 added to it, gives us the date 1914, one of the most important dates in the history of the world. Similarly, (1)703 added to 325 gives us 2028, in which year, Nostradamus tells us, there will be a complete change in the lineup of nations.

3

Fleuve qu'esprouve le nouveau nay Celtique,	The river that makes trial of the new-born Celtic,
Sera en grande de l'Empire discorde;	Shall be at great variance with the Empire,
Le jeune prince par gent Ecclesiastique,	The young prince shall be an Ecclesiastical person,
Ostera le sceptre coronal de concorde.	And have his sceptre taken off, and the crown of concord.

The Rhine River shall be the scene of trial for a new Prince of France.

4

Le Celtique fleuve changera de rivage,	The river Rhine shall change her shores,
Plus ne tiendra la cite d'Agripine;	It shall touch no more the city of Cologne,
Tout trasmue ormis le vieil langage,	All shall be transformed, except the language,
Saturne, Leo, Mars, Cancer en rapine.	Saturn, Leo, Mars, Cancer in rapine.

The borders of Germany shall change so as to no longer include Cologne. A complete upheaval will take place in Germany after a period of great unrest.

5

Si grand famine par une pestifere,	So great a famine with a plague,
Par pluye longue le long du Pole Artique;	Through a long rain shall come along the Arctic Pole,
Samarobryn cent lieux de l'hemisphere,	Samarobryn a hundred leagues from the hemisphere,
Vivront sans loy, exempt de politique.	Shall live without law, exempt from politics.

From the northern hemisphere shall come a devastating plague, followed by a period of anarchy throughout the affected countries.

6

Apparoistra vers le Septentrion,
Non loing de Cancer l'estoille che-
velue;
Suse, Sienne, Boece, Eretrion,
Mourra de Rome grand, la nuit
disperue.

Towards the North shall appear,
Not far from Cancer, a blazing star,
Suza, Sienna, Boetia, Eretrion,
There shall die at Rome a great
man, the night being past.

A light in the sky will appear, and a powerful Italian, unable to live in its glare, shall die.

7

Norvege & Dace, & l'isle Britàn-
nique,
Par les unis freres seront vexees;
Le chef Romain issu du sang Gal-
lique,
Et les copis aux forest repoulsees.

Norway and Dacia, and the British
Island,
Shall be vexed by the brothers
united,
The Roman Captain issued from
French blood,
His forces shall be beaten back to
the forest.

A union of nations will beat back and conquer their common enemy.

8

Ceux qui estoient en regne pour
scavoir,
Au Royal change deviendront a
pouvris,
Uns exilez sans appuy, or n'auoir,
Lettres & lettres ne seront a grand
pris.

Those that were in esteem for their
learning,
Upon the change of a King will
become poor,
Some banished, without help, having no gold,
Learned and learning shall not be
much valued.

A period of oppression against scholars and scientists shall arise.

9

Aux temples saints seront faits grands scandales,	To the holy temples shall be done much scandals,
Comptez seront par honneur & louanges,	That shall be accounted for honors and praises,
D'un que l'on graue d'argent, d'or les medalles,	By one, whose medals are graven in gold and silver,
La fin sera en tourmens bien estranges.	The end of it shall be in very strange torments.

As an adherent of the Roman Catholic Church, Nostradamus could only look with disapproval on the Protestant party under the leadership of the future Henry IV. As the King of Navarre, he had medals and money stamped with his image for use in the holy temples and cathedrals. The last line proved prophetic, when on St. Bartholomew's Day, August 24, 1572, the Protestant Massacre occurred.

10

Un peu de temps les temples de couleurs,	Within a little while the temples of the colours,
De blanc & noir les deux entremeslee;	White and black shall be intermixt,
Rouges & jaunes leur embleront les leurs,	Red and yellow shall take away their colours,
Sang, terre, peste, faim, feu, d'eau affolce.	Blood, earth, plague, famine, fire, water shall destroy them.

After a period of much travail all the races of the world shall lose their prejudices and be as one.

11

Des sept rameaux a trois seront reduits,	The seven branches shall be reduced to three,
Les plus aisnez seront surprins par mort,	The eldest shall be surprised by death,
Fratricider les deux seront seduits,	Two shall be said to kill their brothers,
Les conjures en dormant seront morts.	The conspirators shall be killed being asleep.

Seven brothers shall be reduced to three; of those one shall die suddenly and it will be suspected that he was killed by the other two. And they in turn shall meet violent deaths.

12

Dresser copies pour monter a l'Empire,
Du Vatican le sang Royal tiendra;
Flamans, Anglois, Espaigne aspire,
Contre l'Italie & France contendre.

To raise an army, to ascend the Empire,
Of the Vatican, the Royal blood shall endeavor,
Flemings, English, Spain shall aspire,
And shall contend against Italy and France.

There shall be a great commotion among the nations of Europe over the election of a Pope.

13

Un dubieux ne viendra loing du regne,
La plus grand part le voudra soustenir,
Un captiole ne voudra point qu'il regne,
Sa grande chaire ne pourra maintenir.

A doubtful man shall not come far from the reign,
The greatest part will uphold him,
A capitol will not consent that he should reign,
His great chair he shall not be able to maintain.

Napoleon, after great successes, was finally forced to abdicate.

14

Loing de sa terre roy perdra la bataille,
Prompt eschappe poursuivy suyuant prins,
Ignare prins soubs la doree maille,
Soubs faint habit & l'ennemy surprins.

Far from his country the king shall lose a battle,
Nimble, escaped, followed, following taken,
Ignorantly taken under the gilded coat of mail,
Under a feigned habit the enemy taken.

The Battle of Moscow was the turning point in the career of Napoleon; it was the beginning of the end.

15

Dessous la tombe sera trouve le prince,
Qu'aura le pris par dessus Nuremberg;
L'Espagnol Roy en Capricorn mince,
Feinct & trahy par le grand Vitemberg.

Under the tomb shall be found the prince,
That shall have a price above Nuremberg.
That Spanish King in Capricorn shall be thine,
Deceived and betrayed by the great Lutheran.

A prince shall commit suicide thus foiling the dictates of the Nuremberg judges. There will be a betrayal of a powerful Spaniard by a German ruler.

16

Ce que ravy sera du jeune Milve,
Par les Normans de France & Picardie;
Les noirs du temple du lieu Negrisilve,
Feront aux berg & feu de Lombardie.

That which shall be taken from the young Kite,
By the Normans of France and Picardy,
The black ones of the temple of the Black Forest,
Shall make a rendezvous and a fire in Lombardy.

The Normans shall succeed in overthrowing a young arrogant Prince, and to celebrate their victory they will build a temple in the Black Forest.

17

Apres les livres bruslez les asiniers,
Constraints seront changer habits divers;
Les Saturnins bruslez par les musniers,
Hors la plus part qui ne sera musniers.

After the books shall be burnt, the asses,
Shall be compelled several times to change their clothes,
The Saturnins shall be burnt by the millers,
Except the greater part, that shall not be discovered.

The millers (unlearned persons) shall attempt to annihilate the culture of the Saturnins (studious people) even to the wholesale burning of books. This prophecy was fulfilled in its entirety when the Nazis publicly banned and burned all books that were against their ideology.

18

| Par les physiques le grand Roy delaisse, | The great King being forsaken by the physician, |

Par les physiques le grand Roy de-
laisse,
Par fort non art ne l'Ebrieu est en
vie;
Luy & son genre au regne haut
pousse,
Grace donne a gent qui Christ envie.

The great King being forsaken by
the physician,
Shall be kept alive by power, and
not by the art of a Hebrew,
He, and his kindred shall be put at
the top of the kingdom,
Grace shall be given to a people
that envieth Christ.

A sick King, deserted by his physician, shall be cured by the help of
a Jew, and as a token of the King's gratitude, the Jews of that nation will
enjoy great privileges.

19

La vray flamme engloutira la dame,
Que voudra mettre les innocens a
feu,
Pres de l'assaut l'excercite s'en-
flamme,
Quand dans Seville monstre en
boeuf sera veu.

The true flame shall swallow up
the lady,
That went about to burn the guilt-
less,
Before the assault the army shall be
encouraged,
When in Seville, a monster like an
ox shall be seen.

A monster shall be seen in Seville, similar to the ancient Minotaur
who demanded a tribute of innocent children.

20

L'union feinte sera peu de duree,
Des uns changes reformez la plus-
part,
Dans les caisseaux sera gent en-
dures,
Lors aura Rome un nouveau leo-
part.

The feigned union shall not last
long,
Some shall be changed, others for
the most part reformed,
In the ships people shall be penned
up,
Then shall Rome have a new leopard.

After a short period of peace, there will again be trouble among the
clerical leaders of Rome, and a new Pope will come into power.

21

Quand ceux de Pole Artique unis ensemble,	When those of the Arctic Pole shall be united together,
En Orient grand effrayeur & crainte,	There shall be in the East, great fear and trembling,
Esleu nouveau soustenu le grand temple,	One shall be newly elected, that shall bear the brunt,
Rodes, Bisance de sang Barbare taints.	Rhodes, Constantinople, shall be dyed with Barbarian blood.

The people of northern Europe shall unite against those of the East. The actual battle shall take place near Turkey.

22

Dedans la terre du grand temple celique,	Within the ground of the great celestial temple,
Nepueu a Londres par paix faincte meurtry,	A nephew at London by a feigned peace shall be murdered,
La barque alors deviendra scismatique,	The boat at that time shall become schismatical,
Liberte faincte sera au corne & cry.	A feigned liberty shall be with hue and cry.

In St. Paul's Cathedral, London, the murdered body of a famous person will be found. It will cause great dissension among the churchmen since one of them will be suspected of the crime.

23

D'esprit de Roy munisememens descriees,	Despite the King, the coin will be brought lower,
Et seront peuples esmeus contre leur Roy,	The people shall rise against their King,
Paix, fait nouveau, sainctes loix empirees.	Peace being made, holy laws made worse,
Rapis onc fut en si tresdur arroy.	Paris was never in such a great disorder.

This is a remarkable account of the French Revolution, in proper chronological order—collapse of the financial structure, rising of the people, abandonment of religion and Paris in disorder.

24

Mars & le Sceptre se trouvera con-
  jont,
Dessous Cancer calamiteuse guerre;
Un peu apres sera nouveau Roy
  oingt,
Qui par long temps pacifiera la
  terre.

Mars and the Sceptre, being con-
  joined together,
Under Cancer shall be a calamitous war,
A little while after a new King
  shall be anointed,
Who, for a long time, shall pacify
  the earth.

Nostradamus here speaks of a constellation called the Sceptre. Looking
far into the future, he foretells of a time when this constellation shall be
in conjunction with Mars, and the terrible war that will break out under
this influence. And out of the debacle there will arise a new world leader
and peace will reign for a long time afterward.

25

Par Mars constraire sera la Monarchie,
Du grand pescheur en trouble ruy-
  neux;
Jeune, noire, rouge prendra la hier-
  archie,
Les proditeurs iront jour bruyneux.

By Mars contrary shall the monarchy.
Of the great fisherman, be brought
  into ruinous trouble,
A young, black red shall possess
  himself of the hierarchy,
The traitors shall undertake it on
  a misty day.

The Vatican shall be in a weakened position due to a ruinous war,
and a young cardinal, backed by opponents of the reigning hierarchy, shall
be made Pope.

26

Quartre ans le siege quelque peu
  bien tiendra,
Un surviendra libidineux de vie,
Ravenne & Pise, Veronne sou-
  stiendront,
Pour eslever la croix du Pape envie.

Four years he shall keep the Papal
  seat pretty well,
Then shall succeed one of a libidinous life,
Ravenna, Pisa, shall take Verona's
  part,
To raise up the Pope's cross to life.

A continuation of the preceding stanza, this predicts that the usurper
will reign four years, being then succeeded by a notorious sensualist, whose
main support shall come from those in the above-mentioned cities.

27

Dedans les isles de cinq fleuves a un,	In the islands from five rivers to one,
Par le croissant du grand Chyren Selin;	By the increase of the great emperor Henry,
Par les bruynes de l'air fureur de l'un,	By the frost of the air and the fury of one,
Six eschappez, cachez fardeaux de lyn.	Six shall escape, hidden within bundles of flax.

Again we have a play on words: Chyren meaning Henry, and Selin meaning King. Just what king or ruler Nostradamus refers to is not clear, and it is quite possible that he means by this obscurity to indicate some future world leader.

28

Le grand Celtique entrera dedans Rome,	The great Celtique shall enter into Rome,
Menant amas d'exilez & bannis;	Leading with him a great number of banished men,
Le grand pasteur mettra a mort tout homme	The great shepherd shall put to death every man,
Qui pour le Coq estoit aux Alpes unis.	That was united for the Cock, near the Alps.

The campaign of Napoleon, which culminated in the French victory over Italy, is foretold.

29

La vefue saincte entendant les nouvelles,	The holy widow hearing the news,
De ses rameaux mis en perplex & trouble,	Of her branches put in perplexity or trouble,
Qui sera duict appraiser les querelles,	That shall be skillful in appeasing of quarrels,
Par son pourchas des razes fera comble.	By his purchase shall make a heap of shaven heads.

Nostradamus here discusses a time of interregnum—the period after the death of a Pope until a new one is elected—and refers to the various parts of the Church in his usual obscure manner: by "the holy widow" he means the City of Rome; the "branches" are the clergymen; and the "shaven heads" refer to priests.

30

Par l'apparence de faincte sainctete,
Sera trahy aux ennemis le siege,
Nuict qu'on coidoit dormir en seu-
   rete,
Pres de Braban marcheront ceux du
   Liege.

By the appearance of a feigned
   holiness,
The siege shall be betrayed to the
   enemies,
In a night that everyone thought
   to be secure,
Near Brabant shall march those of
   Liege.

This appears to be a description of some trouble which occurred between the two regions mentioned.

31

Roy trouvera ce qu'il desiroit tant,
Quand le Prelat sera reprins a tort;
Responce au Duc le rendra mal
   content,
Qui dans Milan mettra plusieurs
   a mort.

A King shall find what he so much
   longed for,
When a Prelate shall be censured
   wrongfully,
His answer to the Duke will make
   him discontented,
Who in Milan shall put many to
   death.

Nostradamus discusses one of the many involved quarrels between the State and the Church.

32

Par trahisons de verges a mort
   battu,
Puis surmonte sera par son de-
   sordre;
Conseil frivole au grand captif
   sentu,
Nez par fureur quand Berich
   viendra mordre.

By treason one shall be beaten
   with rods to death,
Then the traitor shall be overcome
   by his disorder,
The great prisoner shall try a frivolous counsel,
When Berich shall bite another's
   nose through anger.

"When traitors fall out amongst themselves, honest men rejoice." Such is the sense of this stanza.

33

Sa main derniere par Alus sanguinaire,	His last hand bloody through all U. S.
Ne se pourra plus la mer garentir;	Shall not save him by sea,
Entre deux fleuves craindre main militaire,	Between two rivers he shall fear the military hand,
Le noir l'ireux le fera repentir.	The black and wrathful one shall be repentant.

A prediction showing the role of the U. S. in the final phase of the career of Mussolini seems to be indicated here.

34

De feu volant la machination,	The contraption of flying fire,
Viendra troubler au grand chef assiegez;	Shall trouble so much the captain of the besieged,
Dedans sera telle sedition,	And within shall be so much rioting,
Qu'en desespoir seront les profligez.	That the besieged shall be in despair.

Although Nostradamus could only dimly sense the import of his prophetic words, we now know all too well the destruction and terror wrought by the airborne weapons described in this quatrain.

35

Pres de Rion & proche Blanchelaine,	Near Rion and towards Blanchelaine,
Aries, Taurus, Cancer, Leo, la Viergge,	Aries, Taurus, Cancer, Leo, Virgo,
Mars, Jupiter, les Sol ardra grand plaine,	Mars, Jupiter, the Sun shall burn a great plain,
Bois & cites lettres cachez au cierge.	Woods and cities, letters hidden in a wax candle.

The first line of this verse is anagrammatic—the word "rion," spelled backwards, becomes noir, black; "blanche" contains the letters blanc, meaning white. Therefore, we must surmise that when the above-mentioned constellations are in conjunction there will be a fire of almost worldwide proportions, the aftermath of which will be a definite division in the world of "black" and "white."

36

Ne bien ne mal par bataille ter- restre, Ne parviendra aux confins de Pe- rouse, Rebeller Pise, Florence voir mal estre, Roy nuict blesse sur mulet a noire housse.	Neither good nor evil by a loud fight, Shall reach to the borders of Pe- rusia, Pisa shall rebel, Florence shall be in a bad way, A King being on his mule shall be wounded in the darkness.

All the cities named are in Italy; the balance should be easy to decipher.

37

L'oeuvre ancienne se parachevera, Du toict cherra sur la grand mal ruyne, Innocent faict mort on accusera, Nocent cache, taillis a la bruyne.	The ancient work shall be finished, From the house tops shall fall great misfortunes, The innocent in fact, shall be ac- cused after his death, The guilty shall be hidden in a wood in misty weather.

King Louis XVI attempted to escape from the rebels, but was apprehended in a forest hiding-place.

38

Aux profilgez de paix les ennemis, Apres avoir l'Italie supperee; Noir sanguinaire, rouge sera com- mis, Feu sang verser, eau de sang col- oree.	To the vanquished the enemies of peace, After they shall have overcome Italy, A bloody Black One shall be com- mitted, Fire and blood shall be discharged, and water coloured with blood.

This is the prognostication of the rape of Italy by the Fascists under the
leadership of Mussolini.

39

L'enfant du regne par paternelle prince,	The child of the kingdom through his father's imprisonment,
Expolie sera pour delivrer;	Shall be deprived of his kingdom for the delivering of his father,
Aupres du Lac Trasimen l'azur prinse,	Near the Lake Trasimene shall be taken in a tower,
La trope hostage pour trop fort s'enyurer.	The troop that was in hostage being drunk.

Lake Trasimene, where Hannibal fought a famous battle with the Romans, is the only clear expression in this otherwise obscurely worded quatrain.

40

Grand de Magonce pour grand soif estaindre,	The great one of Mayence to quench a great thirst,
Sera prive de la grand dignite;	Shall be deprived of his high dignity,
Ceux de Cologne si fort le viendront plaindre,	Those of Cologne shall mourn him so much,
Que le Grand Groppe au Ryn sera jette.	That the Great Groppe shall be thrown into the Rhine.

The German populace shall feel the loss of their great prestige, and shall mourn the loss of their leader, Schickel-GROPPE (Hitler), even to the point of making his name synonymous with the German National Symbol, the River Rhine.

41

Le second chef du regne Dannemarc,	The second head of the Kingdom of Denmark,
Par ceux de Frise & l'isle Britannique,	By those of Holland, and the British Isles,
Fera despendre plus de cent mille marc,	Shall cause to be spent over 100 thousand marks,
Vain exploiter voyage en Italique.	Vainly trying to find a way into Italy.

A signification that Danish, Dutch, and English forces will attempt a costly and ultimately futile invasion of Italy.

42

A l'Ogmyon sera laisse le regne,
Du grand Selin qui plus sera de
faict,
Par l'Italie estendra son enseigne,
Regne sera par prudent contrefait.

Unto l'Ogmion shall be left the
kingdom,
Of great Selyn, who shall do more
than the rest,
Through Italy he shall spread his
ensigns,
He shall govern by prudent for-
geries.

A King of France shall dictate to the Vatican and exert great influence throughout Italy.

43

Long temps sera sans estre habitee,
Ou Seine & Marne autour vient
arrouser,
De la Tamise & martiaux tentee,
Deceus les gardes en evidant re-
pousser.

For a long time shall be unin-
habited
Where the Seine and Marne come
to water about,
From the Thames and martial
people, they shall attempt
To deceive the guards into thinking to resist.

Because of traitors within her gates ruin will fall upon Paris, and the flight of the inhabitants will result in an almost deserted city.

44

De nuict par Nantes l'iris apparoistra,
Des Arcs Marins susciteront la
pluye,
Arabique Goulfre grand classe parfondra,
Un monstre en Saxe naistra d'ours
& truye.

By night in Nantes the rainbow
shall appear,
Arches of the Sea shall cause rain,
The Arabian Gulf shall drown a
great fleet,
A monster shall be in Saxony from
a bear and a sow.

Incendiary bombs shall light up the nights in France; and in Germany, the British shall cause great destruction.

45

Le gouverneur du Regne bien sca- vant, Ne consentir voulant au fait Royal, Mellile classe par le contraire vent, Le remettra a son plus desloyal.	The governor of the Kingdom be- ing wise, Shall not consent to the King's will He shall ponder setting out a fleet by the contrary wind, Which he shall put into the hands of the most disloyal.

The reference here is obviously to the Battle of Trafalgar, that decisive naval victory of the British over the French and Spanish fleets; there is also an indication of the dissension between Napoleon and Admiral Ville-neuve over the disposition of the French fleet.

46

Un juste sera en exil anvoye, Par pestilence aux confins de Non seggle, Response au rouge le fera desvoyer, Roy retirant a la Rane & l'Aigle.	A just person shall be banished, By plague to the borders of Non- Seggle, The answer to the red one shall make him deviate, Retiring himself to the Frog and the Eagle.

Russia, formerly allied against France, shall be privately assured that her best interests lie in deserting her partner and joining France and her allies.

47

Entre deux monts les deux grands assemblees, Delaiseront leur simulte secrette; Bruxelles & Dolle par Langres ac- cablees, Pour a Malignes executer leur peste.	Between two mountains the two great ones shall meet, They shall forsake their secret en- mity, Brussels and Dolle shall be crushed by Langres, To put their plague in execution at Maline.

A long-forgotten incident is here described, and I think it needs no further interpretation than the verse indicates.

48

La sainctete trop saincte & seduc-tive,	The feigned and seducing holiness,
Accompagnee d'une langue diserte;	Accompanied with a fluent tongue,
La cite vieille & Palme trop has-tive,	Shall cause the old city and the too hasty Parma,
Florence & Sienne rendront plus desertes.	Florence and Sienna to be more desert.

The sanctimonious mouthings of a fluent demagogue shall influence many people in Rome and other important Italian cities, and cause them to abet him in his nefarious schemes.

49

De la partie de Mammer grand pontife,	By the project of Mammon, high priest,
Subjuguera les confins du Dan-ube,	They shall subjugate the borders of the Danube,
Chasser les croix par fer raffe ne riffe,	They shall pursue crosses of iron, topsy-turvy,
Captifs, or, bagues, plus de cent mille rubles.	Slaves, gold, jewels, more than a hundred thousand rubles.

The Swastika, crooked-cross emblem of the Nazis, is clearly foreseen by Nostradamus; also the financial origin of their unholy crimes against humanity.

50

Dedans le puits seront trouvez les os,	In the well shall be found the bones,
Sera l'incest commis par la maras-tre;	Incest shall be committed by the stepmother,
L'estat change, on querre bruit les los,	The state being changed, there shall be a great stir about the bones,
Et aura Mars ascendant pour son astre.	And she shall have Mars for her ascending planet.

A stepmother shall have a child by her son-in-law, and will commit infanticide, throwing the body in a well. When the bones are discovered a great furor will take place.

51

Peuple assemble voir nouveau spectacle
Princes & Roys par plusieurs assistans,
Pilliers faillir, murs, mais comme miracle,
Le Roy sauve & trente des instans.

People assembled to see a new show,
Princes and Kings, with many assistants,
Pillars shall fail, walls also, but as a miracle,
The King saved, and thirty of the standers-by.

This pertains to the Congress of Vienna, which convened after the defeat of Napoleon and effected many changes among the nations of Europe.

52

En lieu du grand qui sera condamne,
De prison hors, son amy en sa place;
L'espoir Troyen en six mois joint mort nay,
Le Sol a l'Vurne seront prins fleuves en glace.

Instead of the great one that shall be condemned,
And put out of prison, his friend being in his place,
The Trojan hope in six months united, still-born,
The Sun in Aquarius, then rivers shall be frozen.

To the Trojan hope, viz., the King of France, after being married six months, shall be born a child, delivered before its time.

53

Le grand Prelat Celtique a Roy suspect,
De nuict par cours sortira hors du regne,
Par Duc fertille a son grand Roy Bretagne,
Bisance a Cypres & Tunes insuspect.

The great Celtic Prelate suspected by his King,
Shall in haste by night go out of the government.
By means of a Duke, fruitful to his King, Great Britain,
Turkey to Cyprus, and Tunis shall be unsuspected.

A Prelate of Celtic origin shall be removed from power by his King. Great Britain shall be the gainer.

54

Au poinct du jour second chant du coq,	At the break of day, at the second crowing of the cock,
Ceux de Tunes, de Fez, & le Bugie,	Those of Tunis, and Fez and Bugia,
Par les Arabes captif le Roy Maroq,	By means of the Arabians, shall take prisoner the King of Morocco
L'an mil six cens & sept de Liturgie.	In the year 1607 by liturgy.

Here again we have recourse to Nostradamus' key figure (as noted in quatrain 2, Century VI). By using this number, 325, and adding to it the figure 1607 referred to above, we get 1932. In this instance, the date is approximate, since the inference gathered from the quatrain clearly applies to conditions leading up to the Spanish Civil War which began in 1936.

55

Au Chelme Duc, en arrachant l'esponce,	The Chelme Duke, on throwing the sponge,
Voille Arabesque voir, subit descouverte;	Shall see Arabian Sails suddenly discovered,
Tripolis, Chio, & ceux de Trapesonce,	Tripoli, Chios, and those of Trapesan,
Duc Prins, Marnegro, & sa cite deserte.	The Duke shall be taken, Marnegro, and the city shall be deserted.

The regions mentioned are near or in Turkey. Chelme is a German word signifying a rogue. The meaning here seems to be that there shall be conflict between this wicked Duke and the rulers of these various cities.

56

La crainte armee de l'ennemy Narbon,	The feared army of the enemy Narbonne
Effrayera si fort les Hesperiques;	Shall so much terrify the Spaniards,
Parpignan vuide par L'aveugle d'-Arbon,	That Parpignan shall be left empty by the blind d'Arbon,
Lors Barcelon par mer donra les piques.	Then Barcelona by sea shall give the weapons.

Parpignon, a border town between France and Spain, shall be captured by the French. Barcelona shall come to the rescue by way of the sea.

57

Celuy qu'estoit bien avant dans le regne,	He that was a great way in the kingdom,
Ayant chef rouge proche la hierar-chie;	Having a red head and near the hierarchy,
Aspre & cruel, & se fera tant crain-dre,	Harsh and cruel, shall make himself so dreadful,
Succedera a Sacree Monarchie.	That he shall succeed to the Sacred Monarchy.

A Cardinal of great power—backed by much influence—shall make himself so indispensable to the Vatican, that he will be awarded the Papacy.

58

Entre les deux monarques eslong-nez,	Between the two monarchs that live far from each other.
Lors que Sol par Selin cler perdue;	When the Sun shall be eclipsed by Selene,
Simulte grande entre deux indig-nez,	Great enmity shall be between the two,
Qu'aux Isles & Sienne la liberte rendue.	So that liberty will be restored to the Isles and Sienna.

When the Sun is eclipsed by the Moon, Sienna shall have its liberty restored.

59

Dame en fureur par rage d'adultere,	A lady in fury by rage of an adultery,
Viendra a son prince conjurer non de dire,	Shall come to her prince and conjure him to say nothing,
Mais bref cogneu sera le vitupere,	But soon shall the shameful thing be known,
Que seront mis dixsept a martyre.	So that seventeen shall be put to death.

An explicit statement that should be clear to all.

60

Le prince hors de son terroir Celtique,
Sera trahy, deceu par interprete;
Rouan, Rochelle, par ceux d'Armo-
rique,
Au Port de Blaye deceus par moine
& prestre.

The Prince being out of his Celtic
country,
Shall be betrayed and deceived by
an interpreter.
Rouen, Rochelle, by those of Gascony,
At the Port of Bordeaux shall be
deceived by a monk and priest.

A false interpretation of a political message shall cause an uproar
throughout France.

61

Le grand tapis plie ne monstrera,
Fors qu'a demy la pluspart de l'his-
torie;
Chasse du regne loing aspre apparoistra.
Qu'au fait bellique chacun le viendra eroire.

The great carpet folded shall not
show,
But by half the greatest part of the
history,
The exiles of the kingdom shall
appear sharp afar off.
In warlike matters everyone shall
believe.

The true historical facts concerning an exiled leader, who maintained
his powerful influence even during his banishment, shall be forever concealed from posterity.

62

Trop tard tous deux, les fleurs seront perdues,
Contre la loy serpent ne voudra
faire;
Des ligueurs forces par gallops con-
fondues,
Savone, Albigne, par Monech
grand martyre.

Both the flowers shall be lost too
late,
Against the law the serpent shall
do nothing,
The forces of the leaguers, by gallops, shall be confounded,
Savoy, Albigne, by Monaco shall
suffer great martyrdom.

Nostradamus here expresses his hatred for heretics by referring to them
as serpents. By "gallops" he means horsemen, and the meaning to be drawn
from this stanza is that the heretics of the above-named towns shall be
persecuted and driven out.

63

La dame seule au regne demeuree,
L'unique estaint premier au lict d'-
  honneur,
Sept ans sera de douleur exploree,
Quis longue vie au regne par grand
  heur.

The lady shall be left to reign
  alone,
The unique one being extin-
  guished, first in the bed of honour,
Seven years she shall weep for grief,
After that she shall live long in the
  reign by grandeur.

Catherine de Medici outlived her husband, Henry II of France, by many years. After his death she went into deep mourning for seven years.

64

On ne tiendra pache aucun arreste,
Tous recevans iront par tromperie;
De paix & trefue, terre & mer pro-
  teste;
Par Barcelone classe prins d'indus-
  trie.

No binding agreement shall be
  kept,
Those that admit of it deal in
  trumpery,
There shall be no protestations by
  land and sea,
Barcelona shall take a fleet by ingenuity.

An armed truce with trickery on all sides shall beset the nations, and Spain shall be the gainer.

65

Gris & bureau, demie ouverte
  guerre,
De nuict seront assailliz & pillez;
Le bureau prins passera par la serre,
Son temple ouvert, deux aux plas-
  tres grillez.

Between the grays and the bureaus
  shall be half open war,
By night they shall be assaulted
  and plundered,
The government being taken shall
  put in custody,
His temple shall be opened, two
  shall be put in the grate.

Conflict between lower classes and bureaucrats is foreshadowed ending with the overthrow of a government.

66

Au fondement de la nouvelle secte,
Seront les os du grand Romain
  trouvez,
Sepulchre en marbre apparoistra
  converte.
Terra trembler en Avril, mal en-
  fovez.

At the founding of a new sect,
The bones of the great Roman
  shall be found,
The Sepulchre shall appear covered with marble,
The earth shall quake in April,
  they shall be ill-buried.

A new sect of friars, while digging the foundation for a church, un-
earthed human bones which they believed to be the remains of a famous old
Roman. The last line has no particular connection with this tale, signifying that there will be an earthquake during the month of April, at which
time many graves will be opened and their contents revealed.

67

Au grand Empire par viendra tout
  un autre,
Bonte distant plus de felicite;
Regi par un issu non loing du peau-
  tre,
Corruer Regnes grande infelicite.

To the great Empire quite another
  shall come,
Being distant from goodness and
  happiness,
Governed by one of base parentage,
The Kingdom shall fall, a great
  unhappiness.

The future fate of all empires is here explicated.

68

Lors que soldats fureur seditieuse,
Contre leur chef feront de nuict fer
  livre,
Ennemy d'Albe soit par main fur-
  ieuse,
Lors vexer Rome & principaux se-
  duire.

When the seditious fury of the
  soldiers,
Against their chief shall make the
  iron shine by night,
The enemy d'Albe shall by a furious hand,
Then vex Rome and seduce the
  principal one.

The Duke of Alba, commander of the Spanish Army in the war against
the Roman forces of the Pope, unmercifully forced the war to a successful
conclusion for his master, Emperor Charles V.

69

La grand pitie sera sans long tarder,
Ceux qui donoient seront contraints de prendre,
Nuds affamez de froid, soif, soy
  bander,
Passer les monts en faisant grand
  esclandre.

What a great pity will it be before
  long,
Those that did give, shall be con-
  strained to receive,
Naked, famished with cold, to mutiny,
To go over the mountains making
  great disorders.

A land of plenty shall soon be in want and the people will revolt.

70

Un chef du monde le grand Chyren sera;
Plus outre, apres ayme, craint, re-
  doute;
Son bruit & los les cieux sur passera,
Et du seul titre Victeur, fort content.

A chief of the world, the great
  Henry shall be,
At first, beloved, afterwards feared,
  dreaded,
His fame and praise shall go be-
  yond the heavens,
And shall be contented with the
  title of Victor.

The nations will organize a super-government covering the entire
world. The president will be named Henry.
  "Chyren" by transposition of letters is an anagram for "Henryc," the
then current form of Henry.

71

Quand on viendra le grand Roy
  parenter,
Avant qu'il ait du tout l'ame rendue,
On le verra bien tost apparenter,
D'Aigles, Lions, Crois, Couronne
  vendue.

When they shall come to celebrate
  the obsequies of the great King,
A day before he be quite dead,
He shall be seen presently to be
  allied,
With Eagles, Lions, Crosses,
  Crowns of Rue.

A continuation of the previous stanza; at the end of Henry's reign,
he shall be exposed as being allied with predatory interests, bringing
much sorrow and suffering to mankind.

72

Par fureur faincte d'esmotion divine,
Sera la femme du grand fort violee;
Judges voulants damner telle doctrine,
Victime au peuple ignorant immo-
lee.

By a feigned fury of divine inspiration,
The wife of the great one shall be
ravished,
Judges willing to condemn such a
doctrine,
A victim shall be sacrificed to the
ignorant people.

Marie Antoinette, wife of Louis XVI of France, was condemned to death by the judges of the revolution and guillotined in the presence of a howling mob.

73

En cite grand un moyne & artisan,
Pres de la porte logez & aux murail-
les;
Contre modene secret, cave disant,
Trahis pour faire sous couleur d'es-
pousailles.

In a great city a monk and an
artisan
Dwelling near the gate and walls,
Against woman secrets, beware
further,
A treason shall be plotted under
pretense of marriage.

A monk, an artisan and a woman shall share a secret, relating to a treasonable act; womanlike she shall tell and so betray it.

74

La dechassee au regne tournera,
Ses ennemis trouvez des conjurez;
Plus que jamais son temps triom-
phera,
Trois & septante a mort trop asse-
urez.

The expelled shall come again to
the kingdom,
Her enemies shall be found to be
conspirators,
More than ever his time shall triumph,
Three and seventy appointed by
death.

Exiled anti-Nazi liberals shall again return to the countries of Europe and many of their persecutors shall be marked for death.

75

Le grand Pilot sera par Roy mande,
Laisser la classe, pour plus haut lieu
　attaindre;
Sept ans apres sera contrebande,
Barbare armee viendra Venise
　craindre.

The great Pilot shall be sent for
　by Royal mandate,
To leave the fleet, and be preferred
　to a higher place,
Seven years after he shall be coun-
　termanded,
A barbarian army shall put Venice
　to fear.

A great leader, long absent from public life, shall be recalled to pilot his country's destiny during a time of great stress. The latter part of the stanza indicates his final fall from grace in the face of overwhelming public opposition.

76

La cite antique d'Antenoree forge,
Plus ne pouvant le tyran supporter;
Le manche fainct au temple couper
　gorge,
Les siens le peuple a mort viendra
　bouter.

The ancient city founded by An-
　tenor,
Not being able to bear the tyrant
　any longer.
The feigned handle in the temple
　cut a throat,
The people will come to put his
　servants to death.

The city founded by Antenor, who came to Italy with Aeneas, is Padua. Being a university city, it will not be able to stand the antics of a tyrant any longer. He shall have his throat cut, and his companions will also be put to death.

77

Par la victoire du deceu fraudu-
　lente,
Deux classes une, la revolte Ger-
　mains,
Le chef meurtry & son fils dans la
　tente,
Florence, Imole pourchassez dans
　Romaine.

By the deceitful victory of the de-
　ceived,
One of the two fleets shall revolt to
　the Germans,
The chief and his son murdered
　in their tent,
Florence, Imole, persecuted in
　Romania.

The Germans shall be deceived into thinking that they have won a victory. Trouble in Italy shall hasten their disillusionment and contribute to their final defeat.

78

Crier victoire du grand Selin croissant,	They shall cry at the victory of the great Selin's crescent,
Par les Romains sera l'Aigle clame,	By the Romans the Eagle shall be claimed,
Ticcin, Milan & Gennes ny consent,	Ticin, Milan and Genoa consent not,
Puis par eux mesmes Basil grand reclame.	Then by themselves the great Basil shall be claimed.

The Romans, defeated in a battle with the Turks, will request aid from other Italian cities. Being refused by them, they will then appeal to the great King (Basil from the Greek word *Basileus*).

79

Pres de Tesin les habitants de Logre,	Near the Tesin the inhabitants of Logre,
Garonne & Saone, Siene, Tar & Gironde,	Garonne and Saone, Siene, Tar and Gironde,
Outre les monts dresseront promontoire,	Shall erect a promontory beyond the mountains,
Conflict donne, Pau granci, submerge onde.	Conflict given, the Po passed over, some shall be drowned.

The Italians shall attempt to build an empire beyond their own borders. Eventually they will be defeated in this purpose, and shall suffer great losses.

80

De Fez le Regne parviendra a ceux d'Europe,	The Kingdom of Fez shall come to those of Europe,
Feu leur cite, & lame trenchera;	Fire and sword shall destroy their city,
Le grand d'Asie terre & mer a grand troupe,	The great one of Asia, by land and sea with a great army,
Que bleux, pars, croix a mort dechassera.	So that blues, greens, crosses to death he shall drive.

"A strange prophecy if it prove true," said a 17th century disciple of Nostradamus. And time so proves it—that this is the prediction of the Spanish Civil War, of the uprisings which began in Morocco and spread to Spain; and even indicates the aid that was given the Loyalists by Russia and Franco by Germany.

81

Pleurs, cris, & plaincts, hurlemens, effrayeurs,	Tears, cries and complaints, howlings, fear,
Coeur inhuman, cruel, noir, & transy.	An inhuman heart, cruel black and astonished,
Leman, les Isles, de Gennes les majeurs,	Geneva, the Islands of the great ones of Genoa,
Sang espancher, tochsain, a nul mercy.	Shall spill blood, the bell shall ring and no mercy given.

During the course of a war that shall involve most of the earth's surface, a battle of great importance will be fought with the Dodecanese Islands as the prize.

82

Par les deserts de lieu, libre, & farouche,	Through the deserts of a place free and ragged,
Viendra errer nepueu du grand Pontife;	The nephew of the Pope shall come to wander,
Assomme a sept avec ques lourde souche,	Knocked in the head by seven with a heavy club,
Par ceux qu'apres occuperont le cyphe.	By those who after shall obtain the cipher.

A nephew of the Pope shall be exiled to a desert, where he shall be attacked by seven men, one of which will afterwards gain the Papacy.

83

Celuy qu'aura tant d'honneur & carresses,	He that shall have had so many honors and welcomes,
A son entree en la Gaule Belgique,	At his going into French Belgium,
Un temps apres fera tant de rudesses,	A while after shall commit so many rudenesses,
Et sera contre a la fleur tant bellique.	And shall be against the warlike flower.

This concerns the Duke of Alencon who was sent into the Low Countries as Governor for Henry III, King of France. So entranced was he by the beauty and riches of Antwerp, that he attempted to seize the city, but he was overcome by the citizens and most of his followers were destroyed.

84

Celuy qu'en Sparte Claude ne veut
    regner,
Il fera tant par voye seductive;
Que de court, long, le fera araigner,
Que contre Roy fera sa perspective.

He that Claudius will not have to
    reign in Sparta,
The same shall do so much by a
    deceitful way,
That he shall cause him to be ar-
    raigned short and long,
As if he had made his prospect
    upon the King.

One shall be hindered from reigning, by the machinations of another.

85

La grand cite de Tharse par Gau-
    lois,
Sera destruite, captifs tous a Tur-
    ban,
Secours par mer, du grand Portu-
    galois,
Premier d'este le jour de sacre
    Urban.

The great city of Tharse taken by
    the French,
All who wore the turban shall be
    made slaves,
Help by sea from the great Portu-
    guese,
The first day of summer and the
    installation of Urban.

What is meant by the taking of Tarsus, the birthplace of the Apostle Paul, is not clear to me. The rest of the stanza refers to the persecution and enslavement of non-Christians during the reigns of various early Popes (indicated by "Urban," the name taken by eight different Popes, the last of whom held the office from 1623 to 1644).

86

Le grand Prelat un jour apres son
    songe
Interprete au rebours de son sens;
De la Gascongne luy surviendra un
    monge,
Qui fera eslire le grand Prelat de
    Sens.

The great Prelate the next day
    after his dream,
Interpreted contrary to his sense,
From Gascony shall come to him
    a monk,
That shall cause the great Prelate
    of Sens to be elected.

A lowly monk shall come to a princely churchman, and, following his advice, the Prelate will be elected to a high office.

87

L'election faicte dans Francfort,
N'aura nul lieu, Milan s'opposera;
Le sien plus proche semblera si
grand fort,
Qu'outre le Rhin es mareschs chas-
sera.

The election made at Frankfort,
Shall be void, Milan shall oppose
it;
He of the Milan party shall be so
strong,
As to drive the other beyond the
marshes of the Rhine.

At Frankfort in Germany, the ancient German rulers were elected.
Milan is the place where the Italian Fascist leaders first became powerful.
The rest is plain.

88

Un regne grand demourra desole,
Aupres del Hebrose seront assem-
blees;
Mont Pyrenees le rendront console,
Lors que dans May seront terres
tremblees.

A great king shall be left desolate,
Near the River Hebrus an assembly
shall be made,
The Pyrenean Mountains shall
comfort him,
When in May shall be an earthquake.

A reference to an ancient incident, this concerns a King who, after
being defeated in battle near the River Hebrus (the ancient name for
the River Maritza), loses his kingdom and is forced to flee to the shelter
of the Pyrenees Mountains.

89

Entre deux cymbles pieds & mains
estachez,
De miel face oingt, & de laict sub-
stante;
Geuspes & mouches seront amour
fachez,
Poccilateurs faucer, cyphe tente.

Between two boats one shall be
tied hand and foot,
His face anointed with honey, and
be nourished with milk,
Wasps and bees shall make much
of him mad,
For being treacherous cup bearers,
and poisoning the cup.

A description of a form of ancient torture meted out to poisoners—put
between two troughs called boats, their bodies were daubed with honey,
so that wasps and bees could torment them to death.

90

L'honnissement puant abominable,
Apres le faict sera felicite;
Grand excuse, pour n'estre favor-
    able,
Qu'a paix Neptune ne sera incite.

The stinking and abominable de-
    filing,
After the deed shall be successful,
The great one excused for not be-
    ing favorable,
That Neptune might be persuaded
    to peace.

This refers to an infamous pact, agreed upon by several nations, ostensibly for the preservation of peace. The Munich Pact and the temporary
acclamation of the role played by Chamberlain are clearly indicated.

91

Le conducteur de la Guerre Navale,
Rouge effrene, severe, horrible
    grippe,
Captif eschappe de l'aisne dans la
    baste;
Quand il naistra du grand un fils
    Agrippe.

The leader of the Naval War,
Red, rash, severe, horrible execu-
    tioner.
Being slave, shall escape, hidden
    among the harness,
When shall be born to the great
    one, a son named Agrippa.

Cornelius Agrippa, 1486–1535, a German soldier, philosopher and
alchemist, is here alluded to.

92

Princesse de beaute tant venuste,
Au chef menee, le second faict
    trahy;
La cite au glaive de poudre face
    aduste,
Par trop grand meurtre le chef du
    Roy hay.

A Princess of an exquisite beauty,
Shall be brought to the chief, the
    second fact betrayed,
The city shall be given to fire and
    sword,
By too great a murder, the chief
    man of the King shall be hated.

The sequence of events is plain, the only difficulty is in the naming of
the city.

93

Prelat avare, d'ambition trompe,
Rien ne fera que trop cuider
viendra,
Ses messagers, & luy bien attrape,
Tout au rebours voir qui le bois
fendra.

A covetous Prelate, deceived by
ambition,
Shall do nothing but covet too
much,
His messengers and he shall be
trapped,
When they shall see one cleave the
the wood the contrary way.

Cardinal Richelieu's overweening ambition led him to be the greatest
figure of his day; a prophetic picture of Richelieu and his intrigues is given
here by Nostradamus.

94

Un Roy ire sera aux sedifragues,
Quand interdicts seront hernois de
guerre,
La poison taincte au succre par les
fragues,
Par eaux meurtris, morts disant
serre serre.

A King shall be irate against the
treaty breakers,
When the warlike armour shall be
forbidden,
The poison with sugar shall be put
in the strawberries,
They shall be killed and die, saying, "close, close."

After a trial, held against the treaty breakers, they shall be executed saying, "We came very close."

95

Par detracteur calomnie a puis nay;
Quand istront faict enormes &
martiaux;
La moindre part dubieuse a l'aisne,
Et tost au regne seront faicts par-
tiaux.

The youngest son shall be slan-
dered by a detractor,
When enormous and martial deeds
shall be done,
The least part shall be doubtful to
the eldest,
And soon after they shall both be
equal in the government.

A quarrel between two brothers (princes) will lead to the verge of
civil war. Their differences will be conciliated and both will play an equal
share in the government of their country.

96

Grand cite a soldats abandonnee,
Onc ny eut mortel tumult si
    proche,
O qu'elle hideuse calamite s'ap-
    proche,
Fors une offense n'y sera pardon-
    nee.

A great city shall be abandoned to
    the soldiers,
There never was a mortal tumult
    so near,
Oh! what a hideous calamity ap-
    proaches,
Except one offense, nothing shall
    be pardoned.

A great city shall be pillaged by a barbarian horde; the only ones
spared shall be those of the same race.

97

Cinq & quarante degrez ciel bru-
    slera,
Feu approcher de la grand cite
    neuve,
Instant grand flamme esparse sau-
    tera,
Quand on voudra des Normans
    faire preuve.

The heaven shall burn at five and
    forty degrees,
The fire shall come near the great
    new city,
In an instant a great flame dis-
    persed shall burst out,
When they shall make a trial of
    the Normans.

A cataclysmic fire shall engulf the greatest and newest of the world's
big cities.

98

Ruyne aux Volsques de peur si fort
    terribles,
Leur grand cite taincte, faict pesti-
    lent;
Piller sol, lune, & violer leurs
    temples;
Et les deux fleuves rougir de sang
    coulant.

Ruin shall happen to the Vandals
    that will be terrible,
Their great city shall be tainted, a
    pestilent deed;
They shall plunder sun and moon,
    and violate their temples,
And two rivers shall be red with
    running blood.

The atomic bombing of Hiroshima is foretold by Nostradamus. Its
location, between two rivers, is given, as well as the mention of the temples
of the Japanese.

99

L'ennemy docte se tournera confus,
Grand camp malade, & de faict par
embusches,
Mont Pyrenees & Pernus luy seront faict refus,
Proche du fleuve descouvrant antiques ruches.

The learned enemy shall go back
confounded,
A great camp shall be sick and in
effect through ambush,
The Pyrenean Mountains shall
refuse him,
Near the river discovering the
ancient hives.

An educated yet barbarous nation shall be defeated in its attempt to
foist its culture on other peoples, and its leaders shall be refused sanctuary
wherever they try to flee.

100

Fille de l'Aure, asyle du mal sain,
Ou jusqu'au ciel se void l'ampthi-
teatre;
Prodige veu, ton mal est fort prochain,
Seras captive, & des fois plus de
quatre.

Daughter of Laura, sanctuary of
the sick,
Where to the heavens is seen the
amphitheatre;
A prodigy being seen, the danger
is near,
Thou shalt be taken captive above
four times.

An ingenious stanza, it contains many things. The reference to "Daughter of Laura" concerns the city of Nismes in Languedoc, famous for its
amphitheatre and for being the birthplace of Laura, mistress of the poet
Petrarch. The last two lines contain a warning of approaching civil war
in France, clearly an indication of the far-in-the-future French Revolution.

LEGIS CAUTIO CONTRA INEPTOS CRITICOS

Qui legent hos versus, mature cen-
  sunto;
Prophanum vulgus & inscium ne
  attrectato.
Omnesque Astrologi, Blenni, Bar-
  bari procul sunto,
Qui aliter faxit, is rite sacer esto.

INVOCATION OF THE LAW AGAINST INEPT CRITICS

Those who read these verses, let
  them consider with mature
  mind,
Let not the profane, vulgar and
  ignorant be attracted to their
  study.
All Astrologers, Fools and Barbarians draw not near,
He who acts otherwise, is cursed
  according to rite.

213

[Various quatrains within the following Century were found to duplicate those occurring in the previous Centuries, and therefore have been deleted. The numbering of the quatrains has been maintained according to the original sequence.]

1

L'arc du thresor par Achilles deceu,
Aux procrees sceu la quadrangu-
laire;
Au faict Royal le comment sera
sceu,
Corps veu pendu au veu du popu-
laire.

The arch of the treasure by Achilles deceived,
Shall show to posterity the quadrangle,
In the royal deed the comment
shall be known,
The body seen hung in full view
of the people.

Marshal d'Ancre, Treasurer of France, and favorite of the Queen Regent, Marie de Medici, was exposed by Achilles de Harlay, President of Paris, and convicted for the mishandling of funds. By order of Louis XIII, he was killed in the quadrangle of the Louvre and his body was later hanged in a public place.

2

Par Mars ouvert Arles ne donra
guerre,
De nuict seront les soldats eston-
nez;
Noir, blanc, a l'Inde dissimule en
terre,
Sous la saincte ombre traistre verrez & sonnez.

Arles shall not proceed by open
war,
By night the soldiers shall be astonished,
Black, white, and blue dissembled
on the ground,
Under the feigned shadow will be
proclaimed traitors.

Arles, a city in France, shall be the scene of a mutiny.

3

Apres de France la victoire navale,
Les Barchinons, Sallinons, les Phocens,
Lierre d'or, l'enclume serre dedans
  la balle,
Ceux de Toulon au fraud seront
  consents.

After the naval victory of the
  French,
Upon those of Tunis, Salle, and
  the Phocens,
Keg of gold, the anvil shut up in
  a ball,
Those of Toulon to the fraud shall
  consent.

A naval victory of the French over those of the Barbary Coast shall
be attained by means of a novel weapon, an anvil and a ball, shut up in
a keg of gold.

4

Le Duc de Langres assiege dedans
  Dole,
Accompagne d'Ostin & Lyonnois;
Geneve, Auspourg, joinct ceux de
  Mirandole,
Passer les monts conter les Ancon-
  nois.

The Duke of Langres shall be be-
  sieged in Dole,
Being in company with those of
  Autun and Lion,
Geneva, Augsburg, those of Miran-
  dola,
Shall go over the mountains against
  those of Ancona.

France, Italy, Switzerland, and Germany shall be involved in a military
expedition.

5

Vin sur la table en sera respandu,
Le tiers n'aura celle qu'il preten-
  doit;
Deux fois du noir de Parme des-
  cendu,
Perouse a Pise ce qu'il cuidoit.

Wine shall be spilt upon the table,
By reason that a third person shall
  not have her,
Twice, the black one, descended
  from Parma,
Shall do to Perugia and Pisa what
  he intended.

The all-powerful Black One in Italy shall dominate and ravage Italian
centers of culture at will.

6

Naples, Palerme, & tout la Sicile,
Par main barbare sera inhabitee,
Corsique, Salerne & de Sardeigne,
l'Isle,
Faim, peste guerre, fin de maux
intemptee.

Naples, Palermo and all Sicily,
By barbarous hands shall be depopulated,
Corsica, Salerno and the Island of Sardinia,
In them shall be famine, plague, war and endless evils.

A picture, as foreseen by Nostradamus, of conditions in Italy in the closing years of World War II.

7

Sur le combat des grands chevaus
legers,
On criera le grand croissant confond,
De nuict tuer moutons, habits de
bergers,
Abismes rouges dans le fosse profond.

At the fight of the great light horsemen,
They shall cry out, confound the great crescent,
By night they shall kill sheep dressed as shepherds,
Red abysms shall be in the deep ditch.

A nocturnal sally by the Turks shall cause much damage to defenseless populations.

8

Flora, fuis, fuis le plus proche Romain,
Au Fesulan sera conflict donne;
Sang espandu, les plus grands prins
a main,
Temple ne sexe ne sera pardonne.

Flora, fly, fly from the nearest Roman,
In the Fesulan shall be the fight,
Blood shall be spilt, the greatest shall be taken,
Neither temple nor sex shall be spared.

Flora is the Goddess of Flowers and Agriculture, and Fesulan is a place in Italy. Nostradamus warns the inhabitants of Fesulan that there will be some trouble during a Festival in honor of the Goddess Flora.

9

Dame a l'abscence de son grand capitaine,
Sera priee d'amour du Viceroy,
Faincte promesse & mal'heureuse estraine,
Entre les mains du grand Prince Barroys.

A lady in the absence of her great captain,
Shall be entreated of love by the Viceroy,
A pretended promise and unhappy New Year's gift,
In the hand of the great Prince of Bar.

Bar was a principality adjoining Lorraine, which Henry IV gave as a marriage gift to his sister Catherine, when she married the Duke of Lorraine's son. The rest of this quatrain indicates some unhappiness connected with this match.

10

Par le grand Prince limitrophe du Mans,
Preux & vaillant chef de grand exercite;
Par mer & terre de Gallois & Normans,
Caspre passer Barcelonne pille Isle.

The great Prince dwelling near Le Mans,
Stout and valiant, general of a great army,
Of Britons and Normans by sea and land,
Ravaging Cape Barcelona and plunder the Island.

Le Mans is a city in France, and a French general from this vicinity shall lead an army of Britons and Normans to ravage Barcelona.

11

L'enfant Royal contemnera la mere,
Oeil, pieds blessez, rude, inobeissant,
Nouvelle a dame estrange & bien amere,
Seront tuez des siens plus de cinq cens.

The Royal Infant shall despise his mother,
Eye, feet wounded, rude, disobedient,
News to a lady very strange and bitter,
There shall be killed about five hundred.

In 1615, when Louis XIII, King of France, was about fifteen years of age, he was persuaded to make war against his own mother, Marie de Medici, then Regent of the Kingdom. In the ensuing battle about five hundred of the Queen's soldiers were slain.

12

Le grand puisnay fera fin de guerre,
Aux dieux assemble les excusez,
Cahors, Moissac iront long de la serre,
Rusec, Lectore, les Agenoise rasez.

The great young brother shall make an end of the war,
In two places he shall gather the excused,
Cahors, Moissac, shall go out of his clutches,
Russec, Lectore and those of Agen shall be cut off.

All the places mentioned are in the Province of Guyenne, France; and the incident mentioned concerns an inter-city war involving all these regions.

13

De la cite marine & tributaire,
La teste raze prendra la satrapie;
Chasser sordide qui puis sera contraire,
Par quatorze ans tiendra la tyrannie.

Of the maritime city and tributary,
The shaven head shall take the government,
He shall turn out a vile man who shall oppose him,
During fourteen years he will keep away the tyranny.

A positive assertion concerning Cardinal Richelieu, who actually took over a secular branch of the government, and made himself Governor of Havre de Grace.

14

Faux exposer viendra topographie,
Seront les cruches des monuments ouvertes;
Pulluler secte, sainte philosophie,
Pour blanches, noires, & pour antiques vertes.

They shall show topography falsely,
The urns of the monuments shall be open,
Sects shall multiply and holy philosophy,
Shall give black for white, and green for gold.

A corrupt period in history is foretold, when too many sects will spring up, creating great conflict in the church.

15

Devant cite de l'insubre countree,
Sept ans sera le siege devant mis;
Le tres grand Roy y fera son entree,
Cite puis libre hors de ses ennemis.

Before a city of the lower country,
Seven years of siege shall be laid,
The most great King shall make
  his entry into it,
Then the city shall be full being
  out of the enemies' hands.

A city in the Low Country will be under siege for seven years, after which it will be liberated and the former inhabitants, who had fled from their enemy, will return to enjoy the new freedom.

16

Entree profonde par la grand
  Royne faicte;
Rendra le lieu puissant inacces-
  sible;
L'armee des trois Lyons sera def-
  faicte,
Faisant dedans cas hideux & ter-
  rible.

The deep trench made by the
  Queen,
Shall make the place powerful and
  inaccessible,
The army of the three lions shall
  be defeated,
Doing within a hideous and ter-
  rible thing.

An army, owing allegiance to an alliance of three predatory monarchs, shall be defeated but not before committing hideous crimes against captured civilians.

17

Le Prince rare en pitie & clemence,
Apres avoir la paix aux siens baille,
Viendra changer par mort grand
  cognoissance,
Par grand repos le regne travaille.

The Prince, rare in pity and clemency,
After he shall have given peace to
  his subjects,
Shall by death change his great
  knowledge,
After great rest the kingdom shall
  be troubled.

This concerns Henry IV, peace-loving King of France, who was assassinated on May 14, 1610, by Ravaillac. After his death there was much trouble in the Kingdom caused by the dissension among the Princes.

18

Les assiegez couleront leurs paches,	The besieged shall color their articles,
Sept jours apres feront cruelle issue,	Seven days after they shall make a cruel issue,
Dans repoulez, feu sang, sept mis a l'hache,	They shall be beaten back, fire, blood, seven put to the axe,
Dame captive qu'avoit la paix issue.	The lady shall be prisoner who tried to make peace.

A description of an event which will be the turning point in a war.

19

Le fort Nicene ne sera combatu,	The Nicene fort shall not be fought against,
Vaincu sera par rutilant metal,	By shining metal it shall be overcome,
Son faict sera un long temps debatu,	The doing of it shall a long time be debated,
Au citadins estrange espouvantal.	It shall be a strange fearful thing to the citizens.

Nice, endangered by invaders, shall buy her way to peace by the use of shining metal (gold).

20

Ambassadeurs de la Toscane langue,	The ambassadors of the Tuscan tongue,
Avril & May Alpes & mer passer,	In April and May, shall go over the Alps and the sea,
Celuy de veau exposera l'harangue,	One like a calf, shall make a speech,
Vie Gauloise en voulant effacer.	Attempting to defame French customs.

On May 7, 1938, Mussolini, in a mutual admiration session with the Fuehrer, in Berlin, flamboyantly stated, "Germany and Italy have left behind them the Utopias to which Europe has entrusted her destiny. It is this law which Nazi Germany and Fascist Italy has obeyed, obeys, and will obey."

21

Par pestilente inimitie Volsique,	By a pestilent Italian enmity,
Dissimulee chassera le tyran;	The dissembler shall expel the tyrant,
Au pont de Sorgues se fera la trafique,	The bargains shall be made at Sorgues bridge,
De mettre a mort luy & son adherent.	To put him and his adherent to death.

Premier Pierre Laval, cohort of Mussolini, was eventually expelled, captured and executed, thus fulfilling the prophecy.

22

Les Citoyens de Mesopotamie,	The citizens of Mesopotamia,
Irez encontre amis de Tarraconne,	Being angry with the friends of Tarrogona,
Jeux, Ris, banquets, toute gent endormie,	Sport, laughter, banquets, everybody being asleep,
Vicaire au Rhosne, prins cite, ceux d'Ausone.	The vicar being in Rhone, the city taken by those of Bordeaux.

This concerns a region of France which lies between two rivers, and its long since forgotten quarrel with the citizens of Bordeaux.

23

Le Royal Sceptre sera contrainct de prendre,	The Royal Sceptre shall be constrained to take
Ce que ses predecesseurs voint engage;	What his predecessors had mortgaged,
Puis que l'aigneau on fera mal entendre,	After that they shall misinform the lamb,
Lors qu'on viendra le palais saccager.	When they shall come to plunder the palace.

Clearly this refers to a palace scandal, but it is worded so obscurely that it is too difficult to discern what royal family is involved.

24

L'ensevely sortira du tombeau,	The buried shall come out of his grave,
Fera de chaines lier le fort du pont,	The fort of the bridge shall be tied with chains,
Empoisonne avec oeufs de Barbeau,	Poisoned with the roe of a Barbel,
Grand de Lorraine par le Marquis du Pont,	Shall a great one of Lorraine be, by the Marquis Dupont.

The first part of this verse has no importance or relationship to the prophecy, which concerns the poisoning of the Duke of Lorrain by the Marquis Du Pont.

25

Par guerre longue tout l'exercite espuiser,	By a long war, all the army drained dry,
Que pour soldats ne trouveront pecune,	So that to raise soldiers, they shall find no money,
Lieu d'or, d'argent, cuir on viendra cuser,	Instead of gold and silver, they shall stamp leather,
Gaulois aerain, signe croissant de Lune.	The French copper, marked with the signs of the crescent moon.

Before the discovery of the West Indies, and the consequent expansion and exploitation of the colonies, many European countries were forced to use substitutes for the usual gold and silver coins.

26

Fustes galees autour de sept navires,	Flying boats and galleys round about seven ships,
Sera livree une mortelle guerre;	Shall be in the livery of deadly war,
Chef de Madrid, recevra coup de vires,	The chief of Madrid shall receive blows of oars,
Deux eschapees, & cinq menees a terre.	Two shall escape, and five carried to land.

A Spanish Admiral shall suffer great losses in a naval battle. Of his entire fleet only two ships shall manage to escape. The rest will be taken as prizes, among them the ship which the Admiral personally commanded.

27

Au coin de vast la grand cavalerie,
Proche a Ferrare empeshce au ba-
    gage,
Pompe a Turin feront tel volerie,
Que dans le fort raviront leur hos-
    tage.

In a corner of the wasted, the great
    cavalry,
Near Ferrara, shall be busy about
    the baggage,
Pomp at Turin, they shall make
    such a robbery,
That in the fort they shall ravish
    their hostage.

During a war the people of the country will sustain great losses and suffer greatly, while their leaders will lead lives of luxury in a fortified city.

28

Le captaine conduira grande proye,
Sur la montagne des ennemis plus
    proche,
Environne, par feu fera telle voye.
Tous eschappez, or trente mis en
    broche.

The captain shall lead a great prey,
Upon the mountain, that shall be
    nearest to the enemies,
Being encompassed with fire, he
    shall make such a way,
All shall escape, except thirty that
    shall be spitted.

A leader, surrounded by enemy soldiers, shall contrive to lead his men out of danger, except thirty who will be taken and tortured by their captors.

29

Le grand duc d'Albe se viendra re-
    beller,
A ses grands peres fera le tradi-
    ment;
Le grand de Guise le viendra de-
    beller,
Captif mene & dresse monument.

The great Duke of Alba shall rebel,
To his grandfathers he shall make
    the plot,
The great Guise shall vanquish
    him,
Led prisoner, and a monument
    erected.

The Duke of Alba was sent to Rome by Charles V of Spain, to lend his aid to others of the Spanish Party in that city.

30

Le sac s'approche, feu, grand sang espandu,	The sack draws near, fire, abundance of blood spilt,
Pau, grand fleuve, aux bouvirs l'entreprinse,	Pau, a great river, an enterprise by churls,
De Gennes, Nice, apres long attendu,	Of Genoa, Nice after they shall have stayed long,
Foussan, Turin, a Savillan la prinse.	Fossan, Turin, the prize shall be at Savillan.

For four years, 1555–59, there was constant fighting among various cities in Italy, especially those near the River Pau (Po).

31

De Langeudoc, & Guienne plus de dix,	From Languedoc and Guienne more than 10,000
Mille voudront les Alpes repasser;	Would be glad to repass the Alps,
Grans Allobroges marcher contre Brundis,	Great Allobroges shall march against Brundis,
Aquin & Bresse les viendront recasser.	Aquin and Bresse shall beat them back.

A French army passing over the Alps into Italy will regret this maneuver.

32

Du Mont Royal naistra d'une casane,	Out of Montreal shall be born in a cottage,
Qui duc, & compte viendra tyranniser,	One that shall tyrannize over duke and earl,
Dresser copie de la marche Millane,	He shall raise an army in the land of the rebellion,
Favence, Florence d'or & gens espuiser.	He shall empty Favence and Florence of their gold.

A Canadian leader, of lowly birth, shall be raised to great power and eventually assume command over men of the nobility.

33

Par fraude, regne, forces expolier,
La classe obsesse, passages a l'es-
pie;
Deux faicnts amis se viendront
t'allier,
Esueiller haine de long temps as-
soupie.

By fraud a kingdom and army shall
be despoiled,
The fleet shall be possessed, passages shall be made to spies,
Two feigned friends shall agree
together,
They shall raise up a hatred that
had long been dormant.

The alliance between Hitler and Mussolini is predicted. The infiltration
by propaganda, the rousing of Anti-Semitism and their "divide and conquer" technique are described.

34

En grand regret sera la gent Gauloise,
Coeur vain, leger croira temerite;
Pain, sel, ne vin, eau, venin ne cer-
voise,
Plus grand captif, faim, froid, ne-
cessite.

In great regret shall the French
nation be,
Their vain and light heart shall believe rashly,
They shall have neither bread, salt,
wine nor beer,
Moreover, they shall be prisoners
and shall suffer hunger, cold and
need.

This continuation of the preceding stanza tells of conditions in France
under the heel of the Axis invader.

35

Le grand poche viendra plaindre,
pleurer,
D'avoir esleu, trompez seront en
l'aage,
Guiere avec eux ne voudra demeu-
rer;
Deceu sera par ceux de son lan-
gage.

The great pouch shall bewail and
bemoan,
Having elected one, they shall be
deceived,
His age shall not stay long with
them,
He shall be deceived by those of
his own language.

This continues the previous prediction of conditions in France, under
Hitlerism; and goes on to outline the sabotaging, by the French underground movement, of the Vichy regime under Marshal Petain.

36

Dieu, le ciel tout le divin verbe a l'onde,
Porte par rouges sept razes a Bizance,
Contre les oingts trois cens de Trebisonde,
Deux loix mettront, & horreur, pluis credence.

God, Heaven all the divine world in water,
Carried by red ones, seven shaved heads at Stamboul,
Against the anointed, three hundred of Trebizond,
They shall put two laws, and horror, and afterwards believe.

A great disputation is to take place in Constantinople, seven priests against three hundred unbelievers.

37

Dix envoyez, chef de nef mettre a mort,
D'un adverty, en classe guerre ouverte;
Confusion chef, l'un se picque & mord,
Le ryn, stecades nefs, cap dedans la nerte.

Ten shall be sent to put the captain of the ship to death,
He shall have notice by one, the fleet shall be in open war,
Great confusion shall be, by pricks and bites,
The Rhine, dung boats, within the north cape.

A mutiny shall take place within the German Navy.

38

L'aisne Royal sur coursier voltigeant,
Picquer viendra si rudement courir;
Cueulle, lipee, pied dans l'estrain pliegnant,
Traine, tire, horriblement mourir.

The eldest Royal, prancing upon a horse,
Shall spur, and run fiercely,
Open mouth, the foot in stirrup, complaining,
Drawn, pulled, die horribly.

The eldest son of a King shall die a horrible death as the result of being thrown from a horse.

39

Le conducteur de l'armee Fran-
coise,
Cuidant perdre le principale phalange;
Par sus pave de l'Avaigne & d'ar-
doise,
Soy parfondra par Gennes gent
estrange.

The leader of the French army,
Hoping to rout the principal pha-
lanx,
Upon the pavement of Avaigne
and slate,
Shall sink in the ground by Genoa,
a strange nation.

A French General shall meet with disaster in his attempt to attack
the strongest flank of the enemy. The land being strange to him, he shall
lead his men into swampy territory and they shall flounder and sink into
the ground, and thus be routed.

40

Dedans tonneaux hors oingts d'-
huile & gresse,
Seront vingt un devant le port fermez,
Au second guet par mort feront
prouesse,
Gaigner les portes, & du guet as-
sommez.

In empty tuns slippery with oil
and grease,
Before the harbor, one and twenty
shall be shut,
At the second watch by death they
shall do great feats of arms,
To win the gates, and be killed by
the watch.

By a stratagem, twenty-one men shall attempt to sneak through the
gates of an enemy harbor but shall fail and be killed.

41

Les os des pieds & des mains enserrez,
Par bruit maison long temps inhabitee,
Seront par songes concavant de-
terrez,
Maison salubre & sans bruit habitee.

The bones of the feet and hands
in shackles,
By a noise a house shall be a long
time deserted,
By a dream the buried shall be
taken out of the ground,
The house shall be salubrious, and
inhabited without noise.

A ghost shall inhabit a house, wherein a skeleton is shackled. After
decent burial of the remains the house shall again be at rest.

42

Quand Innocent tiendra le lieu de Pierre,	When Innocent shall hold the place of Peter,
Le Nizaram Sicilian se verra,	The Sicilian Nizaram shall see himself,
En grands honneurs, mais apres il cherra,	In great honors, but after that he shall fall,
Dans le bourbier d'une civil guerre.	Into the dirt of a civil war.

This prognostication is remarkable for its clarity of wording and the exactness of its fulfillment. Setting the period of time, our first reference is to Innocent X who was elected Pope in 1644. His noted contemporary, the French Cardinal Mazarin (anagrammatically referred to here as Nizaram) was of Italian origin. Under the sponsorship of Richelieu he became a citizen of France and eventually the successor of the great Cardinal. He was one of the most powerful figures of his time and led the fortunes of France during the closing years of the Thirty Years' War.

43

Lutece en Mars, Senateurs en credit,	Lutetia in Mars, Senators shall be in credit,
Por une unit Gaule sera troublee,	In a night France shall be troubled,
Du grand Croesus l'Horoscope predit,	The Horoscope of the Great Croesus predicts,
Par Saturnus, sa puissance exilee.	That by Saturn his power shall be put down.

Lutetia is the Latin word for Paris. After the death of Henry IV, King of France, the Parliament of Paris began to check on the activities of various noblemen, among them the Marquis d'Ancre. His fate is described in Quatrain 1, Century VII.

44

Deux de poison saisis nouveaux Venus,	Two by poison provided by the new Venus,
Dans la cuisine du grand Prince verser;	To pour in the kitchen of the great Prince,
Par le souillard tous deux au faict cogneus,	By the scullion the fact shall be known,
Prins qui cuidoit de mort l'aisne vexer.	And be taken, that thought by death to vex the elder.

A woman shall provide poison, in a plot to do away with a great Prince. A cook's boy shall discover the plot when tasting the King's dish.

73

Renfort de sieges manubis & man-
    iplis,
Changez le sacre & passe sur le
    Pronsne,
Prins & captifs n'arreste les priz
    triples,
Plus par fonds mis, esleve, mis au
    trosne.

Recruit of sieges, spoils and prizes,
Holy day shall be changed and
    passed over the Pronsne,
Taken, made captive and not held
    in the triple field,
Moreover, one from the bottom
    shall be raised to the throne.

A period of military unrest will take place, resulting in the raising of a little Corporal to the throne.

80

L'Occident libres les Isles Britan-
    niques,
Le recogneu passer le bas, puis
    haut,
Ne content trist Rebel, corff, Esco-
    tiques,
Puis rebeller par plui & par nuict
    chaut.

The West shall be free, and the
    British Isles,
The discovered shall pass low, then
    high,
Scotch Pirates shall be, who shall
    rebel,
In a rainy and hot night.

John Paul Jones, called by the British "the Scotch Pirate and Rebel," is here referred to by Nostradamus, as is the fact that the West (America) shall be free.

82

La stratageme simulte sera rare,
La mort en voye rebelle par con-
    tree,
Par le retour du voyage Barbare,
Exalteront la protestante entree.

The simulated stratagem shall be
    scarce,
Death shall be in a rebellious way
    through the country,
By the return from the Barbarian
    voyage,
They shall exalt the Protestant en-
    trance.

A political stratagem shall result in the triumph of the Protestants.

83

Vent chaut, conseil, pleurs, timi-
dite,
De nuict au lit assailly sans les
armes,
D'oppression grande calamite,
L'Epithalame converty pleurs &
larmes.

Hot wind, counsel, tears, fearful-
ness,
He shall be assaulted in his bed by
night without arms,
From that oppression shall be
raised a great calamity,
The Epithalamium shall be converted into tears.

The Epithalamium, a nuptial song or poem in praise of the bride
or bridegroom, is referred to here. The connected event can be gathered
from the text of the stanza.

EPISTLE TO HENRY II

To the most invincible, most high, and most Christian King of France, Henry the Second: Michael Nostradamus, his most obedient servant and subject, wishes victory and happiness.

By reason of that singular observation, O most Christian and victorious King, my face, which had been cloudy a great while, did present itself before your immeasurable Majesty. I have been ever since perpetually dazzled, continually honoring and worshipping that day, in which I presented myself before it, as before a singular and humane Majesty. Now seeking after some occasion whereby I might make appear the goodness and sincerity of my heart and extend my acquaintance toward your most excellent Majesty, and seeing that it was impossible for me to declare it by effects, as well as because of the darkness and obscurity of my mind, even for the enlightening it did receive from the face of the greatest Monarch in the world. It was a great while before I could resolve to whom I should dedicate these three last Centuries of my Prophecies, which make the complete thousand. After I had a long time considered, I have with a great temerity made my address to your Majesty, being no way daunted by it, as the great author Plutarch related in the Life of Lycurgus, that, seeing the offerings and gifts that were sacrificed in the temples of their heathen gods, many came no more, lest the people should wonder at the expense.

Notwithstanding, seeing your royal splendor joined with an incomparable humanity, I have made my address to it, not as to the Kings of Persia, of

---

This dedicatory letter was used by Nostradamus as the preface to his second edition which contained new prophecies.

The following notation appeared, on the page preceding the above epistle, in the 1672 edition of *The Prophecies or Prognostications of Michael Nostradamus,* translated and annotated by Theophilus de Garencieres.

Friendly Reader,

Before you read the following epistle, I would have you be warned of a few things: One is, that according to my opinion, it is very obscure and intelligible (sic) in most places, being without any just connection, and besides the obscurity of the sense, the crabbedness of the expression is such, that had not the importunity of the Bookseller prevailed, I would have left it out, but considering the respect due to Antiquity, the satisfaction we owe to curious persons, who would perhaps have thought the Book imperfect without it, we let it go, trusting to your candor and ingenuity.

231

whom to come near it was forbidden, but as to a most prudent and wise prince. I have dedicated my nocturnal and prophetical calculations, written rather by a natural instinct and poetical furor than by any rules of poetry; and the most part of it written and agreeing with the years, months and weeks, of the regions, countries and most of the towns and cities in Europe; touching also something of Africa, and of a part of Asia, by the change of regions that come near to those climates, and compounded in a natural fashion. But some may answer (who hath need to blow his nose) that the rhyme is as easy to be understood, as the sense is hard to get at. Therefore, O most humane King, most of the prophetical stanzas are so difficult, that there is no way to be found for the interpretation of them. Nevertheless, being in hope of setting down the towns, cities, and regions, wherein most of those shall happen, especially in the year 1585, and in the year 1606, beginning from this present time, which is the 14th of March, 1557.

Going further to the fulfilling of those things, which shall be in the beginning of the seventh millenary, according to my astronomical calculation and other learning which I could reach (at which time the adversaries of Christ and of His Church shall begin to multiply), all has been composed and calculated in days and hours of election, and well disposed, and all as accurately as was possible for me to do. And the whole "*Minerva libera et non invita*," * calculating almost as much of the time that is come, as of that which is past, comprehending it in the present time, and what by the course of the said time shall be known to happen in all regions punctually as it is here written, adding nothing superfluous, although it be said "*Quod de futuris non est determinata omnino veritas*." ** It is very true, Sir, that by my natural instinct given me by my progenitors, I did think I could foretell anything; but having made an agreement between this said instinct of mine, and a long calculation of art, and by a great tranquility and repose of mind, by emptying my soul of all care, I have foretold most part of these ex *tripode œneo* (by the brass tripod), though there be many who attribute to me some things that are no more mine than what is nothing at all. Only the eternal God, who is the searcher of men's hearts, being pious, just, and merciful, is the true Judge of it; Him I beseech to defend me from the calumny of wicked men, who would as willingly question how all your ancient progenitors, the Kings of France, have healed the disease called the Kings-evil; how some other nations have cured the biting of venomous beasts; others have had a certain instinct to foretell things that are to come, and of others too tedious to be here inserted. Notwithstanding those in

---

* "When Minerva was free and favorable."
** "There can be no truth entirely determined for certain which concerns the future."

whom the malignancy of the wicked spirit shall not be suppressed by length of time, I hope that after my decease my work shall be in more esteem than when I was alive.

However, if I should fail in the calculation of times, or should not please some, may it please your most imperial Majesty to forgive me, protesting before God and His Saints, that I do not intend to insert anything in writing in this present Epistle that may be contrary to the true Catholic faith, while consulting the astronomical calculations, according to my learning. For the space of times of our fathers that have been before us are such, submitting myself to the correction of the most learned, that the first man Adam was before Noah, about one thousand two hundred and forty-two years, not computing the time according to the Gentile records, as Varro did, but only according to the Sacred Scriptures, taking them as a guide to my astronomical calculations, and to the best of my understanding. After Noah and the universal flood, about a thousand and fourscore years, came Abraham, who was a supreme astrologer, according to most men's opinion, and did first invent the Chaldean letters; after that came Moses, some five hundred and fifteen or sixteen years after. And between the time of David and Moses there passed about five hundred and seventy years. After which, between the time of David and that of our Saviour and Redeemer Jesus Christ, born of the Virgin Mary, there passed (according to some chronographers) a thousand three hundred and fifty years.

Some may object, that this calculation is not true; because it differs from that of Eusebius. And from the time of human redemption, to that of the execrable seduction of the Saracens, have passed six hundred and four and twenty years or thereabouts. From that time hitherto, it is easy to gather what times are past. If my computations be not good among all nations, however, all has been calculated by the course of the celestial bodies joined with emotion infused in me at certain loose hours, the emotion which has been handed down to me by my ancient progenitors. But the danger at this time (most excellent King) requires that such secret events should not be manifested except by an enigmatical sentence, having but one sense and only one intelligence, without having mixed with it any ambiguous or amphibological calculation. But rather under a cloudy obscurity, through a natural infusion, coming near to the sentence of one of the thousand and two Prophets, that have been since the Creation of the world, according to the calculation and Punic Chronicle of Joel: "*Effundum spiritum meum super omnem carnem, et prophetabunt filii vestri, et filiae vestrae.*" * But such a prophecy did proceed from the mouth of the Holy Spirit, who was the supreme and eternal power, which being

_____

* See Joel ii.28.

come with that of the celestial bodies, has caused some of them to predict
great and wonderful things.

For my part I challenge no such thing in this place, God forbid. I
confess truly, that all comes from God, for which I give Him thanks,
honor, and praise, without having mixed anything of that divination which
proceeds à fato, but à Deo, à natura (which proceeds from fate, but from
God, and nature). And most of it is joined with the motion and course
of the celestial bodies, much as if seeing in a lens, and through a cloudy
vision, the great and sad events, the prodigious and calamitous accidents
that shall befall the worshippers. First upon the temples of God, and
secondly upon those who draw their support from earth, this draws near,
with a thousand other calamitous accidents, which shall be known in the
course of time.

For God will take notice of the long barrenness of the great Dame,
who afterwards shall conceive two principal children. But, being in danger,
she will give birth with risk at her age of death in the eighteenth year, and
not able to go beyond thirty-six, shall leave behind her three males and
one female, and he will have two who never had any of the same father.
The differences between the three brothers shall be such, though united
and agreed, that the three and four parts of Europe will tremble. By the
lesser in years shall the Christian monarchy be upheld and augmented;
sects shall rise and presently be put down again; the Arabians shall be put
back; kingdoms shall be united and new laws made. Concerning the other
children, the first shall possess the furious crowned Lions, holding their
paws upon the escutcheons. The second, well attended by the Latins,
will go so deep among the Lions, that a second trembling and furious
descent will be made, to get upon the Pyrenees Mountains. The ancient
monarchy shall not be transferred, and the third inundation of human
blood shall happen; also for a good while Mars shall not be in Lent.

The daughter shall be given for the preservation of the Church, the
dominator of it falling into the Pagan sect of the new unbelievers, and
she will have two children, one from faithfulness, and the other from
unfaithfulness, by the confirmation of the Catholic Church. The other,
who to his confusion and late repentance, shall go about to ruin her,
shall have three regions over a wide extent of leagues, that is to say, the
Roman, the German, and the Spanish, and it will take a military hand
to adequately take care of the area stretching from the 50th to the 52nd
degree of latitude. And all those remote regions north above the 48th
degree, who by vain fright shall quake, and then those of the west, south
and east shall tremble because of their power, and the power of that
what shall be done cannot be undone by warlike power. They shall be
equal in nature, but much different in faith.

After this the barren Dame, of a greater power than the second, shall be admitted by two people, by the first made obstinate by him that had power over the others; by the second, and by the third, that shall extend his circuit to the east of Europe; there his forces will stop and be overcome, but by sea he will make his excursions into Trinacria and the Adriatic with his myrmidons. Germany shall fall, and the Barbarian Sect shall be wholly driven from among the Latins. Then the great Empire of Antichrist shall begin in the Attila, and Xerxes come down with an innumerable multitude of people, so that the coming of the Holy Ghost, proceeding from the 48th degree, shall transmigrate, driving away the abomination of the Antichrist, who made war against the royal person of the great vicar of Jesus Christ and against His Church, and His Kingdom, and reign *per tempus, et in occasione temporis* (for a time, and to the end of time). And before this shall precede a solar eclipse, the most dark and obscure that was since the creation of the world, till the death and passion of Jesus Christ, and from Him until now. There shall be in the month of October, a great revolution made, such that everybody will think that the earth has lost its natural motion and has gone down into perpetual darkness. In the spring before and after this, shall happen extraordinary changes, reversals of kingdoms, and great earthquakes; all this accompanied with the procreation of the New Babylon, a miserable prostitute large with the abomination of the first holocaust. And this shall last only seventy-three years and seven months.

Then from that stock that has been so long time barren, proceeding from the 50th degree, one will issue who will renovate all the Christian Church. Then shall be a great peace, union and concord, between some of the children of races long wandering and separated by diverse kingdoms; and such peace shall be made that the instigator and promoter of military function by diversity of religions, shall be tied to the bottom of the deep, and united to the kingdom of the furious who shall counterfeit the wise. The countries, towns, cities and provinces that had deserted their first ways to free themselves, captivating themselves more deeply, shall be secretly angry at their liberty and religion lost, and shall begin to strike from the left, to return once more to the right.

Then restoring the holiness, so long beaten down with their former writings, afterwards will come the great dog, the irresistible mastiff (war) who shall destroy all that was done before. Churches shall be built up again as before, the clergy shall be restored to its former state, until it falls back again into whoredom and luxury, and commits a thousand crimes. And being near to another desolation, when she shall be in her higher and more sublime dignity, there shall rise powers and military hands, who shall take away from her the two swords, and leave only the resemblance, after which, tired of the crookedness that is about them, the people will cause these things to straighten. Not willing to submit unto them by the end opposite to the sharp hand that touches the ground they shall provoke. To the branch long barren, will proceed one who shall deliver the people of the world from that meek and voluntary slavery; putting themselves under the protection of Mars, depriving Jupiter of all his honors and dignities, for the free city established and seated in another little Mesopotamia. And the chief governor shall be thrust out of the middle, and set in the high place of the air, being ignorant of the conspiracy of the conspirators, with the second Thrasibulus, who long before did prepare for this thing. Then shall the impurities and abominations be objected with great shame, and made manifest to the darkness of the veiled light, and shall cease toward the end of the change of his kingdom, and the chief men of the Church shall be put back from the love of God and many of them shall apostatize from the true faith.

Of the three sects (Lutheran, Catholic, and Mahometan), that which is middlemost, by the actions of its worshippers, shall be thrown into ruins. The first, wholly in all Europe, and the most part of Africa undone by the third, by means of the poor in spirit, who by madness elevated shall, through libidinous luxury, commit adultery. The people will rise and maintain it, and shall drive away those that did adhere to the legislators, and it shall seem, from the kingdoms spoiled by the Eastern men, that God the Creator has loosed Satan from his infernal prison, to cause to be born the great Dog and Dohan (Gog and Magog), who shall make so great and abominable a breach in the Churches, that neither the reds nor the whites, who are without eyes and without arms, shall not judge of it, and their power shall be taken away from them.

Then shall there be a greater persecution against the Church than ever was, and in the meantime shall be so great a plague, that two parts of three in the world shall fail, so much so that no one shall be able to know the true owners of fields and houses, and there shall happen a total desolation to the clergy, and martial men shall usurp what shall come from the City of the Sun, and from Malta, and from the Islands of Hières, and the great chain of the port shall be open which takes its name from a sea ox (Bosphorus).

A new incursion shall be made from the sea coasts, willing to deliver the Castulan Leap from the first Mahometan taking, and the assaulting shall not altogether be in vain, and that place where the habitation of Abraham was, shall be assaulted by those who shall have reverence for the Jovials. The great eastern city of Achem shall be encompassed and assaulted on all sides by a great power of armed men. Their sea forces shall be weakened by the western men, and to that kingdom shall happen great desolation, and the great cities shall be depopulated, and those that shall come in shall be comprehended within the vengeance of the wrath of God. The Holy Sepulchre, held in great veneration for so long a time, shall remain a great while open to the universal aspect of the heavens, sun and moon. The sacred place shall be converted into a stable for cattle small and large, and put to profane uses. O what a calamitous time shall be then for women with child! For then the principal Eastern Ruler, being for the most part moved by the Northern and Western men, shall be vanquished and put to death, beaten, and all the rest put to flight, and the children he had by many women put in prison. Then shall be fulfilled the prophecy of the Royal Prophet. "*Ut audiret gemitus compeditorum, et solveret filios interemptorum.*" *

What great oppression shall be made then upon the princes and governors of kingdoms, and especially on those that shall live eastward and near the sea, their languages intermixed with all nations. The language of the Latin nations mixed with Arabic and North African communication. All the Eastern kings shall be driven away, beaten and brought to nothing, not altogether by means of the strength of the kings of the North, and the drawing near of our age, but by means of three secretly united, seeking for death by ambushes one against another. The renewing of the triumvirate shall last seven years, while the fame of such a sect shall be spread all the world over, and the sacrifice of the holy and immaculate host shall be upheld. And then shall the lords be two in number, victorious in the North against the Eastern ones, and there shall be such a great noise and warlike tumult that all the East shall quake for fear of those two brothers of the North who are yet not brothers. And because, Sir, by this discourse, I put all things confusedly in these predictions as to the time concerning the event of them; for the account of the time which follows, very little is conformable, if at all, to that I have done before, being by astronomic rule and according to the Sacred Scriptures, in which I cannot err.

I could have set down in every quatrain the exact time in which they shall happen, but it would not please everybody, and much less the interpretation of them, till, Sir, your Majesty has granted me full power so to do, that my calumniators may have nothing to say against me. Nevertheless, reckoning the years since the creation of the world to the birth of Noah, there passed 1506 years, and from the birth of Noah to the building of the ark at the time of the universal flood, 600 years passed (whether solar years, or lunar, or mixed), for my part according to the Scriptures, I hold that they were solar. And at the end of those 600 years Noah entered into the ark to save himself from the flood, which flood was universal upon the earth and lasted a year and two months; and from the end of the flood to the birth of Abraham did pass 295 years; and from the birth of Abraham to that of Isaac did pass 100 years;

---

* "Let the sighing of the prisoner come before thee, to release the children of death" (Ps. lxxviii. 11).

from Isaac to Jacob, sixty years; and from the time he went into Egypt until he came out of it, did pass 130 years; and from the time that Jacob went into Egypt until his posterity came out of it did pass 430 years; and from the coming out of Egypt to the building of Solomon's Temple in the fortieth year of his reign did pass 480 years; and from the building of the Temple to Jesus Christ, according to the computations of the chronographers, did pass 490 years. And thus by this calculation, which I have gathered out of the Holy Scriptures, the whole comes to about 4173 years and eight months more or less. But since the time of Jesus Christ hitherto, I leave it because of the diversity of opinion. Having calculated these present prophecies in accordance to the order of the chain which contains the revolution, and all by astronomical rule, and according to my natural instinct; after some time, and including in it the time Saturn takes to turn to come in on the 7th of the month of April until the 25th of August; Jupiter from the 14th of June to the 7th of October; Mars from the 27th of April till the 22nd of June; Venus from the 9th of April to the 22nd of May; Mercury from the 3rd of February to the 24th of the same; afterwards from the 1st of June to the 24th of the same; and from the 25th of September to the 16th of October, Saturn in Capricorn, Jupiter in Aquarius, Mars in Scorpio, Venus in Pisces, Mercury within a month in Capricorn, Aquarius in Pisces, the moon in Aquarius, the Dragon's head in Libra, the tail opposite to her sign. Following a conjunction of Jupiter and Mercury, with a quadrin aspect of Mars to Mercury, and the head of the Dragon shall be with a conjunction of Sol and Jupiter; the year shall be peaceful without eclipse.

Then the beginning of that year shall see a greater persecution against the Christian Church than ever was in Africa, and it shall be in the year 1792,* at which time everyone will think it a renovation of the age. After that the Roman people shall begin to stand upright again, and to put away the obscure darkness, receiving some of its former light, but now without great divisions and continual changes. Venice, after that, with great strength and power will lift up her wings so high that she will not be much inferior to the strength of ancient Rome. And at that time great Byzantine sails, joined with the Italians by the help and power of the North, shall hinder them so that those of Crete shall not keep their faith. The ships built by the ancient martial men will keep company with them under the waves of Neptune. In the Adriatic there shall be a great discord, what was united shall be put asunder, and what was before a great city shall become a house, including the Pampotan and Mesopotamia of Europe, in (19)45, and others to 41, 42, and 47. And

---

* Date of French Revolution.

in that time and those countries the infernal power shall rise against the Church of Jesus Christ. This shall be the second Antichrist, which shall persecute the said church and its true vicar by the means of the power of temporal kings, who through their ignorance shall be seduced by tongues more sharp than any sword in the hands of a madman.

The said reign of Antichrist shall not last but till the ending of him who was born of Age, and of the other in the city of Plancus (Lyons), accompanied by the elect of Modena, Fulcy by Ferrara, maintained by the Adriatic, Liguriens, and the proximity of the great Trinacria (Sicily). Afterwards the Gallic Ogmion shall pass the Mount Jovis (Barcelona), followed with such a number that even from afar off the Empire shall be presented with its grand law, and then and for some time after, shall be profusely spilled the blood of the innocents by the guilty raised on high. Then by great floods the memory of those things contained in such instruments, shall receive incalculable loss, even to the letters themselves. This will happen to the Northerns. By the Divine Will Satan will be bound once more, and universal peace shall be among men, and the Church of Jesus Christ shall be free from all tribulation, although the Azostains (debauchees) would desire to mix with the honey their pestilent seduction. This shall happen about the seventh millenary, when the sanctuary of Jesus Christ shall no more be trodden down by the unbelievers that shall come from the North. The world will then be near its great conflagration, although by the calculations of my prophecies, the course of time goes much further.

In the epistle that some years ago I dedicated to my son Caesar Nostradamus, I have openly enough declared some things without prognosticating. But here, Sir, are comprehended many great and wonderful events, which those that come after us shall see. And during the said astrological computation, in harmony with the Sacred Scriptures, the persecution of the clergy shall have its beginning in the power of the Northern Kings joined by the Eastern ones. And that persecution shall last eleven years, or a little less, at which time the chief Northern king shall fail, which years being ended, shall come in his stead a united Southern one, who shall yet more violently persecute the clergy of the Church for the space of three years by the apostolical seduction of one that shall have absolute power over the militant Church of God. The holy people of God and keepers of His law, and all order of religion, shall be grievously persecuted and afflicted, so much that the blood of the true ecclesiastical men shall flow all over. One of these horrid kings shall be praised by his followers for having spilt more human blood of the innocent clergymen than anybody has done to wine. The said king shall commit incredible crimes against the Church; human blood shall run through public streets and Churches, as water coming from an impetuous rain. Next, rivers shall be red with blood. In a sea fight the sea shall be red, so that one king will say to another, "*Bellis rubuit navalibus aequor.*" * After that in the same year, and those following, shall happen the most horrible pestilence, caused by the famine preceding, and so great tribulations as ever did happen since the first foundation of the Christian Church throughout all the Latin regions, some marks remaining in some countries under Spain.

Then the third Northern king (Russia?), hearing the complaint of the people of his principal title, shall raise up so great an army, shall go through the limits of his last ancestors and progenitors, that they will all be set up again in their first state. The great Vicar of the Cope shall be restored in his former estate, but desolate and altogether forsaken, shall then go back to the sanctuary that was destroyed by Paganism, when the Old and New Testament will be thrust out and burnt. After that shall the Antichrist be the infernal prince. And in this last era all the kingdoms of Christianity and also of the unbelievers shall quake for the space of years, and there shall be more grievous wars and battles; towns, cities, castles and other buildings shall be burnt, desolated and destroyed with a great effusion of vestal blood, married women and widows ravished, sucking children dashed against the walls of towns, and so many evils shall be committed by the means of the infernal prince, Satan, that almost the entire world shall be undone and desolate.

Before these events many unusual birds shall cry through the air, crying, "Huy, huy." ("Now, now.") A little while after they shall vanish. After this shall have lasted a good while, there shall be renewed a reign of Saturn and a golden age. God the Creator shall say, hearing the affliction of His people, Satan shall be put and tied in the bottom of the deep, and there shall begin an age of universal peace between God and man. The ecclesiastical power shall return in force and Satan shall be bound for the space of a thousand years, and then shall be loosed again.

All these figures are justly fitted by the Sacred Scriptures to the celestial things, that is to say, Saturn, Jupiter and Mars, and others joined with them, as may be seen more at large in some of my quatrains. I would have calculated it more deeply, and coordinated one with the other, but seeing, O most excellent King, that some stand ready to censure me, I shall now withdraw my pen to its nocturnal repose.

"*Multa etiam, O Rex potentissime proeclara, et sane in brevi ventura, sed omnia in hac tua Epistola, innectere non possumus, nec volumus, sed ad intellegenda quoedam facta, horrida fata pauca libanda sunt, quamvis tanta sit in omnes tua amplitudo et humanitas homines, deosque pietas, ut*

---

* "The sea blushed red with the blood of naval fights."

solos amplissimo et Christianissimo Regis nomine, et ad quem summa totius religionis auctoritas deferatur dignus esse videare." * But I shall only beseech you, O most merciful King, by your singular and prudent goodness, to understand rather the desire of my heart, and the earnest desire I have to obey your most excellent Majesty, ever since my eyes were so near to your royal splendor, than the greatness of my word can attain to or deserve.

Faciebat Michael Nostradamus
Solonoe Petrae Provincae

From Salon this 27th June, 1558

---

* "So many things, O most potent King of all, of the most remarkable kind are to happen soon, that I neither would nor could incorporate them all into this epistle; but in order to intelligently comprehend certain facts, a few horrible fated events must be set down in extract, although your amplitude and humanity toward mankind is so great, as is your piety to God, that you alone seem worthy of the great title of the most Christian King, and to whom the highest authority in all religion should be deferred."

1

Pau, nay, loron plus feu qu'a sang
    sera,
Laude nager, fuir grand aux surrez,
Les aggassas entree refusera,
Pampon, Durance, les tiendra en-
    serrez.

Pau, nay, loron, more in fire their
    blood shall be,
Seen to swim, great ones shall run
    to their surreys,
The aggassas shall refuse the entry,
Pampon, Durance shall keep them
    enclosed.

This seemingly obscure and unintelligible quatrain conceals a complex play on words by means of which Nostradamus predicts the advent of Napoleon, viz., nay-pau-loron.

2

Condon & Aux & autour de Mi-
    rande,
Je voy du ciel feu qui les environne,
Sol, Mars, conjoint au Lion, puis
    Marmande,
Foudre, grand guerre, mur tombe
    dans Garonne.

Condon and Aux, and about Mi-
    rande,
I see a fire from heaven that sur-
    rounds them,
Sol, Mars, in conjunction with the
    lion, and then Marmande
Lightning, great war, wall falls into
    the Garonne.

Cities in France are named, all of which will suffer much military destruction.

3

Au fort chasteau de Vigilanne &
    Resviers,
Sera serre le puisnay de Nancy;
Dedans Turin seront ards les pre-
    miers,
Lors que de dueil Lyon sera transy.

In the strong castle of Vigilanne
    and Resviers,
Shall be kept close the youngest
    son of Nancy,
Within Turin, the first shall be
    burnt up,
When Lyons shall be overwhelmed
    with sorrow.

Contemporary politics, that loomed large at the time but which have since lost their significance, are here recorded.

4

Dedans Monech le Coq sera receu,
Le Cardinal de France apparoistra,
Par Logarion Romain sera deceu,
Foiblesse a l'Aigle, & force au Coq
    naistra.

Within Monaco the Cock shall be
    received,
The Cardinal of France shall ap-
    pear,
By Logarion Roman shall be de-
    ceived,
Weakness   to   the   Eagle,   and
    strength to the Cock shall grow.

Monaco, then an Italian possession, admitted the French for the first time, persuaded by the policy of Cardinal Richelieu, the Gallic Cock being the gainer thereby.

5

Apparoistra temple luisant orne,
La lampe & cierge a Borne & Bre-
    tueil,
Pour la Lucerne le canton des-
    torne,
Quand on verra le grand Coq cer-
    cueil.

A brilliantly adorned temple shall
    appear,
The lamp and wax candle of Borne
    and Bretueil,
For Lucerne the canton is turned,
When the great Cock shall be seen
    in his coffin.

After the death of a French King the glory of France will be at its zenith.

6

Charte fulgure a Lyon apparente
Luysant, print Malte, subit sera
estrainte,
Sardon, Mauris traitera decevante,
Geneve a Londres a Coq trahison
fainte.

A thundering light at Lyons appearing,
Brightly, Malta instantly shall be put out,
Sardon shall treat Mauris deceitfully,
From Geneva to London, the Cock a pretended treason.

Tremendous aerial bombardments shall devastate France and extend even to Malta and Sardinia. The French shall pretend to be unfaithful to Geneva and London.

7

Verceil, Milan donra intelligence,
Dedans Tycin sera fait la paye,
Courir par Seine eau, sang feu par
Florence,
Unique choir d'haut en bas faisant
maye.

Verceil, Milan shall give intelligence,
In the Ticin shall the peace be made,
Run through Seine water, blood, fire through Florence,
Only one shall fall from top to bottom making friends.

Italian cities in northern Italy shall make peace with the French; only one person shall suffer by this act.

8

Pres de Linterne dans de tonnes
fermez,
Chivaz fera pour l'Aigle la menee,
L'esleu casse, luy ses gens enfermez,
Dedans Turin rapt espouse em-
menee.

Near Linterne, enclosed within the farms,
Chivas shall drive the plot for the Eagle,
The elect dismissed, he and his men shut up,
Within Turin, the bride raped and carried away.

Linterne and Chivas are small towns in Italy. In a plot to gain power, the local government will be overcome and the prize seized.

9

Pendant que l'Aigle & le Coq a
  Savone
Seront unis, Mer, Levant & Hon-
  grie,
L'armee a Naples, Palerme, Mar-
  que d'Ancone,
Rome, Venise, par barbe horrible
  crie.

While the Eagle and Cock at Sa-
  vonna
Shall be united, Sea, Levant and
  Hungary,
The army at Naples, Palermo,
  Mark of Ancona,
Rome, Venice, cry because of a
  horrid barb.

The American Eagle and the French Cock shall be in a united campaign against the Italians, Hungarians, etc., and the Italian armies shall
be in great distress because of a new and punishing weapon used against
them.

10

Puanteur grande sortira de Lausanne,
Qu'on ne scaura l'origine du fait,
L'on mettra hors tout la gent loing-
  taine,
Feu veu au ciel, peuple estranger
  deffait.

A great stink shall come forth from
  Lausanne,
So that no one shall know the ori-
  gin of it,
They shall put out all the foreign-
  ers,
Fire seen in heaven, a strange peo-
  ple defeated.

The presages contained in this quatrain are now *faits accomplis*, written
with a bloody pen on the pages of History. The Conference of Lausanne
is predicted and the signing of many diplomatic instruments, including
the Treaty of Peace itself. Cynically Nostradamus refers to the "stink that
shall come forth from Lausanne," indicating the cynicism of the partici-
pants; he even shows the blind faith with which these documents were
accepted by the people of the world. He foretells that the "peace" shall
be short-lived; that minorities shall be persecuted; that the fires of war
shall be rekindled and again sweep over the earth.

11

Peuple infiny paroistra a Vicence,
Sans force feu brusler la basilique,
Pres de Lunage deffait grande de
  Valence,
Lors que Venise par mort prendra
  pique.

Infinite number of people shall appear at Vincenza,
Without force, fire shall burn in
  the basilick,
Near Lunage the great one of Va-
  lencia shall be defeated,
When Venice by death shall be
  piqued.

Basilick is the name of an old Italian fort which was heavily fortified
by cannon. The sense of this verse then is that Italy will be engaged in
a war.

12

Apparoistra aupres de Buffalore
L'haut & procere entre dedans Mi-
lan,
L'Abbe de Foix avec ceux de Sainct
Maure,
Feront la forbe habillez en vilain.

Near the Bufalore shall appear
The high and tall, come into Mi-
lan,
The Abbot of Foix with those of
Saint Maure,
Shall make the deceit, being
clothed like a villain.

Foix and St. Mauve are towns in France. This concerns a debate among the clergymen of these communities.

13

Le croise frere par amour effrenee,
Fera par Praytus Bellerophon
mourir,
Classe a mil ans la femme forcenee,
Beu le bruvage, tous deux apres
perrir.

The crossed brother through un-
bridled love,
Shall cause Bellerophon to be killed
by Praytus,
Fleet to thousand years, the women
frantic,
The drink being drunk, both after
that shall perish.

Bellerophon was a hero of Greek mythology. He fell from his steed Pegasus and perished, while attempting to fly to heaven.

14

Le grand credit, d'or, d'argent,
l'abundance,
Aveuglera par libide l'honneur;
Cogneu sera d'adultere l'offense,
Qui parviendra a son grand des-
honneur.

The great credit, of gold, of silver,
great abundance,
Shall blind honor by lust,
The offense of the adulterer shall
be known,
Which shall come to his great dis-
honor.

A period of inflation accompanied by laxity of morals shall sweep the civilized world.

15

Vers Aquilon grands efforts par hommasse
Presque l'Europe & l'univers vexer,
Les deux eclipses mettre en telle chasse,
Et aux Pannons vie & mort renforcer.

Towards the North great endeavours by a masculine woman,
To trouble Europe, and almost all the world,
The two eclipses shall be put to flight,
And shall reinforce life, and death to the Poles.

Catherine the Great, 1729–96, Empress of Russia, is here indicated. She was a disciple and friend of the Encyclopaedists, especially of Voltaire, and although she started out with the intention of following their principles in the matters of domestic reform, it was short-lived and completely shattered by the advent of the French Revolution. During her reign she engineered the shameless partitions of Poland, to the great detriment of that nation.

16

Au lieu que Jieson feit sa nef fabriquer,
Si grand deluge sera & si subite,
Qu'on n'aura lieu ne terres s'ataquer,
L'onde monter Fesulan Olympique.

In the place where Jason carried his ship to be built,
So great a flood shall be and so sudden,
That there shall be neither place nor land to save themselves,
The waves shall climb upon the Olympic Fesulan.

Mount Olympus, the mythical home of the gods, is where Jason built his ship, for the Argonauts' voyage. The sense of this stanza is that an inexorable movement shall engulf all those in authority and a new order be created.

17

Les bien aisez subit seront desmis,
Le monde mis par les trois freres en trouble,
Cite marine saisiront ennemis,
Faim, feu, sang, peste, & de tous maux le double.

Those that were at ease shall be put down,
The world shall be put in trouble by three brothers,
The maritime city shall be seized by its enemies,
Hunger, fire, blood, plague, and double of all evils.

Social conditions are to change; world wide repercussions with an abundance of misfortunes shall beset all, due to the machinations of three brothers.

18

De Flore issue de sa mort sera cause,	Issued from Flora, shall be the cause of her death,
Un temps devant par jeusne & vielle bueyre,	A time before, by fasting and stale drink,
Car les trois lys luy feront telle pause,	For the three lilies, shall make her such a pause,
Par son fruit sauve comme chair crue mueyre.	Saved by her fruit, as raw flesh dead.

The three lilies represent the Fleur de Lys, symbol of France. After a period of want and suffering France will be succored by the sacrifices of her patriots.

19

A soustenir la grand cappe troublee,	To maintain up the great troubled cloak,
Pour l'esclaireir les rouges marcheront,	The red ones shall march to clear it,
De mort famille sera presque accablee,	A family shall be almost crushed to death,
Les rouges rouges, le rouge assommeront.	The red reds, shall knock down the red one.

A conspiracy of cardinals against the Pope is here described.

20

Le faux message par election feinte,	The false message, by a fraudulent election,
Courir par urban rompue pache arreste,	Shall be stopped from going about the town,
Voix aceptees, de sang chapelle tainte,	Voices shall be bought, and a chapel tinted with blood,
Et a un autre l'empire contraincte.	By another, who contests the rule.

By bribery a fraudulent rumor shall be perpetrated, and a bloody struggle will arise in the church.

21

Au port de Agde trois fustes entre-
ront,
Portant infection avec foy & pestilence,
Passant le pont mil milles emble-
ront,
Et le pont rompre a tierce resistance.

In the Port of Agda, three ships
shall enter,
Carrying with them infection and
pestilence,
Going beyond the bridge, they
shall carry away thousands.
At the third resistance the bridge
shall be broken.

Agda, a city in France, shall be the entering point for foreign propaganda, eventually conquering the country thereby.

22

Gorsan, Narbonne, par le sel ad-
vertir,
Tucham, la grace Parpignan trahie,
La ville rouge n'y voudra consentir,
Par haulte Voldrap gris vie faillie.

Gorsan, Narbonne, by the salt shall
give notice,
To Tucham, the grace Perpignan
betrayed,
The red city will not give consent
to it,
By high Voldrap, gray life ended.

French cities are named; by an edict from the "red city" (Rome) help
will be given to their inhabitants.

23

Lettres trouvees de la Royne les
coffres,
Point de subscrit sans aucun nom
d'autheur,
Par la police seront cachez les of-
fres,
Qu'on ne scaura qui sera l'amateur.

Letters found in the Queen's cof-
fers,
No superscription, no name of author,
By the police shall be concealed
the offers,
So that no one shall know who
shall be the lover.

The affair of The Diamond Necklace, involving Cagliostro, the master
swindler, Cardinal Rohan, and the Queen of France, is here indicated.

24

Lieutenant a l'entree de l'huys
Assommera la grand de Perpignan,
En se cuidant sauver a Montper-
tuis,
Sera deceu bastard de Lusignan.

The lieutenant shall at the entrance
of the door,
Knock down the great one of Perpignan,
Thinking to save himself at the
mountain straits,
And the bastard of Lusignan shall
be deceived.

Perpignan, at the frontier between Spain and France, shall be the scene of many disgraceful events.

25

Coeur de l'amant ouvert d'amour
furtive,
Dans le ruisseau fera ravir la Dame,
Le demy mal contrefera lascive,
Le pere a deux privera corps de
l'ame.

The lover's heart, being by a furtive love
Shall cause the lady to be ravished
in the brook,
The lascivious shall counterfeit
half a discontent.
The father shall deprive them both
of their souls.

A father, discovering his mistress and his son in a compromising situation, shall kill both of them.

26

De Carones trouvez en Barcelonne,
Mys descouvers, lieu terrouers &
ruyne,
Le grand qui tient ne voudra Pam-
plonne,
Par l'abbaye de Montferrat bruyne.

From Carons found in Barcelona,
Found discovered, in place of soil
and ruin,
The great that hold, will not Pam-
pelone,
By the abbey of Montserrat, a fine
rain.

This evidently refers to the discovery of some sort of plant, which eventually becomes one of the staple foods of the poor people of Europe.

27

La voye Auxelle l'un sur l'autre fornix,	The way Auxelle, one arch upon another,
Du muy de ser hor mis brave & genest,	Being brave and gallant put out the iron vessel,
L'escript d'Empereur le Phoenix,	The writing of the Emperor, the Phoenix,
Veu en celuy ce qu'a nul autre n'est.	In it shall be seen, what nowhere else is.

The return of Napoleon from Elba is here compared to the rising of the phoenix from its ashes.

28

Les simulachres d'or et d'argent enflez,	The idols swollen with gold and silver,
Qu'apres le rapt, lac au feu furent jettez,	Which after the rape were thrown into the lake and fire,
Au descouvert estaincts tous & troublez,	Being discovered after the putting out of the fire,
Au marbre escripts, perscripts interiettez.	Shall be written in marble, precepts being inserted.

An incident of antiquity is described here: the stealing of gold and silver idols from a temple, their desecration by fire and water, and the subsequent erection of a marble monument inscribed in their honor.

29

Au quart pilier l'on sacre a Saturne,	At the fourth pillar where they sacrifice to Saturn,
Par tremblant terre & deluge fendu,	Shaken by an earthquake and a flood,
Sous l'edifice Saturin trouves urne,	A funeral urn shall be found under that Saturnin edifice,
D'or Capion, ravy & puis rendu.	Full of gold, stolen, and then returned.

A funeral urn, in which the ancient Romans kept the ashes of their great ones, shall be uncovered by an upheaval, but gold will be found in it instead.

30

Dedans Tholose non loing de Belu-
zer,
Faisant un puis loing, palais d'es-
pectacle
Thresor trouve un chacun ira vexer,
Et en deux locs tout & pres des
vesacle.

Within Toulouse not far from Be-
luzer,
Digging a well, for the palace of
spectacle,
A treasure found that shall vex
everyone,
In two parcels and near the Basacle.

In Toulouse, in the industrial part of the city called the Basacle, a
Pandora's box will be found.

31

Premier grand fruict le Prince de
Pesquiere;
Mais puis viendra bien & cruel
malin,
Dedans Venise perdra sa gloire
fiere,
Et mis a mal par plus joyue Celin.

The first great fruit the Prince of
Pescaire,
But he shall become very cruel and
malicious,
He shall lose his fierce pride in
Venice,
And shall be put to evil by the
young Turks.

Pescaire, a town near Naples, will be the birthplace of a statesman.
Rising to power at an early age, he will become arrogant and over-confident.
At the height of his career he will be killed in a duel with a Turk.

32

Garde toy roy Gaulois de ton ne-
pveu,
Qui fera tant que ton unique fils,
Sera meurtry a Venus faisant voeu,
Accompagne denuict que trois &
six.

Take heed, O French King, of thy
nephew,
Who shall cause that thine only
son,
Shall be murdered making a vow
to Venus,
Accompanied with three and six.

Napoleon III, nephew of Napoleon Bonaparte, is referred to here;
the significance being the complete disintegration of Napoleonic prestige
under his reign.

33

Le grand naistra de Veronne &
    Vincense,
Qui portera un surnon bien in-
    digne,
Qui a Venise voudra faire ven-
    geance,
Luy mesme prins homme du guet
    & signe.

The great one of Verona and Vin-
    cenza shall be born,
Who shall bear a very unworthy
    name,
Who shall endeavor at Venice to
    avenge himself,
But he shall be taken by a police-
    man.

Another reference to Mussolini, this retells the sordid details of his
ignoble fate.

34

Apres victoire du Lion au Lion,
Sur la montagne de Jura Seca-
    tombe,
Delues, & brodes septiesme mil-
    lion,
Lyon, Ulme a Mausol mort &
    tombe.

After the victory of the Lion
    against the Lion,
Upon the mountain of Jura, Heca-
    tombe,
Of them decorated, the seventh
    million,
Lyons, Ulme fall dead at Mausol.

The mention of places in Switzerland, France, Germany, and the word
"lion" taken as meaning Great Britain, we believe that these things in
connection with the phrases "seventh million" and "fall dead" refer to
the world wars and their casualties.

35

Dedans l'entree de Garonne &
    Blaye,
Et la forest non loing de Damazan,
Du Marsaves gelees, puis gresle &
    bize,
Dordonnois gelle par erreur de Me-
    zan.

Within the entrance of Garonne
    and Blaye,
And the forest not far from Dama-
    zan,
Of Marsaves frosts, then hail and
    north wind,
Dordonois frozen by the error of
    Mezan.

This describes an unusually bad winter in Europe—rivers frozen solid,
terrible winds and hailstorms raging throughout the land.

36

Sera commis contre Oinde a Duche,	The Duche shall be committed against Oinde,
Se Saulne, & sainct Aubin & Beloeuvre,	Of Saulne and Saint Aubin and Beloeuvre,
Paver de marbre, de tous loing espluche,	To have with marble and of towers well picked,
Non Bleteran resister & chef d'oeuvre.	Not Bleteran to resist, and master stroke.

In these latter-day prophecies, we find a few obscure and unintelligible verses. This quite apparently is one of them.

37

Le forteresse aupres de la Thamise,	The fortress near the Thames,
Cherra par lors, le Roy dedans serre,	Shall fall, then the King that was kept within
Aupres du pont sera veu en chemisee,	Shall be seen near the bridge in his shirt,
Un devant mort, puis dans le fort barre.	One dead before, then in the fort kept close.

The execution of Charles I of England is here predicted. He was beheaded in the city of London on January 30, 1649.

38

Le Roy de Bloys dans Avignon regner,	The King of Blois in Avignon shall reign,
Un autre fois le peuple emonopole,	Another time the people do murmur,
Dedans le Rhosne par murs fera baigner,	He shall cause in the Rhone to be bathed through the walls,
Jusques a cinq, le dernier pres de Nolle.	As many as five, the last shall be near Nole.

A King of France shall occupy Avignon, a city in France belonging to a Pope. Some of the inhabitants, objecting to this seizure, shall be thrown over the city walls into the river.

39

Qu'aura este par prince Bizantin,
Sera tollu par prince de Tholose,
Lay foy de Foix, par le chef Tho-
lentin,
Luy faillira ne refusant l'espouse.

What shall have been by a Byzantine prince,
Shall be taken away by the prince
of Tholose,
The faith of Foix by the chief Tho-
lentin,
Shall fail him, not refusing the
spouse.

The French shall occupy territory in the Near East, formerly ruled by the Mohammedans.

40

Le sang du juste par Taur & la
Dorade,
Pour se venger contre les Saturnins
Au nouveau lac plongeront la
Mainade,
Puis marcheront contre les Alba-
nins.

The blood of the just by Taur and
Dorade,
To avenge themselves against the
Saturnins,
In the new lake shall plunge the
Mainade,
Then shall march against the Al-
banins.

It is an almost impossible task to attempt to place geographically the cities and people named, since they bear no resemblance to any known historical references. The event evidently pertains to a quarrel and a revenge.

41

Esleu sera Renard ne sonnant mot,
Faisant le saint public, vivant pain
d'orge,
Tyrannizer apres tant a un cop,
Mettant la pied des plus grands
sur la gorge.

A fox shall be elected that said
nothing,
Making a public saint, living with
barley bread,
Shall tyrannize after upon a sudden
And put his foot upon the throat
of the greatest.

A prediction regarding a Pope to be elected, who, reputedly a saint, after attaining power shall be a great tyrant.

42

Par avarice, par force & violence,
Viendra vexer les siens chefs
   d'Orleans,
Pres Sainct Memire assault & resistance,
Mort dans sa tente, diront qu'il
   dort leans.

By avarice, and force and violence,
Shall come to vex his own chief of
   Orleans,
Near St. Memire, assault and re-
   sistance,
Dead in his tent, they shall say, he
   sleepeth there.

At St. Memire, a French town, a mutiny against the tyrannical local government chiefs shall result in the murder of one of them. To protect the murderer, the inhabitants shall, for a long time, attempt to conceal the body from the authorities.

43

Par le decide de deux choses bas-
   tars,
Nepveu du sang occupera le regne,
Dedans lectoure seront les coups de
   dards,
Nepveu par pleira l'enseigne.

By the decision of two things, bastards,
Nephew of the blood shall occupy
   the government,
Within Lectore shall be blows of
   darts,
Nephew through fear shall fold up
   his ensigns.

A forecast of conditions in France, during a period of unrest, when low-born persons shall seize power.

44

Le procree naturel l'Ogmion,
De sept a neuf du chemin de-
   storner,
A roy de longue & amy au my
   hom,
Doit a Navarre fort de Pau pros-
   terner.

The natural begotten of Ogmion,
From seven to nine shall be put
   out of the way,
To king of long, and friend to
   half man,
Ought to Navarre prostrate the
   fort of Pau.

An illegitimate son of a great monarch shall attempt to murder the king.

45

La main escharpe & la jambe
    bandee,
Louis puisne de palais partira,
Au mot du guet la mort sera tar-
    dee,
Puis dans le temple a Pasques
    saignera.

The hand on a scarf and the leg
    bandaged,
The younger Louis shall depart
    from the palace,
At the watchword his death shall
    be protracted,
Then afterwards at Easter he shall
    bleed in the temple.

The younger, meaning the last great one of the line of Kings named
Louis (Louis XVI), shall be executed.

46

Pol Mensolee mourra trois lieues
    du Rhone,
Fuis les deux prochains Tarare
    destrois;
Car Mars fera le plus horrible
    throsne,
De coq & d'aigle, de France freres
    trois.

Paul Mensolee shall die leagues
    from the Rhone,
Avoid the two straits near the
    Tarara,
For Mars shall keep such a horrible
    throne,
Of cock and eagle, of France three
    brothers.

Paul Mensolee is warned to avoid the roads to Mt. Tarare, as they are
infested with thieves and murderers.

47

Lac Trasmenian portera tesmoig-
    nage,
Des conjurez sarez dedans Perouse,
Un despolle contrefera le sage,
Tuant Tedesq de Sterne & Minuse.

Trasmenian Lake shall bear wit-
    ness,
Of the conspirators shut up in
    Perugia,
A Des Polle shall simulate the pru-
    dent,
Killing Germans of Sterne and
    Minuse.

A reference to the victory of Hannibal at Lake Trasimenus near the
town of Perugia, Italy.

48

Saturne en Cancer, Jupiter avec Mars,
Dedans Fevrier, Caldondon, salva-terre,
Sault, Castallon, assailly de trois pars,
Pres de Verbiesque, conflit mortelle guerre.

Saturn in Cancer, Jupiter with Mars,
In February Caldondon, ground saved,
The Republic assaulted on three sides,
Near Verbiesque, fight and mortal war.

The oft-repeated warning of a great war is here contained.

49

Satur au beuf, Jove en l'eau, Mars en fleiche,
Six de Fevrier mortalite donra,
Ceux de Tardaigne a Bruge si grand breche,
Qu'a Ponterose chef Barbarin mourra.

Saturn in bull, Jupiter in water, Mars in arrow,
The sixth of February shall give mortality,
Those of Tardaigne shall make in Bruges so great a breach,
That the chief Barbarin shall die at Ponterose.

The event indicated shall occur under the influence of these planets, when Saturn is in Taurus, Jupiter in Aquarius, and Mars in Sagittarius. By the death of the chief Barbarin is meant the death of Pope Urban VIII.

50

La pestilence l'entour de Capadille,
Une aurte faim pres de Sagone s'appreste
Le chevalier bastard de bon senille,
Au grand de Thunes fera tranche la teste.

The plague shall be round about Capadillo,
Another famine cometh near to that of Sagunce,
The knight bastard of the good old man,
Shall cause the great one of Tunis to be beheaded.

Plague and famine shall cause great suffering in both Italy and Spain. Political unrest will set in during this time of stress.

51

Le Bizantin faisant oblation,	The Byzantin, making an offering,
Apres avoir Cordube a soy reprinse;	After he hath taken Cordova to himself again,
Son chemin long, repos pamplation,	His road long, rest, contemplation,
Mer passant proy par la Cologne prinse.	Crossing the sea hath a prey by Cologne.

The reference here is to the abdication of Charles V, King of Spain. He retired to a small house on the grounds of a monastery and spent the last years of his life in study and contemplation.

52

Le roy de Bloys Avignon regner,	The King of Blois shall reign in Avignon,
D'Amboise & seme viendra le long de Lyndre,	He shall come from Amboise and Seme, along the Linden,
Ongle a Poitiers sainctes aisles ruyner	A nail at Poitiers shall ruin his holy wing,
Devant Bony.	Before Bony.

One must delve deeply into this quatrain to gather its full meaning. It depicts the phenomenal rise of Napoleon, and even refers to the unprecedented procedure of the Pope's journey to Paris to crown Napoleon as Emperor.

53

Dedans Bologne voudra laver ses fautes,	Within Boulogne, he shall want to wash himself of his faults,
Il ne pourra au temple du soleil,	In the church of the sun, but he shall not be able,
Il volera faisant chose si hautes,	He shall fly, doing things too high,
En hierarchie n'en fut oneq un pareil.	That in the hierarchy was never the like.

This predicts that Cardinal Richelieu, who attained greater secular heights than any other man of the church, shall wish to go on a holy pilgrimage, but shall defer it too long and shall be prevented from doing so by his death.

54

Soubs la couleur de traicte mariage,
Fait magnanime par grand Chyren Selin,
Quintin, Arras recouvrez au voyage,
D'Espagnols fait second banc Macelin.

Under the pretense of a treaty of marriage,
A magnanimous act shall be done by Henry the Great,
St. Quentin and Arras, recovered in the journey,
Of Spaniards shall be made a second Macelin bench.

A King of France, Henry the Great, through a pretended treaty of marriage, shall acquire new territories. The word Macelin is from the Latin word *Macellum* which means shambles. And the meaning here is that there will be a war and subsequent havoc in Spain.

55

Entre deux fleuves se verra enserre,
Tonneaux a caques unis a passer outre,
Huict ponts rompus chef a tant enferre,
Enfans parfaicts sont jugulez en coultre.

Between two rivers he shall find himself shut up,
Tuns and casks put together to pass over,
Eight bridges broken, the chief at last in prison,
Perfect children shall have their throats cut.

A commander of an army, about to launch an attack, shall be temporarily stopped by the destruction of all bridges across the river near which the enemy is encamped. Causing a pontoon bridge to be built, he and his men will cross over and by a surprise attack will overcome and capture the enemy.

56

La bande foible le terre occupera,
Ceux du haut lieu feront horribles cris,
Le gros troupeau d'estre coin troublera,
Tombe pres D. nebro descouvert les escrits.

The weak party shall occupy the ground,
Those of the high places shall make horrible cries,
It shall trouble the great flock in the right corner,
He falleth near D. nebro discovereth the writings.

The continuing struggles between "left" and "right" political parties are here predicted. The obscurely worded last line leads us to believe that Nostradamus purposely wished to withhold his views as to the ultimate outcome.

57

De souldat simple parveindre en empire,	From a simple soldier, he shall come to have supreme command,
De robe courte parviendra a la longue,	From a short gown he shall come to a long one,
Vaillant aux armes, en eglise ou plus pire,	Valiant in arms, no worse man in the church,
Vexer les prestres comme l'eau faict l'esponge.	He shall vex the priests, as water does a sponge.

A perfect picture of Oliver Cromwell: From a simple soldier he rose to be Lord Protector; from a student in the university he became a graduate of Oxford; and as for vexing the clergy, there was no one of his day who caused them more trouble.

58

Regne en querelle aux freres divise,	A kingdom in dispute and divided between the brothers,
Prendre les armes & le nom Britannique,	To take the arms and the Britannic name,
Tiltre d'Anglican sera tard advise,	And the English title, he shall advise himself late.
Surprins de nuict, mener a l'air Gallique.	Surprised in the night and carried into the French air.

This predicts the abdication of King Edward VIII, and the accession to the throne of his brother, Duke of York, who became George VI.

59

Par deux fois haut, par deux fois mis a bas,	Twice set up high, and twice brought down,
L'Orient aussi l'Occident foiblira,	The East also the West shall weaken,
Son adversaire apres plusieurs combats,	His adversary after many fights,
Par mer chasse au besoing faillira.	Expelled by sea, shall fail in need.

The role of Germany in World Wars I and II is predicted. Both times the goal of that country was world domination, and both times she was defeated by the combined efforts of East and West.

60

Premier an Gaule, premier en Romanie,	The first in France, the first in Romania,
Par mer & terre aux Anglois & Paris,	By sea and land to the English and Paris,
Merveilleux faits par celle grand mesnie,	Wonderful deeds by that great company,
Violant, Terax perdra le Norlaris.	By ravishing, Terax shall ruin Norlaris.

The rapidity of the Nazi expansion (the "blitz" technique) both East and West during the dark days of World War II, the wonderful yet vain resistance of the conquered peoples, the ravishing of the countries—all is here prognosticated.

61

Jamais par le decouvrement du jour	Never by the discovering of the day
Ne parviendra au signe sceptrifere	He shall attain to the scepter bearing sign,
Que tous ses siege ne soient en sejour,	Till all his martial trials be settled,
Portant au coq don du Tag amisere.	Carrying to the cock, a gift from Der Tag of misery.

Three factors in this verse—the use of the alien word "Tag," the warning of war, and the reference to the "Cock" (France)—lead us to believe that here is a prognostication of the now infamous words "Der Tag," which was Germany's rallying cry for the day of vengeance and hoped-for triumph over the democracies.

62

Lors qu'on verra expiler le sainct temple,	When one shall see spoiled the holy temple,
Plus grand du Rhosne & sacres prophaner,	The greatest of the Rhone, and sacred things profaned,
Par eux naistra pestilence si ample,	From them shall come so great a pestilence,
Roy faict injuste ne fera condamner.	That the King being unjust shall not condemn them.

When the city of Lyons, the greatest on the Rhone River, is invaded and pillaged, a pestilence will descend upon the city, destroying both inhabitants and invaders.

63

Quand l'adultere blesse sans coup aura	When the adulterer wounded without a blow,
Meurdry la femme & le fils par despit,	Shall have murdered the wife and son by spite,
Famme assoumes l'enfant estranglera;	The woman knocked down, shall strangle the child,
Huict captifs prins s'estouffer sans respit.	Eight taken prisoners, and stifled without tarrying.

A tragic story is told here, of an adulterer who, through his philandering, contracts a contagious disease and in turn infects his wife and child. Being upbraided by his wife, he attempts to murder her and his son and then flees from the scene. She, dying, strangles her child. Without attempting to investigate the facts of the case, eight innocent persons are hanged for these two murders.

64

Dedans les Isles les enfans transportez,	In the Islands the children shall be transported,
Les deux de sept seront en desespoir;	The two of seven shall be in despair,
Ceux du terrouer en seront supportez,	Those of the company shall be supported by
Nom pelle prins, des ligues fuy l'espoir.	Nompelle taken, avoid the hope of the league.

Two royal children (of a family of seven) shall be exiled from their country, and despite the attempts of a current movement to recall them, they shall not return for many years.

65

Le vieux frustre du principal espoir,	The old man frustrated of his chief hope,
Il parviendra au chef de son empire;	He shall attain to the head of the empire,
Vingt mois tiendra le regne a grand pouvoir,	Twenty months he shall keep the kingdom with great power,
Tiran, cruel en delaissant un pire.	Tyrant, cruel, and leaving a worse one.

Louis XVIII, long frustrated in his ambition to rule France, finally gained the throne in 1814 (at the age of 59) after the downfall of Napoleon.

66

Quand l'escriture D. M. trouvee,	When the writing D. M. shall be found,
Et cave antique a lamp descouverte,	And an ancient cave discovered with a lamp.
Loy, Roy & Prinse Ulpian esprouvee,	Law, King, and Prince Ulpian tried,
Pavillon Royne & Duc sous la couverte.	Tent, Queen and Duke under the cover.

Nostradamus here predicts the event of the re-discovery of his writings and the great new meanings that will be found contained in them.

67

Par. Car. Nersas, a ruine grand discorde,	Par. Car. Nersas, to ruin great discord
Ne l'un ne l'autre n'aura election,	Neither one nor the other shall be elected,
Nersas du peuple aura amour & concorde,	Nersas shall have of the people love and concord,
Ferrare, Collone grand protection.	Ferrara, Colonna shall have great protection.

A great variance of opinion shall lead to strife over the election of a Pope, and as a result the two leading candidates will be defeated and a hitherto unknown will gain that high honor.

68

Vieux Cardinal par le jeune deceu,	An old Cardinal, by a young one shall be deceived,
Hors de sa charge se verra desarme,	And shall see himself out of his position,
Arles ne monstres double soit aperceu,	Arles do not show, a double strength perceived,
Et l'Aqueduct & le Prince embaume.	And the Aqueduct, and the embalmed Prince.

Intrigue and vying for power shall flourish among Princes of the Church, and French cities will take sides in the struggle.

69

Aupres du jeune se vieux Ange baisser, *Et le viendra sur monter a la fin;* *Dix ans esgaux aux plus vieux rabaisser,* *De trois deux l'un huictiesme Sera-phin.*	Near the young one the old angel shall bow, And shall at last overcome him, Ten years equal, to make the old one stoop, Of three, two, one, the eighth a Seraphin.

An old man (referred to as an angel) shall humbly defer to a young man, even through he is aware that he is being cheated. After ten years the old one shall turn upon and overcome the young villain. (The mythical allusions in the last line seem to have no particular meaning.)

70

Il entrera vilain, meschant, infame *Tyrannisant la Mesopotamie* *Tous amis faict d'adulterine dame,* *Terre horrible noir de physiogno-mie.*	He shall come in villain, wicked, infamous, To tyrannize Mesopotamia, He maketh all friends by an adulterous lady, Foul, horrid, black, in his physiognomy.

The country near Babylon shall be terrorized by a person of the Negro race.

71

Croistra le nombre si grand des Astronomes, *Chassez, bannis & livres censurez,* *L'an mil six cens & sept par sacre glomes,* *Que nul aux sacres ne seront as-seurez.*	The number of Astronomers shall grow so great, Driven away, banished, books censured, The year one thousand six hundred and seven years by Glomes, That none shall be secure in sacred places.

Nostradamus dates all events from A. D. 325 (Council of Nicaea); thus 1607 plus 325 equals 1932. On January 30, 1933 Hitler became Chancellor of Germany, ushering in the era of the burning of books, the banishment of men of science, religion and art, the crushing of all culture that did not concur with Nazi doctrines.

72

Champ Perusin O l'enorme deffaite
Et le conflict tout aupres de
Ravenne,
Passage sacre lors qu'on fera la
feste,
Vainqueur vaincu, cheval manger
l'avenne.

Perugian field, O the enormous defeat,
And the fight about Ravenna,
Sacred passage when the feast shall
be celebrated,
The victorious vanquished, the
horse to eat up his oats.

Perugia and Ravenna are cities in Italy, where a decisive battle will be
fought on a holiday.

73

Soldat barbare le grand roy frappera,
In justement non eslongne de
mort,
L'avare mere du faict cause sera,
Conjurateur & regne en grand
remort.

A barbarous soldier shall strike the
king,
Unjustly, not far from death,
The covetous mother shall be the
cause of it,
The conspirator and kingdom in
great remorse.

The meaning is so plain, that to interpret it would be superfluous.

74

En terre neuve bien avant Roy
entre,
Pendant subges luy viendront faire
acueil,
Sa perfidie aura tel recontre,
Qu'aux citadins lieu de feste &
receuil.

In a new land, well after a King
enters,
Whilst his subjects shall come to
welcome him,
His perfidy shall find such an accident,
To the citizens it shall be received
instead of feasts.

An unpopular ruler shall die while on tour in a conquered land. The
citizens shall be joyful thereat.

75

Le pere & fils seront meurdris en-semble,	The father and son shall be mur-dered together,
Le prefecteur dedans son pavillon	The governor shall be so in his tent,
La mere a Tours du fils ventre aura enfle,	At Tours the mother shall be got with child by her son,
Cache verdure de fueilles papillon.	Conceal the greenness with butter-fly leaves.

This depicts murder, violence and incest in the city of Tours—and the fruit of the incest shall be strangled at birth and secretly buried, the small grave covered with grass and leaves and left forever unmarked.

76

Plus Macelin que Roy en Angle-terre,	More Macelin than King in Eng-land,
Lieu obscur nay par force aura l'empire,	Born in obscure place, by force shall rule the empire,
Lasche, sans foy, sans loy, seignera terre,	Of loose morals, without faith, without law, the ground shall bleed.
Son temps s'approche si pres que je souspire.	His time is drawing so near that I sigh.

Macelin is from the Latin word *Macellum*, meaning shambles. A ruler of England is to come, who will be one of the world's worst tyrants and will bring about the near ruin of his country.

77

L'Antechrist trois bien trois anni-chilez,	By Anti-Christ, three shall be brought to nothing,
Vingt & sept ans sang durera sa guerre,	His war shall last seven and twenty years,
Les heretiques morts; captifs exilez,	The heretics dead, prisoners exiled, exiled,
Son corps humain eau rougie, gresler terre.	Blood, human body, water made red, earth shrunk.

In 1918, defeated Germany (Anti-Christ) laid the foundations for her dream of world conquest, which came to an end exactly as Nostradamus predicted, twenty-seven years later in 1945.

78

Un Bragamas avec la langue torte	A Bragamas with his harmful tongue,
Viendra des dieux rompre le sanc-tuaire,	Shall come and break the God's sanctuary,
Aux heretiques il ouvrira la porte,	He shall open the gates to heretics,
En suscitant l'eglise militaire.	By raising the militant church.

The word "Bragamas" denotes a braggard, and the meaning of the verse is that he shall cause great harm to God's sanctuary (the Roman Catholic Church) by his boastful and false claims of great power.

79

Qui par fer pere perdra, nay de Nonnaire,	He who by iron shall destroy his father, born in Nonnaire,
De gorgon sur la fera sang per-fetant,	Shall in the end carry the blood of the gorgon,
En terre estrange fera si tout de taire,	Shall in a strange country make all so silent,
Qui bruslera luy mesme & son entante.	That he shall burn himself, and his double talk.

The reference here is to a man of ruthlessness and cunning who, by these traits, shall gain power over a great country. Suppressing all individual opinion and freedom of speech, he shall rule with an all-powerful hand.

80

Des innocens le sang de vefue & vierge,	The blood of the innocent widow and virgin,
Tant de maux faicts par moyen de grand Roge,	Much evil committed by the means of that great rogue,
Saints simulachres trempez en ar-dant cierge,	Holy images, dipped in burning wax candles,
De frayeur crainte ne verra nul que boge.	For fear, nobody shall be seen to stir.

A band of marauders shall roam the countryside, despoiling the innocent. Church property shall be unsafe and the populace shall be in great fear.

81

Le neur empire en desolation	The new empire in desolation,
Sera change du pole aquilonaire,	Shall be changed from the North-
De la Sicile viendra l'emotion,	ern Pole,
Troubler l'emprise a Philip, tribu-	The commotion shall come from
taire.	Italy,
	To trouble the undertaking, tribu-
	tary to Phillip.

The empire of Germany shall be laid waste by invaders from both the north and south. Spain, her spiritual ally, shall be troubled at the same time.

82

Ronge long, sec, faisant du bon	Long devourer, dry, cringing and
vallet,	fawning,
A la parfin n'aura que son congie.	In conclusion shall have nothing,
Poignant poyson, lettres au collet,	but leave to be gone,
Sera saisi, eschappe, en dangie.	Piercing poison and letters in his
	collar,
	Shall be seized, escape and in
	danger.

This depicts the downfall, capture and escape of a tyrant, before whom people had cringed in fear for many years. Although he is never apprehended, he lives out his years in constant fear and danger and dies a miserable death.

83

Le plus grand voile hors du port de	The greatest sail out of the port of
Zara,	Zara,
Pres de Bisance fera son entreprise,	Near Turkey shall make his under-
D'ennemy perte & l'amy ne fera,	taking,
Le tiers a deux fera grand pille &	There shall be no loss of foes or
prise.	friends,
	The third shall make a great pillage
	upon the two.

The Venetians (Zara) shall take the Island of Tenedos, near Constantinople, without loss of life on either side.

84

Paterne aura de la Sicile crie,
Tous les aprests due Goulphre de Trieste,
Qui s'entendra jusques a la Trinacria,
De tant de voiles, fuy, fuy, l'horrible peste.

Paterno shall have out of Sicily screaming,
All the preparations of the Gulf of Trieste,
That shall be heard as far as Trinacria,
Of so many sails, fly, fly, the horrible plague.

There seems to be a misspelling here in the word Paterno. We believe it refers to Palermo, and warns of a plague that shall strike around that vicinity.

85

Entre Bayonne & a Saincte Jean de Lux,
Sera pose de Mars le promottoire;
Aux Hanix d'Aquilon, Nanar hostera Lux,
Puis suffoque au lict sans adjutoire.

Between Bayonne and St. Jean of Lux,
Shall be put down the promoting of Mars,
From the Hunix of the North, Nanar shall take away Lux,
Then shall be suffocated in bed without help.

After many years of war between France and Spain, peace was declared and a marriage arranged between the King of France and the Infanta of Spain. The last two lines have no significance and we believe they were put in merely to make up the rhyme.

86

Par Arnani, Tholose, Ville Franque,
Bande infinie par le Mont Adrian,
Passe riviere, hutin par pont la planque,
Bayonne entrer tous Bichoro criant.

By Arnani, Toulouse and Villefranche,
An infinite number of people by Mont Adrian,
Cross rivers, noise upon the bridges and planks,
Come all into Bayonne crying Bichoro.

"Bichoro" is an old French word for Victory. Bayonne, on the border of Spain, shall be successfully invaded by the French.

87

Mort conspiree viendra en plein effect,
Charge donnee & voyage de mort,
Esleu, cree, receu, par siens deffaict,
Sang d'innocence devant soy par remort.

A conspired death shall come to an effect,
Charge given, and a journey of death,
Elected, created, received, by his own defeated,
Blood of innocence before him by remorse.

A conspiracy against an elected one is here foreshadowed.

88

Dans le Sardaigne un noble Roy viendra,
Qui ne tiendra que trois ans le Royaume,
Plusieurs couleurs avec soy conjoindra,
Luy mesme apres soin matriscome.

Into Sardinia shall come a noble King,
Who shall hold the Kingdom only three years,
He shall join many colors to his own,
Himself afterwards, care, sleep, repentance come.

A King of Sardinia shall not be in power long, in spite of his strong mercenary army.

89

Pour ne tomber entre mains de son oncle,
Qui les enfans par regner trucidez,
Orant au peuple mettant pied sur Peloncle,
Morts & traisne entre chevaux barbez.

That he might not fall into the hands of his uncle,
That had murdered his children for to rule,
Taking away from the people, and putting his foot on the bald-headed one,
Killed and drawn among horses.

A bald-headed tyrant shall be killed in a dishonorable manner after having misruled the country.

90

Quand des croisez un trouve de sens trouble,	When of the crossed, one of a troubled mind,
En lieu du sacre verra boeuf cornu,	In a sacred place, shall see a horny ox,
Par vierge porc son lieu lors sera double	By virgin swine then shall his place be double,
Par Roy plus ordre ne sera soustenu.	By King henceforth, order shall not be sustained.

A madman, whose symbol is a strange cross, shall be aided in his schemes of conquest by unmitigated scoundrels (pure swine), but his power will be short-lived.

91

Parmy les champs de Rodanes entrees,	Through the fields where the Rhone meanders,
Ou les croisez seront presque unis,	Where the crossed shall be almost united,
Les deuz Brassiers en Pisces rencontrees,	The two Brassiers met in Pisces,
Et un grand nombre par deluge punis.	And a great number punished by a flood.

This quatrain continues from the preceding one, indicating the near-success of the plots of the "madman" and his cohorts and predicting their final overthrow.

92

Loin hors du regne mis en hazard voyage,	Far from the kingdom a hazardous journey undertaken,
Grand ost duyra, pour soy l'occupera,	He shall lead a great army, which he shall make his own,
Le Roy tiendra les siens captif, ostage,	The King shall keep his prisoners and pledges,
A son retour tour pays pillera.	At his return he shall plunder all the country.

A General shall mutiny against a King. In retaliation, the King shall hold his relatives hostage; but on the General's return he shall pillage the country.

93

Sept mois sans plus obtiendra pre- lature	Seven months and no more he shall obtain the prelacy,
Par son decez grand scisme fera naistre,	By his decease he shall cause a great schism,
Sept mois tiendra un aurte la pre- ture,	Another shall be seven months gov- ernor,
Pres de Venise paix union renaistre.	Near Venice peace and union shall grow again.

A sharp division of opinion will occur on the death of a Pope after only seven months in office. It will be further aggravated by the death of a governor who also held office for only seven months. When both offices are again filled, to the satisfaction of the dissenting parties, peace will reign once more.

94

Devant le lac ou plus cher fut gette,	Before the lake, wherein most dear was thrown,
De sept mois, & son ost desconfit,	Of seven months and his army dis- comfited,
Seront Hispans par Albannois gastez,	Spaniards shall be spoiled by Albanians,
Par delay perte en donnant le con- flit.	By delaying, loss in giving the battle.

The League of Nations at Lake Geneva is meant here. Spain shall delay giving battle to the English and be the loser thereby.

95

Le seducteur sera mis dans la fosse,	The deceiver shall be put into the dungeon,
Et estache jusques a quelque temps,	And bound fast for a while,
Le clerc uny, le chef avec sa crosse,	The clergy united, the chief with his cross emblem,
Pycante droite attraira les contens.	Pointing upright, shall draw in the contented.

Those of the party of the Cross shall be supported by the rich. Dissenters shall be thrown into jail in order to keep them from spreading their doctrines of heresy.

96

La Synagogue sterile sans nul fruit,
Sera receue entre les infideles,
De Babylon la fille du persuit,
Misere & triest luy trenchera les aisles.

The Synagogue barren, without fruit,
Shall be received among the infidels,
In Babylon, the daughter of the persecuted,
Miserable and sad shall cut her wings.

There will be a period of great persecution of the Jews, and their Synagogues will become empty and desolate because of it.

97

Aux fine du var changer le pempotans,
Pres du rivage, le trois beaux enfans naistre,
Ruyne au peuple par aage competans
Regne au pays charger plus croistre.

At the finish of the war, to change the glory,
Near the shore shall three fair children be born,
Ruin to the people, by competent age,
To change that country's Kingdom and see it grow no more.

The entire course of a Kingdom shall be changed by the appearance of three brothers, who shall enter into and take over the branches of government.

98

Des gens d'Eglise sang sera espanche,
Comme de l'eau en si grand abondance
Et d'un long temps ne sera restranche,
Veue au clerc ruine & doleance.

The blood of churchmen shall be spilt,
As water in such great abundance,
And for a long time shall not be stayed,
Ruin and grievance shall be seen to the clergy.

This refers to the various religious wars that plagued France and during which numerous clergymen were killed. We believe that it might also indicate the Thirty Years' War, which was primarily a religious conflict.

99

Par la puissance de trois Roys temporels,
En autre lieu sera mis le Saint Siege;
Ou la substance de l'esprit corporel,
Sera remis & receu pour vray siege.

By the power of three temporal Kings,
The Holy See shall be put in another place,
Where the substance of the corporeal spirit,
Shall be restored, and admitted for a true seat.

A coalition of three temporal rulers shall attempt to change the location of the Holy City.

100

Pour l'abundance de l'arme respandue,
Du haut en bas, par le bas au plus haut,
Trop grande foy par jeu vie perdue,
De soif mourir par abondant deffaut.

Through the abundance of the army scattered,
High will be low, low will be high,
Too great a faith, a life lost in jesting,
To die by thirst, through abundance of want.

Nations will increase their military might and great armies will be scattered throughout the world. The people, burdened with the increased taxes for the maintenance of these armies, will finally rebel, and world-wide revolution will follow.

1*

Seront confus plusieurs de leurs attente,	Many shall be confounded in their expectation,
Aux habitants ne sera pardonne,	The people shall not be pardoned,
Qui bien pensoient perseverer l'attente,	Who thought to persevere in their resolution,
Mais grand loisir ne leur sera donne.	But there shall not be given them a great leisure for it.

The collaborationists shall not escape; they shall be sought out and prosecuted.

2

Plusieurs viendront, & parleront de paix,	Many shall come and talk of peace,
Entre Monarques & Seigneurs bien puissans,	Between Monarchs and Lords very powerful,
Mais ne sera accorde de si pres,	But it shall not be agreed to it so soon,
Que ne se rendent, plus qu'autres obeissans.	If they do not show themselves more obedient than others.

We are just on the verge of the fulfillment of this prophecy; relations between powerful industrialists and leaders of the labor organizations shall not be settled soon, unless a greater spirit of cooperation develops.

3

Las quelle fureur, helas quelle pitie,	See! what fury, alas what pity,
Il y aura entre beaucoup de gens!	There shall be betwixt many people,
On ne vit onc une telle amitie,	There never was seen such a friendship,
Qu'auront les loups a courir diligens.	As the wolves shall have in being diligent to run.

Under the guise of political organizational activity, various elements of society shall be set at each other's throats.

* These six stanzas have heretofore been included with Century VIII.

4

Beaucoup de gens viendront parle-
    menter,
Aux grands seigneurs qui leur
    feront la guerre,
On ne voudra en rien les escouter,
Helas! si Dieu n'enuoye paix en
    terre.

Many peoples shall come to speak,
To great lords that shall make war
    against them,
They shall not be admitted to a
    hearing,
Alas! If God does not send peace
    upon earth.

This needs no explanation.

5

Plusieurs secours viendront de tous
    costez,
De gens loingtains qui voudront
    resister;
Ils seront tout a coup bien hastez,
Mais ne pourront pour celte heure
    assister.

Many helps shall come on all sides,
Of peoples far off, that would want
    to resist,
They shall be upon a sudden all
    very hasty,
But for the present they shall not
    be able to assist.

At a time of need, when a great emergency threatens, the nations of the
world will promise to aid the needy, but will not be in a position to give
immediate help.

6

Las quel plaisir ont Princes estrang-
    ers!
Garde toy bien qu'en ton pays ne
    vienne,
Il y auroit de terribles dangers,
En maints contrees, mesme en la
    Vienne.

Ha! Pleasure take foreign Princes,
Guard thyself lest any should come
    into thy country,
There should be terrible dangers,
In several countries, and chiefly in
    Vienna.

A clear warning to the nations of the world to profit by the example
of Austria, and to arm themselves against subversive foreign propaganda.

1

Dans la maison du traducteur de
  Boure,
Seront les lettres trouvees sur la
  table,
Borgne, roux blanc, chenu tiendra
  de cours,
Qui changera au nouveau Connes-
  table.

In the house of the translator of
  Boure,
The letters shall be found upon the
  table,
Blind of one eye, red, white, hoary,
  shall keep its course,
Which shall change at the coming
  of the new constable.

A disseminator of subversive propaganda will be exposed upon the election of a new local governor.

2

Du haut du Mont Aventin voix
  ouye,
Vuides, vuidez de tous les deux
  costez,
Du sang des rouges sera l'ire as-
  somie,
D'Arimin, Prato, Columna de-
  botez.

From the top of Mount Aventine,
  a voice was heard,
Get you gone, get you gone on all
  sides,
With the blood of the red one, the
  passions shall be glutted,
From Arimini and Prato, the
  Colonnas shall be driven away.

Mt. Aventine is one of seven hills of Rome. A fratricidal struggle shall take place in Italy resulting in the ruin of the Colonna family.

278

3

La magna vaqua a Ravenne grand
  trouble,
Conduicts par quinze enserrez a
  Fornase;
A Rome naistra deux monstres a
  teste double,
Sang, feu, deluge, les plus grands
  l'espase.

The magna vaqua great trouble at
  Ravenna,
Conducted by fifteen, shut up at
  Fornase,
At Rome, shall be born two mon-
  sters with a double head,
Blood, fire, flood, the greater ones
  astonished.

The expression "magna vaqua" is a derisive term, meaning a great
nothing. The significance of the quatrain lies in the prediction of the monstrous Rome-Berlin Axis, and the indication of its short but bloody period
of existence.

4

L'an ensuyvant descouverts par
  deluge,
Deux chefs esleuz, le premier ne
  tiendra,
De fuyr ombre a l'un d'eux le refuge,
Saccagee case qui premier main-
  tiendra.

The year following being discovered by a flood,
Two chiefs elected, the first shall
  not hold,
To fly from shade, to one shall be a
  refuge
That house shall be plundered
  which shall maintain the first.

A follow-up of the preceding stanza, this predicts the flight of Mussolini
to Germany, after the crumbling of his power, and the eventual ruin of
both him and Hitler.

5

Tiere doibt du pied au premier
  semblera
A un nouveau Monarque de bas
  haut
Qui Pise & Luiques tyran occupera,
Du precedent corriger le deffault.

The third toe shall be like the first,
To a new high monarch come from
  a low estate,
Who being a tyrant shall occupy
  Pisa and Lucca,
To correct the faults of him that
  preceded him.

One of low estate, pretending to improve conditions in Italy, shall seize
power and become a dictator.

6

Par la Guyenne infinite d'Anglois
Occuperont par nom d'Angle
Aquitaine,
Du Languedoc, I, palme Bour-
delois,
Qu'ils nommeront apres Barboxi-
taine.

There shall be in Guyenne an in-
finite number of English,
Who shall occupy it by the name
of Aquitanian England,
On Languedoc, near the land of
Bordeaux,
Which afterwards they shall call
Barboxitain.

The prediction here is that the English will invade and occupy the west
coast of France near Bordeaux.

7

Qui ouvrira le monument trouve,
Et ne viendra le serrer prompte-
ment,
Mal luy viendra, & ne pourra
prouve,
Si mieux doit estre Roy Breton ou
Normand.

He that shall open the found
sepulchre,
And shall not close it again
promptly,
Evil will befall him, and he shall
not be able to prove
Whether is best, a British or Nor-
man King.

The discovery and opening of the tomb of Tutankhamen brought sudden and mysterious death to the discoverer and to members of his family.

8

Puisnay Roy fait son pere mettre a
mort,
Apres conflict de mort tres in hon-
este;
Escrit trouve soupcon, donra
remort,
Quand loup chasse pose sur la
couchette.

A Younger King causeth his father
to be put
To a dishonest death, after a battle,
Writing being found shall give suspicion and remorse,
When a hunted wolf shall pose on
the cot.

A young prince, during the action of a battle, shall turn and, unseen
by others, shall kill his father. However, after a short time, documents will
turn up in which his murderous intentions are clearly outlined, and he
shall be overthrown.

9

Quand lampe ardente de feu inextinguible	When a lamp burning with an unquenchable fire,
Sera trouvee au Temple des Vestales,	Shall be found in the Temple of the Vestals,
Enfant trouve, feu, eau passant par crible;	A child shall be found, water running through a sieve,
Nismes eau perir, Tholose cheoir les hales.	Nismes to perish by water, the city hall shall fall at Toulouse.

There was a custom among the Vestal Virgins of ancient Rome, pertaining to the punishment of those among them who had forfeited their honor. They were buried alive in a cave, with some bread and water and a lamp with an infinitesimal amount of oil. Beyond this reference, this quatrain holds no greater meaning.

10

Moine, Moinesse d'enfant mort expose,	Monk and Nun having exposed a dead child,
Mourir par ourse ravy par verrier,	To be killed by a bear and be carried away by a glazier,
Par Foix & Panniers le camp sera pose,	The camp shall be pitched at Foix and Panniers,
Contre Tholose, Carcas, dresser sorrier.	Against Toulouse, Carcassone shall be against them.

Neglect of the teaching of spiritual values shall cause innocent children to fall prey to false doctrines.

11

Le just a tort a mort l'on viendra mettre	The just shall be put to death wrongfully,
Publiquement, & du milieu estaint;	Publicly, and being taken out of the midst,
Si grand peste en ce lieu viendra naistre,	So great a plague, shall break into that place,
Que les jugeans fouyr seront contraints.	That the judges shall be compelled to run away.

This has some relation to the preceding stanza, involving an extension of those conditions mentioned.

12

Le tant d'argent de Diane & Mercure,	The so much silver of Diana and Mercury,
Les simulachres au lac seront trouvez;	The statues shall be found in the lake,
Le figulier cherchant argille neuve,	The potter seeking for a new clay,
Luy & les siens, d'or seront abbreuvez.	He and his, shall be filled with gold.

A smooth-tongued demagogue, ever seeking new victims under the pretense of reform, shall be shown to have betrayed and looted all.

13

Les exilez autour de la Solongne	The exiles in the tower of Sologne,
Conduicts de nuict pour marcher en l'Auxois,	Being conducted by night to go into Auxois,
Deux de Modene truculent de Bologne,	Two of Modena, the cruel of Bologna,
Mis, descouverts par feu de Burancois.	Shall be discovered by the fire of Burancois.

Pertaining to a local incident of Nostradamus' time, this merely describes the escape and eventual capture of some criminals.

14

Mis en planure chauderon d'infecteurs,	On the plain shall be put a great dyers vat,
Vin, miel, & huyle, & bastis sur fourneaux,	Filled with wine, honey and oil and built on a furnace,
Seront plongez, sans mal dit malfacteurs,	In it shall be plunged without evil, those called malefactors,
Sept, fum, extaint au canon des Bordeaux.	Seven, summoned, at the law of Bordeaux.

Boiling in oil, a favorite punishment reserved for counterfeiters in ancient France, shall be meted out to seven persons at Bordeaux.

15

Pres de Parpan les rouges detenus,
Ceux du milieu parfondrez menez
   loing;
Trois mis en pieces, & cinq mal
   soustenus,
Pour le Seigneur & Prelat de Bour-
   boing.

Near unto Parpan, the red ones
   detained,
Those of the middle sunk and carried far away,
Three cut in pieces and five ill sus-
   tained,
For the Lord and Prelate of Bur-
   going.

One of the many feuds among the cardinals and lesser clergymen is
herein described.

16

De Castel Franco sortira l'assemblee,
L'ambassadeur non plaisant fera
   scisme;
Ceux de Riviere seront en la
   meslee,
Et au grand goulphre desnier ont
   l'entree.

From Spanish Franco shall come
   the assembly,
The Ambassador not pleased, shall
   make a separation,
Those of the Riviera, shall be in
   the melee,
And shall deny entry into the great
   gulf.

This quatrain is remarkable in that it exactly names the protagonist
involved. The reference is, of course, to Franco, the Spanish Civil War
and its repercussions.

17

Le tiers premier, pis que ne fit
   Neron,
Vuidez vaillant que sang humain
   respandre,
R'edificer fera le Forneron,
Siecle d'or, mort, nouveau Roy
   grand esclandre.

The third first, worse than ever did
   Nero,
Go out of the valiant, he shall
   spill much human blood,
He shall cause the Forneron to be
   rebuilt,
Golden age dead, new King great
   troubles.

This points directly to King Charles IX, third son of Henry II. The
most notorious event of his reign was the infamous Massacre of St. Bartholomew.

18

Le lys Dauffois portera dans Nancy,
Jusques en Flandres Electeur de
l'Empire,
Neufve obturee au grand Mont-
morency,
Hors lieux prouvez delivre a clere
peyne.

The Dauphin shall carry the lily
into Nancy,
As far as Flanders the Elector of
the Empire,
New hindrance to great Mont-
morency,
Out of proved places, delivered to
a clear pain.

An incident in the reign of Louis XIII when Nancy was conquered by the Dauphin.

19

Dans le milieu de la Forest May-
enne,
Sol au Lyon la fourdre tombera,
Le grand bastard issu du grand du
Maine,
Ce jour Fougere pointe en sang en-
trera.

In the middle of the Forest of
Mayenne,
Sol being in Leo, the lightning shall
tumble,
The great bastard, begat by the
great du Main,
That day Fougeres shall enter its
point into blood.

An incident pertaining to one of the noble families of ancient France, this needs no further interpretation.

20

De nuict viendra par la forest de
Reines,
Deux pars Voltorte Herne, la pierre
blanche,
Le moine noir en gris dedans
Varennes,
Esleu cap. cause tempeste, feu,
sang tranche.

By night shall come through the
forest of Reines,
Two parts Voltorte Herne, the
white stone,
The black monk in gray within
Varennes,
Elected captain, causeth tempest,
fire, blood running.

At Varennes, Louis XVI, disguised in a monk's cloak, was intercepted as he attempted to escape from the Revolutionists.

21

Au temple haut de Bloys sacre Salonne,	At the high temple of Blois sacred Salon,
Nuict pont de Loyre, Prelat, Roy pernicant;	In the night the bridge of Loire, Prelate, King pernicious,
Cuiseur victoire aux marests de la Lone,	A poignant victory in the marshes of Lone,
D'ou Prelature de blancs abormeant.	Whence Prelature of white shall be abortive.

During the course of one night, both a Prelate and a King will meet their deaths on a bridge, much to the rejoicing of the lesser clergy of the region.

22

Roy & sa court au lieu de langue halbe,	King and his court in the place of half language,
Dedans le temple vis a vis du palais,	Within the church, near the palace,
Dans le jardin Duc de Mantor & d'Albe,	In the garden, Duke of Mantor and of Alba,
Albe & Mantor, poignard, langue & palais.	Alba and Mantor, dagger, tongue in the palace.

This continues the story of the previous quatrain, describing the intrigue and scandal that prevailed in both the church and the palace.

23

Puisnay jouant au fresch dessous la tonne,	The youngest son playing under the tun,
Le haut du toit du millieu sur la teste,	The top of the house shall fall on his head,
Le pere Roy au temple sainct Salonne,	The king, his father, in the temple of Saint Soulaine,
Sacrifiant sacrera fum de feste.	Sacrificing shall make festival smoke.

A young prince shall be injured by the cave-in of a house. No greater significance can be gathered from this obscure verse.

24

Sur le palais au rocher des fenestres *Seront ravis les deux petits royaux,* *Passer Aurelle, Lutece, Denis clois-* *tres,* *Nonnain, Mallods avalle verts* *noyaux.*	Upon the palace at the rock of the windows, Shall be carried the two little royal ones, To pass Aurele, Lutece, Denis cloisters, Nonnain, Mollods to swallow green kernels of fruit.

The journey of two children of a royal household is herein described.

25

Passant les Ponts, venir pres des *rosiers,* *Tard arrive plustost qu'il cuydera,* *Viendront les noves Espagnols a* *Besiers,* *Qui icelle chasse emprinse cassera.*	Going over the bridge, to come near the rose-trees, Arriving late, much sooner than he thought, Shall come the news of Spaniards to Beziers, Who shall chase this hunting un- dertaking.

In this particular section Nostradamus seems concerned merely with trivial events of his day; this quatrain continues in that vein, describing an incident in a hunting expedition.

26

Nice sortie sur nim des lettres *aspres,* *La grand cappe fera present non* *sien;* *Proche de vultry aux murs de vertes* *capres* *Apres Plombin le vent a bon* *escient.*	A foolish going out, caused by sharp letters, The great cap shall give what is not his, Near Vultry by the walls of green capers, About Piombino the wind shall be in good earnest.

The Pope is here referred to as "the great cap," and the meaning is that he shall be the arbitrator in a dispute between the Italian cities of Velitrum and Piombino.

27

De bois la garde, vent clos rond
pont sera,
Haut le receu frappera de Dauphin,
Le vieux Teccon bois unis passera,
Passant plus outre du Duc le droict
confin.

The fence being of wood, close
wind, bridge shall be broken,
He that is received high, shall strike
at the Dauphin,
The old Teccon shall pass over
smooth wood,
Going to the right on the side of
the Duke.

Malcontents shall attempt to form a conspiracy against the government, but it shall be put down almost immediately due to the leaders betraying their cause and going over to the side of the Duke.

28

Voille Symacle, Port Massiliolique,
Dans Venise port marcher aux Pannons,
Partir du goulfre & Synus Illyrique,
Vast a Sicille, Ligurs coups de
canons.

Symaclian Sail, Massillion port,
In Venice to march towards the
Hungarians,
To go away from the Gulf and
Illyrian Straits,
Towards Sicily, the Genoese, with
cannon shots.

A great expedition from Marseilles, arriving at Venice, shall march towards the Hungarians. The Genoese will be driven from Sicily by cannon shots.

29

Lors que celuy qu'a nul ne donne
lieu,
Abandonner voudra lieu prins non
pris;
Feu, nef, par saignes, bitument a
Charlieu,
Seront Quintin, Balez reprins.

When he that giveth place to nobody,
Shall forsake the place taken and
not taken,
Fire, ship, by bloody bitumen at
Charlieu,
Then St. Quentin and Calais shall
be taken.

The powerful dictator shall retreat from northern France, and Calais shall be retaken from him.

30

Au port de Puola & de Saincte Nicolas,	At the harbor of Puola and St. Nicolas,
Perir Normandie au Goulfre Phanatique,	A Norman ship shall perish in the Fanatic Gulf,
Cap de Bizance rues crier helas!	At the Cape of Byzantia, the streets shall cry "Alas!"
Secors de Gaddes & du grand Philippique.	Help from Cadiz and from the Spanish King.

The reference here is to the port of Malta, which was besieged by the Turks. Philip II, King of Spain, sent an army to relieve it, which caused a great commotion among the people of Constantinople.

31

Le tremblement de terre a Mortars,	There shall be an earthquake by mortars,
Cassich, Sainct Georges a demy perfondrez,	Cassich, St. George shall be half swallowed up,
Paix assoupie, la guerre esueillera,	The war shall awake the sleeping peace,
Dans temple a Pasques abysmes enfondrez.	On Easter Day, shall be a great hole sunk in the temple.

Terrific artillery fire shall shake the earth; England (St. George) shall be almost defeated; the war shall spread to the ends of the earth; and on Easter Day, a great cathedral will be hit by a bomb.

32

De fin porphire profond collon trouvee	A deep column of fine Porphyry shall be found,
Dessous la laze escripts capitolin;	Under whose base shall be important writings,
Os, poil retors, Romain force prouvee,	Bones, hairs twisted, Roman force tried,
Classe agiter au port de Methelin.	A fleet about the port of Methelin.

Porphyry (A. D. 233–305), a Neoplatonic philosopher, wrote many treatises against Christianity.

33

Hercules Roy de Rome & Dannemarc,	Hercules, King of Rome, and Denmark,
De Gaule trois Guion surnomme,	Of France three Guyon surnamed,
Trembler l'Italie & l'un de sainct Marc,	Shall cause Italy to quake and one of Venice,
Premier sur tous Monarque renomme.	He shall be above all a famous monarch.

We believe that the "Hercules" referred to indicates the powerful and famous Napoleon, before whom all Europe quaked.

34

La parte solus mary sera mittre.	The separated husband shall wear a mitre,
Retour conflict passera sur la tuille;	Returning, battle, he shall go over the tiles,
Par cinq cens un trahye sera tiltre,	By five hundred, one dignified shall be betrayed,
Narbon & Saulce par coutaux avons d'huille.	Narbon and Saulce shall have oil by Quintal.

Here is one of the most famous and most discussed prophecies of Nostradamus, and the most remarkable for its mention of so many actual names—Narbon (Narbonne), Louis XVI's minister of war; Saulce, oilman and mayor of Varennes; and the reference to "over the tiles" (Tuileries), which was not a palace when Nostradamus was alive, but was the location of kilns for tiles. The interpretation, then, is that the king and queen were arrested at Varennes because Saulce betrayed them to the soldiers when they came to his shop. The five hundred men were the Marseillais who attacked the palace of Tuileries and formally put the king under arrest. At that time the king was wearing the red "miter" of the Revolution.

35

Et Ferdinand blonde sera descorte,	And Ferdinand having a troop of blond men,
Quitter la fleur, suyure le Macedon,	Shall leave the flower to follow the Macedonian,
Au grand Besoing defaillira sa routte,	At his great need his road shall fail him,
Et machera contre le Myrmidon.	And he shall go against the Myrmidon.

King Ferdinand, of Bulgaria, with a German Army at his command, shall campaign against the Greeks and Macedonians, but he shall fail to conquer them.

36

Un grand Roy prins entre les mains d'un jeune,	A great King taken in the hands of a young one,
Non loin de Pasques, confusion, coup cultre,	Not far from Easter, confusion, of a knife,
Perpet. cattif temps, que foudre en la hune,	Shall commit, pitiful time, the fire at the top of the mast,
Trois freres lors se blesseront, & meurtre.	Three brothers then shall wound one another, and murder done.

The reference here is to the execution of Louis XVI, on January 21, 1793; and also indicating the confusing state of affairs in France at that time.

37

Pont & molins en Decembre versez	Bridges and mills in December overturned,
En si hault lieu montera la Garonne;	In so high a place the Garonne shall come,
Murs, edifice, Tholose renversez,	Walls, buildings, Toulouse overturned,
Qu'on ne scaura son lieu autant matronne.	So that no one shall know its place, so much Matrone.

A tremendous overflowing of the Garonne River shall occur in December with disastrous destruction of life and property.

38

L'entree de Blaye par Rochelle & l'Anglois,	The entrance of Blaye, by Rochelle and the English,
Passera outre le grand Aemathien,	Shall go beyond the great Aemathien,
Non loing d'Agen attendra le Gaulois,	Not far from Agen shall expect the French,
Secours Narbonne deceu par entretien.	Help from Narbonne deceived by entertainment.

The English will attempt an invasion of France by way of Bordeaux (Blaye). The French will issue a call for help to the people of Southern France, but, spurred on by traitors in their midst, they shall refuse to aid their countrymen.

39

En Arbissela, Vezema & Crevari
De nuict conduicts par Savone
attraper,
Le vif Gascon, Giury & la Charry.
Derrier mur vieux & neuf palais
gripper.

By Arbisella, Vezema and Crevari,
Being conducted by night to take
Savonna,
The quick Gascon, Giury and the
Charry,
Behind old walls and new palaces
to grapple.

An incident concerning the minor disturbances between the Italians
and Gascons in Nostradamus' day is described.

40

Pres de Quentin dans la forest
Bourlis.
Dans l'Abbaye seront Flamens
tranchez,
Les deux puisnais de coups my
estourdis,
Suitte oppressee & garde tous
haches.

Near St. Quentin in the forest of
Bourlis.
In the Abbey the Flemish shall be
slashed,
The two younger sons half aston-
ished with blows,
The followers oppressed, and the
guards cut to pieces.

An incident during the war in the Flemish lowlands between Flamans
and the Spaniards, this concerns a peculiar accident which caused much
talk at that time.

41

Le grand Chyren soy saisir d'Avignon,
De Rome lettres en miel plein
d'amertume,
Lettre ambassade partir de Chanignon,
Carpentras pris par Duc noir
rouge plume.

The great Henry shall seize upon
Avignon,
Letters from Rome shall come full
of bitterness,
Letters and embassies shall go to
Chanignon,
Carpentras taken by a black Duke
with a red feather.

This prophecy was fulfilled when Avignon, the one time seat of Papal
power, was seized by the French King.

42

De Barcelonne, de Gennes &
Venise,
De la Sicille pres Monaco unis,
Contre Barbare classe prendront la
vise,
Barbar poulse bien loing jusqu'a
Thunis.

From Barcelona, from Genoa and
Venice,
From Sicily near Monaco united,
Against the Barbarians the fleet
shall take her aim,
The Barbarian shall be driven back
as far as Tunis.

Spain and Italy united in war, shall be driven back in Africa as far as Tunis.

43

Proche a descendre l'armee cru-
cigere,
Sera guettee par les Ismaelites,
De tous costez batus par nef
Raviere,
Prompt assaillis de dix galeres
d'eslites.

The crusading army being about
the land,
Shall be watched by the Ismaelites,
Being beaten on all sides, the ship
carried away,
Presently assaulted by ten chosen
warships.

A crusading (Christian) army shall attempt an incursion against non-believers. They shall meet with great resistance and will be forced to withdraw.

44

Migrez, migres de Geneve tres-
tous,
Saturne d'or en fer se changera,
Le contre Raypoz exterminera tous,
Avant l'advent le Ciel signes fera.

Leave, leave, go forth out of
Geneva, all
Saturn of gold, shall be changed
into iron,
The contrary of the positive ray
shall exterminate all,
Before it happens, the Heavens
shall show signs.

Startling! Nostradamus here foretells the advent of atomic power. He indicates clearly that this force can be used for useful or destructive purposes. But, with terrifying finality, he warns of the eventual destruction of our civilization by means of the release of atomic energy—holding out but one ray of hope, "the Heavens shall show signs," meaning that we will be given one final chance to determine our destiny.

45

Ne sera soul jamais de demander,	He shall never be weary of asking,
Grand Mendosus obtiendra son empire	Great Liar shall obtain his dominion,
Loing de la court fera contre·mander,	Far from the court he shall be countermanded,
Piedmont, Picart, Paris, Tyrhen le pire.	Piedmont, Picardy, Paris, Tyrhenia the worse.

This points to the doctrine of lies and deceit which was the cornerstone of the Nazi philosophy; and indicates the final downfall of the regime.

46

Vuydez, fuyez de Tholose les rouges,	Get you gone, fly from Toulouse, ye red ones,
Du sacrifice faire expiation,	There shall expiation be made of the sacrifice,
Le chef du mal dessous l'ombre des courges,	The chief cause of the evil under the shadow of the gourds,
Mort estrangler carne omination.	Shall be strangled, a presage to the destruction of much flesh.

In Toulouse, the red ones (cardinals) are warned of an imminent on-slaught against members of the clergy.

47

Les soub signez d'indigne delivrance,	The undersigned to a worthless deliverance,
Et de la multe auront contre advis,	Shall have from the multitude a contrary advice,
Change monarque mis en perille pence,	Changing their monarch and put him in peril,
Serrez en cage se verront vis a vis.	They shall see themselves shut up in a cage.

A petition to deliver a monarch from imprisonment shall be against the will of the people; and for this, the petitioners themselves shall be jailed.

48

La grand cite d'ocean maritime,
Environnee de marets en crystal;
Dans le solstice hyemal & la prime,
Sera tentee de vent espouvental.

The great maritime city of the ocean,
Encompassed with marshes of crystal,
In the winter solstice and the spring,
Shall be tempted with a fearful wind.

The people of London are warned of the approach of a great hurricane which will cause much damage to the city.

49

Gand & Bruxles marcheront contre Anvers,
Senat de Londres mettront a mort leur Roy,
Le sel & vin luy seront a l'envers,
Pour aux avoir le regne en desarroy.

Ghent and Brussels shall march against Antwerp,
The Senate of London shall put their King to death,
The salt and wine shall not be able to do him good,
That they may have the kingdom into ruin.

This is a most remarkable prophecy, for here we have a concatenation of circumstances starting with the number of the quatrain itself, 49; and the unmistakable event referred to was the execution of King Charles 1 in the year 1649.

50

Mendosus tost viendra a son haut regne,
Mettant arriere un peuple Norlaris,
Le rouge blesme, le mesle a l'interregne,
Le jeune crainte & frayeur Barbaris.

Mendosus shall soon come to his high government,
Putting aside a little the Norlaris,
The red pale, the male at the inter-reigne
The young fear, and dreadful barbarism.

The great liar (see Quatrain 45) shall gain supremacy, being especially successful in operations among young people.

51

Contre les rouges sectes se ban-
deront,
Feu, eau, fer, corde, par paix se
minera,
Au point mourir ceux qui machi-
neront,
Fors un que monde sur tout ruynera.

Against the reds, sects shall gather
themselves,
Fire, water, iron, rope, by peace it
shall be destroyed,
Those that shall conspire shall be
put to death,
Except one, who above all shall
ruin the world.

Many peoples will join in a coalition against the "reds"; and even
during a so-called period of peace there will be much bloodshed due to
the bitterness of the dissenting groups.

52

La paix s'approche d'un coste & la
guerre,
Oncques ne fut la poursuite si
grande,
Plaindre homme, femme, sang
innocent par terre,
Et ce sera de France a toute bande.

Peace is coming on one side, the
war on the other,
There never was so great a pursuit,
Man, woman, shall bemoan, inno-
cent blood shall be spilt,
It shall be in France at all sides.

The events depicted came to pass during the reign of Charles IX,
when France was embroiled in a series of wars, and was torn internally
by the constant struggles between the Protestant and Catholic factions
of the population.

53

Le Neron jeune dans les trois
cheminees,
Fera de paiges vifs pour ardoir
jetter,
Heureux qui loing sera de tels
menees,
Trois de son sang le feront mort
guetter.

The young Nero in the three chim-
neys,
Shall cause pages to be thrown to
be burnt alive,
Happy shall be he, who shall be far
from this doing.
Three of his own blood shall cause
him to be put to death.

A tyrannical leader (here referred to as a Nero) shall cause much
destruction of life and property. Three men of his own class shall
destroy him.

54

Arrivera au port de Corsibonne,	There shall come into the port of
Pres de Ravenna qui pillera la dame,	Corsibonne
En mer profonde legat de la Ulisbonne,	Near Ravenna, those that shall plunder the lady,
Sous roc cachez raviront septante ames.	In the deep sea shall be the Ambassador of Lisbon,
	The hidden under the rock, shall carry away seventy souls.

Corsica shall be the birthplace of one (Napoleon) who shall plunder Italy and cause great damage to the whole of Europe.

55

L'horrible guerre qu'en occident s'appreste;	The horrible war is in preparation in the west,
L'an ensuivant viendra la pestilence,	The year following shall come the plague,
Si fort terrible, que jeune, vieil, ne beste,	So strangely terrible, that young, old, nor beast shall escape.
Sang, feu, Mercu, Mars, Jupiter en France.	Blood, fire, Mercury, Mars, Jupiter in France.

In the western area, a horrible war is in preparation; following this will come a terrible plague, such as the world has never seen before.

56

Camp pres de Noudam passera Goussanville,	A camp shall by Noudam pass Goussanville,
Et a Maiotes laissera son enseigne,	And shall leave its flag at Maiotes,
Convertira en instant plus de mille,	And shall in an instant convert more than a thousand,
Cherchant les deux remettre en chaine & legne.	Seeking to put the two parties in good understanding.

Events and towns related here are of no importance now, but had local significance in Nostradamus' day.

57

Au lieu de Drux un roy reposera,
Et cherchera loy changeant d'an-
atheme,
Pendant le ciel si tresfort tonnera,
Portee neufue Roy tuera soy-
mesme.

In the place of Drux a king shall
repose,
And shall seek a law changing
anathema,
In the meanwhile the heaven shall
thunder so strongly,
That a new gate shall kill the King
himself.

Drux is a city in Normandy; and in this region the King shall attempt
to alter the local religious customs, without success.

58

Au coste gauche a l'endroit de
Vitri,
Seront guettez les trois rouges de
France,
Tous assoumez rouge, noir non
meurdry,
Par les Bretons remis en asseurance.

On the left coast over against
Vitry,
The three red ones of France shall
be watched for,
All the red shall be beaten to death,
the black not murdered,
By the Britons set up again in secu-
rity.

The British shall re-establish a government in France; radicals shall
be eliminated from any participation in it.

59

A la Ferte prendra la Vidame,
Nicol tenu rouge qu'avoit produit
la vie,
La grand Loyse naistra que fera
clame,
Donnant Bougongne a Bretons par
envie.

In the Ferte the Vidame shall take,
Nicol, reputed red, who is the
product of life,
The great Louis shall be born, who
shall lay claim,
Giving Burgundy to the Britons
through envy.

The reds shall be beaten by the opposite party, with the aid of a British
leader named Louis, who will ask for payment in the form of an alliance
between France and England.

60

Conflict barbare, en la cornere noire,
Sang espandu trembler la Dalamatie,
Grand Ismael mettra son promontoire,
Ranes trembler, secours Lusitanie.

A barbarous fight in the black corner,
Blood shall be spilt, Dalamatia shall tremble for fear,
Great Ishmael shall set up his promontory,
Frogs shall tremble, Portugal shall bring succour.

Inter-sectional warfare among the Mohammedans is here predicted.

61

La pille faite a la coste marine,
Incite nova & parens amenez,
Plusieurs de Malte par le fait de Messine,
Estroit serrez seront mal guerdonnez.

The plunder shall be made on the sea coast,
Incited by new people and friends brought up,
Many of Malta, for the fact of Messina,
Being kept close, shall be ill rewarded.

A coalition of small nations, hitherto considered peaceful and harmless, shall attempt to gain control of Europe.

62

Au grand de Cheramonagora,
Seront croisez par rangs tous attachez,
Le Pertinax Oppi, & Mandragora,
Raugon d'Octobre le tiers seront laschez.

To the great one of Cheramonagora,
Shall be crossed by ranges, all tied up.
The Pertinax Oppi, and Mandragora,
Raugon the third of October shall be set loose.

There is a warning implicit in the words of this quatrain, of a world-shaking event that will take place on October third.

63

Plainctes & pleurs, cris & grands hurlements,
Pres de Narbon a Bayonne & en Foix,
O quel horribles, calamitez, changemens,
Avant que Mars revolu quelquefois.

Complaints and tears, cries and great howlings,
Near Narbonne, Bayonne and in Foix,
O what horrid calamities and changes,
Before Mars has made somewhat his revolution.

Much disturbance in France is foreseen, with many changes taking place, leading to a completely reorganized government.

64

L'Aemathion passer monts Pyrenees,
En Mars Narbon ne fera resistance,
Par mer & terre fera si grand menee,
Cap. n'ayant terre seure pour demeurance.

The invader shall pass the Pyrenean Mountains,
In March Narbonne shall make no resistance,
By sea and land he shall make so much ado,
Cap. shall not have safe ground to live in.

An invasion shall come to France, by way of the Spanish Frontier.

65

Dedans le coing de Luna viendra rendre,
Ou sera prins & mis en terre estrange,
Les fruicts immeurs seront a grand esclandre,
Grand vitupere, a l'un grande louange.

He shall come into the corner of Luna,
Where he shall be taken and put in a strange land,
The green fruits shall be in great disorder,
A great shame, to one shall be great praise.

This stanza has a relation to the preceding one, in that the invaded land shall be despoiled.

66

Paix, union sera & changement,
Estats, Offices, bas hault, & hault
bien bas,
Dresser voyage, le fruict premier,
torment,
Guerre cesser, civils proces, debats.

Peace, union, shall be and profound changes,
Estates, offices, the low high and
the high very low,
A journey shall be prepared for, the
first fruit, pains,
War shall cease, also civil processes
and strife.

A Utopian age shall come into being in the course of time, but not
without pain.

67

Du hault des monts a l'entour de
Dizere,
Port a la roche Valent, cent assem-
blez,
De Chasteau-Neuf, Pierrelate, en
Douzere,
Contre le Crest, Romains for as-
semblez.

From the top of the mountains
about Dizere,
Gate at the rock Valence, a hun-
dred gathered together,
From Chateau Neuf, Pierrelate, in
Douzere,
Against the Crest, Romans shall be
assembled.

This prophecy, obscure and meaningless to us, was directed to the people in the provinces of Dauphine and Languedoc, in which all the towns
and rivers mentioned were situated.

68

Du mont Aymar sera noble obscur-
cie,
Le mal viendra au joinct de Saone
& Rhosne,
Dans bois cachez soldats jour de
Lucia,
Que ne fut onc un si horrible
throsne.

From Mount Aymar shall proceed
a noble obscurity,
The evil shall come to the joining
of the Saone and Rhone,
Soldiers shall be hid in the wood
on St. Lucia's Day,
So that there was never such a horrible throne.

A group of men, banded together in a conspiracy to overthrow the
local government, shall attempt a march on the city of Lyons, but shall be
overcome by soldiers during a battle in the forest just outside the city.

69

Sur le mont de Bailly & la Bresse,
Seront cachez de Grenoble les fiers,
Outre Lyon, Vien, eulx si grand
    gresle,
Langoult en terre n'en restera un
    tiers.

Upon the Mount of Bailly and the
    country at Bresse,
Shall be hidden the fierce ones of
    Grenoble,
Beyond Lyons, Vienna, upon them
    shall fall such a hail,
That languishing on the ground,
    not even a third shall be left.

A fearful hail (bombardment) shall fall on parts of Italy and Austria,
destroying two-thirds of the population.

70

Harnois trenchans dans les flam-
    beaux cachez
Dedans Lyon le jour de Sacrement,
Ceux de Vienne seront trestour
    hachez,
Par les Cantons Latins, Mascon
    eront.

Sharp weapons shall be hidden in
    burning weapons,
In Lyons the day of the Sacrament,
Those of Vienna shall be cut to
    pieces,
By the Latin Cantons, after the ex-
    ample of Mascon.

This foretells the advent of terrible incendiary weapons; and deplores
the rise of a science that may lead mankind to ultimate destruction.

71

Aux lieux sacrez, animaux veu a
    Trixe,
Avec celuy qui n'osera le jour,
A Carcassonne pour disgrace pro-
    pice,
Sera pose pour plus ample sejour.

The place of sacred objects shall be
    seen at Trixe,
With him that shall not dare in
    the day,
In Carcassone for a favourable dis-
    grace,
He shall be set to make a longer
    stay.

Holy objects in France shall be defiled, by temporary invaders.

72

Encor seront les saincts temples pollus,
Et expillez par Senat Tholosain,
Saturne deux trois siecles revollus,
Dans Avril, May, gens de nouveau levain.

Once more shall the Holy Temple be polluted,
And depredated by the Senate of Toulouse,
Saturn two, three cycles revolving,
In April, May, people of a new leaven.

According to this prophecy, there will be a complete revision of the basic concepts of religion about the year 2150 (600 years after it was written), and a new world order will arise (possibly one religion for all).

73

Dans Fois entrez Roy cerule Turban,
Et regnera moins evolu Saturne,
Roy turban blanc, Bizance coeur ban,
Sol, Mars, Mercure, pres la hurne.

In Foix shall come a King with a blue Turban,
And shall reign before Saturn is revolved,
Then a King with a white turban shall make Turkey quake,
Sol, Mars, Mercury being near the top of the mast.

Foix, a city in southern France, shall be the center of military disturbances, culminating in the selection of a ruler who will bring great prosperity.

74

Dans la cite de Fertsod homicide,
Fait & fait multe beuf arant ne macter,
Retours encores aux honneurs d'Artemide,
Et a Vulcan corps morts sepulturer.

In the city of Fertsod, murder shall be done,
Causing a fine to be laid for killing a plow ox,
There shall be a return of the honors due to Artemide,
And Vulcan shall bury dead bodies.

In this quatrain, Nostradamus pays honor to a spiritual "contemporary," the writer Artemidorus (100 B.C.), who was widely known in his day for his writings on augurs, and whose books on dream interpretation are still extant.

75

De l'Ambraxie & du pays de
  Thrace,
Peuple par mer, mal & secours
  Gaulois,
Perpetuelle en Provence la trace,
Avec vestiges de leur coustumes &
  loix.

From Ambraxia, and from the
  country of Thracia,
People by sea, evil and French as-
  sistance,
The trace of it shall be perpetual in
  Provence,
The footsteps of their customs and
  laws remaining.

Provence is shown here by Nostradamus, to have been settled originally by Thracians, with vestiges of the original laws and customs still remaining.

76

Avec le noir rapax & sanguinaire,
Yssu de peaultre de l'inhumain
  Neron,
Emmy deux fleuves main gauche
  militaire,
Sera meurtry par Joyne Chaul-
  veron.

With the black and rapacious near
  a bloody peace,
Descended from the hide of the in-
  human Nero,
Between two rivers, by the left
  military hand,
He shall be murdered by Joyn
  Caulveron.

One of a like character to Nero, black and rapacious, shall meet a violent death at the hands of revolutionaries.

77

Le regne prins le Roy conviera,
La dame prinse a mort jurez a sort,
La vie a Royne fils on desniera,
Et la pillex au fort de la consort.

The Kingdom being taken the King
  shall invite,
The lady taken to death,
The life shall be denied unto the
  Queen's son,
And the Pellex shall be at the
  height of her ease.

The Latin word Pellex means a concubine. The signification here is that a King, having taken another country, puts his Queen and her son to death, taking his concubine as wife and crowning her Queen of his enlarged kingdom.

78

La Dame Greque de beaute laydique,	The Grecian Lady of exquisite beauty,
Heureuse faicte de proces innumerable,	Made happy from innumerable quarrels,
Hors translatee au Regne Hispanique,	Being translated into the Spanish Kingdom,
Captive prinse mourir mort miserable.	Shall be made a prisoner, and die a miserable death.

The reference here is to Elizabeth of Valois who was married to King Philip II of Spain. According to historical gossip she was in love with another and never found any happiness in her royal liaison.

79

Le chef de classe, par fraude stratageme,	The commander of the fleet by fraud and stratagem
Fera timides sortir de leurs galleres,	Shall cause the timid ones to come out of their galleys,
Sortis meurtris chef renieux de cresme,	Come out murdered, chief renouncer of baptism,
Puis par l'embusche luy rendront les saleres.	After that, by an ambush, they shall give him his salary.

The story of a mutiny on board ship is here related. The commander of the fleet, promising clemency to the mutineers, persuades them to give up the ship over which they have won control; but, reneging on his promise, he attacks and kills many of them. The survivors, enraged at this treatment, turn on and kill him.

80

Le Duc voudra les siens exterminer,	The Duke shall endeavor to exterminate his own,
Envoyera les plus forts, lieux estranges,	And shall send away the strongest of them into strange places,
Par tyrannie Bize & Luc ruyner,	By tyranny Pisa and Lucca will be ruined,
Puis le Barbares sans vin feront vendanges.	The Barbarians shall make vintage without wine.

The ruthless plans for conquest of an Italian Duke are here described.

81

Le Roy ruse entendra ses em-
  busches,
De trois quartiers ennemis assaillir,
Un nombre estrange larmes de
  coqueluches,
Viendra Lamprin de tracteur faillir.

The King by a ruse, shall hear of
  the ambushes,
And shall assail his enemies on
  three sides,
A strange number of friars, tears,
Shall cause Lamprin to desert the
  traitor.

The King shall use strategy to defend himself, and the influence of the clergy shall cause the "Light Prince" to come to the King's aid.

82

Par le duluge & pestilence forte,
La cite grande de long temps as-
  siegee,
La sentinelle & garde de main
  morte,
Subite prinse, mais de nul outragee.

By the deluge and violent plague,
The great city having been long
  besieged,
The sentinal and watch being surprised,
Shall be taken suddenly, but hurt
  by nobody.

Paris shall be taken over by an alien company by means of a bloodless invasion.

83

Sol vingt de Taurus si fort terre
  trembler,
Le grand theatre remply ruinera,
L'air, ciel & terre, obscurcir &
  troubler,
Lors l'infidele Dieu, & saincts
  voguera.

The sun being in the 20th of
  Taurus, the earth shall so quake,
That it shall fill and ruin the great
  theatre,
The air, the heaven and the earth
  shall be so obscured and
  troubled,
That unbelievers shall call upon
  God, and his saints.

The tenth of May is foretold as the exact day of the great Cataclysm.

84

Roy espose parfaira l'Hecatombe,
Apres avoir trouve son origine,
Torrent ouvrir de marbre & plomb
la tombe,
D'un grand Romain d'enseigne
Medusine.

The King exposed shall fulfill the
Hecatomb,
After he has found out his off-
spring,
A torrent shall open the sepulchre,
made of marble and lead,
Of a great Roman, with a Medusian
design.

A so-called revolutionary movement, based on the ideas advocated in Ancient Rome, is here compared to the Medusa's head, in that it turns the beholders thereof into stone, meaning that its concepts will lead to a static and unprogressive society.

85

Passer Guienne, Languedoc & le
Rhosne,
D'Agen tenans de Marmande & la
Reole,
D'ouvrir par for parroy, Phocen
tiendra son throsne,
Conflict aupres sainct Pol de Man-
seole.

They shall pass over Gascony, Lan-
guedoc, and the Rhone,
From Agen keeping Marmande,
and the Reale,
To open the wall by faith Phocen
shall keep his throne,
A battle shall be by St. Paul of
Manseole.

Armies shall pass through all the above-mentioned French towns, during the course of a great war.

86

Du bourg Lareyne parviedrot droit
a Chartes
Et feront pres du Pont Anthony
pause,
Sept pour la paix cauteleux comme
Martres
Feront entree d'armes a Paris
clause.

From Bourge, La Reyne they shall
come straight to Chartres,
And shall make a stand near Anthony's Bridge,
Seven for peace as crafty as Martres,
They shall enter in Paris besieged
with an army.

This continues the story in the preceding stanza, and foretells a march on Paris, culminating in its taking.

87

Par la forest de Touphon essartée
Par hermitage sera pose le temple,
De Duc d'Estampes par sa ruse inventee,
De Montleheri prelat donra exemple.

By the forest of Touphon cut off,
At the hermitage shall the temple be set,
The Duke of Prints by his invented ruse,
Shall give an example to the prelate of Montleheri.

By the ruse of inflated money, the temporal governments shall overcome the authority of the Church.

88

Calais, Arras secours a Theroanne,
Paix & semblant simulera l'escoute,
Soul de d'Alobrox descendre par Roane,
Destornay peuple qui defera la routte.

Calais, Arras shall give help to the Theroanne,
Peace or the like, shall dissemble the hearing,
Soldiers of Allobrox shall descend by Roanne,
People persuaded, shall spoil the march.

An incident in a war between France and Spain, concerning the Netherlands.

89

Sept ans sera Philip, fortune prospere,
Rabaissera des Barbares l'effort,
Puis son midi perplex, revours affaire,
Jeune Ogmion abysmera son fort.

Seven years of prosperous fortune shall Philip have,
And shall beat down the attempt of the Barbarians,
Then in his heyday, perplexed with misdirections,
Young Ogmion shall pull down his strength.

The story here is clearly that of the career of Philip II of Spain.

90

Un grand Capitaine de la grand Germanie,	A Captain of great Germany,
Se viendra rendre par simule secours,	Shall come to yield himself by simulating help,
A Roy des Roys, ayde de Pannonie,	To the Kings of Kings, with the help of Hungary,
Que sa revolte fera de sang grand cours.	So that his revolt shall cause great bloodshed.

Hitler, offering help to Hungary, shall involve her in the general ruin that follows.

91

L'horrible peste Perynthe & Nico-polle,	The horrid pestilence shall be in Corinth and Nicopol,
Le Chersonnez tiendra & Marce-loune,	The Crimeans and the Mace-donians also,
La Thessalie vestera l'Amphipolle,	It shall waste Thessaly and Amphi-polis,
Mal incogneu, & le refus d'An-thoine.	An unknown evil and the refusal of Anthony.

A great plague shall befall the places mentioned.

92

Le Roy voudra dans cite neufve entrer,	The King shall desire to enter into the New City,
Par ennemis expugner l'on viendra,	With foes they shall come to over-come it,
Captif libere faulx dire & perpetrer,	The prisoner being freed, shall speak and act falsely,
Roy dehors estre, loin d'ennemis tiendra.	The King being gotten out, shall keep far from enemies.

The New City shall be besieged by a powerful person helped by spies within.

93

Les ennemis du fort bien esloig-nez, Par chariots conduict le Bastion, Par sur les murs de Bourges esgrongnez Quand Hercules battra l'Haema-thion.	The enemies being a good way from the fort, By chariots shall be conducted to the Bastion, From the top of Bourges' walls they shall be cut less, When Hercules shall beat the Bloody One.

Bourges, a city in France, south of Paris, shall be in the direct path of a march on Paris, and shall be devastated by the invading army.

94

Foibles galeres seront unis ensem-ble, Ennemis faux, le plus fort en rem-part, Foible assaillies Vratislave tremble, Lubecq & Mysne tiendront Bar-bare part.	Weak ships shall be united to-gether False enemies, the strongest shall be fortified, Weak assaults, and yet Bratislava quakes for fear. Lubeck and Misne shall take the part of the Barbarians.

Weak nations, although not trusting each other, shall be forced to unite. Bratislava, a Czecho-Slovakian city, Lubeck and Misne shall be in the hands of the Germans.

95

Le nouveau faict conduira l'exer-cite, Proche Apame jusqu'aupres du rivage, Tendant secours de Milanoise eslite, Duc yeux prive, a Milan fer de cage.	The New Man shall lead up the Army, Near Apame, till near the bank, Carrying aid of elite forces from Milan, The Duke deprived of his eyes, and an iron cage at Milan.

A mob of rebellious soldiers aided by civilians captured and lynched Mussolini and his paramour at Milan in April, 1945.

96

Dans cite entrer exercit desniee,
Duc entrera par persuasion,
Aux foibles portes clam armee
   amenee,
Mettront feu, mort, de sang effu-
   sion.

Being denied entrance into the city,
The Duke shall enter by persuasion,
To the weak gates, secretly the
   army being brought,
Shall put all to fire and sword.

Because of the clarity of the English verse, we feel that this needs no
further interpretation.

97

De mer copies en trois parts
   divisees,
A la seconde les vivres failleront,
Desesperez cherchant Champs
   Elisees,
Premiers en breches entrez victoire
   auront.

A fleet being divided into three
   parts,
The living shall fail the second
   part,
Being in despair, they shall seek
   the Champs Elysées,
And entering the breach first, shall
   obtain victory.

Three armies shall converge at Paris; the second one will enter it first,
and parade on the Champs Elysées.

98

Les affligez par faut d'un seul taint,
Contremanant a partie opposite,
Aux Lygonnois mandera que con-
   traint,
Seront de rendre le grand chef de
   Molite.

The afflicted by fault of one, only
   died,
Carrying against the opposite part,
Shall send word to those of Lyons,
   they shall be compelled,
To surrender the great chief of
   Molite.

The reference here, we believe, is to Laval and the role he played in
the betrayal of France.

99

Vent Aquilon fera partir le siege,
Par murs jetter cendres, chaulx, &
poussiere,
Par pluye apres qui leur fera bien
piege,
Dernier secours encontre leur frontiere.

The North Wind shall cause the
siege to be raised
They shall throw ashes, lime and
dust,
By a rain after they shall be a trap
to them,
It shall be the last help against the
frontier.

The siege of a city will be lifted and an enemy driven back by a wind storm of such ferocity as to make it impossible for the armies to make use of their weapons.

100

Navalle pugne nuict sera superee,
Le feu, aux naves a l'Occident
ruine;
Rubriche neuve, la grand nef
coloree,
Ire a vaincu, & victoire en bruine.

In a sea fight night shall be overcome,
By fire, to the ship of the west,
ruin shall happen,
A new stratagem, the great ship
coloured,
Anger to the vanquished, and victory in a fog.

This tells of a naval battle which took place at night, in which the firing from both sides was so constant and fierce, that it literally turned night into day.

CENTURY X

A l'ennemy, l'ennemy foy promise,
Ne se tiendra, les captifs retenus;
Prins preme mort, & le reste en
chemise,
Donnant le reste pour estre
secourus.

To the enemy, the enemy faith
promised,
Shall not be kept, the captives will
be detained,
The first taken, put to death, and
the rest stripped,
Giving the rest that they may be
rescued.

The enemy, capturing many by the promise of fair treatment, shall vio-
late his pledge.

2

Voile gallere voil de net cachera,
La grande classe viendra sortir la
moindre,
Dix naves proches le tourneront
poulser,
Grand vaincue, unies a soy joindre.

The galley and the ship shall hide
their sails,
The great fleet shall make the little
ones come out,
Ten ships approaching shall turn
and push it,
The great being vanquished, they
shall unite together.

This is a prophetic description by Nostradamus of the defeat of the
Spanish Armada, August, 1588.

3

| En apres cinq troupeau ne mettra hors, | After five he shall not put out his flock, |

En apres cinq troupeau ne mettra
hors,
Un fuytif pour Penelon laschera,
Faux murmurer secours venir par
lors,
Le chef, le siege lors abandonnera.

After five he shall not put out his
flock,
He will let loose a runaway for
Penelon,
There shall be a false rumor, help
shall then come,
The commander shall forsake the
siege.

A small group of men, defending their city against a large enemy army, sends out a scout who succeeds in getting through the enemy lines and in bringing back enough reinforcements to drive back the enemy and lift the siege.

4

Sur la minuict conducteur de
l'armee.
Se sauvera subit esvanovy,
Sept ans apres la fame non blasmee,
A son retour ne dira oncq ouy.

About midnight the leader of the
army,
Shall save himself, vanishing suddenly,
Seven years after his fame shall not
be blamed,
And at his return he shall never
say yes.

This puts forth the prophecy that Hitler will return alive seven years after his supposed death in 1945.

5

Albi & Castres seront nouvelle
ligue,
Neuf Arriens, Lisbon & Portuges.
Carcas, Tholose consurmeront leur
brigue.
Quand chef neuf monstre de Laura-
gues.

Albi and Castres shall make a new
league,
Nine Aryans, Lisbon and Portu-
guese,
Carcasonne, Thoulouse, shall make
an end of their confederacy,
When the new chief shall come
from Lauragais.

Although this verse is most obscurely worded and weighted down with many seemingly unconnected names, we gather from it the prognostication of the rise of the theory of Aryan supremacy which was one of the basic concepts of the Hitler regime.

6

Gardon a Nemans, eaux si hault
  desborderont,
Qu'on coidera Deucalion renaistre,
Dans le colosse la plus part fuyront,
Vesta sepulchre feu estaint apparo-
  istre.

Gardon at Nismes, waters shall
  overflow so high,
That they think Deucalion be born
  again,
Most of them will run into the
  colossus,
And a sepulchre, and fire extin-
  guished, shall appear.

The description here is of the great flood of the River Gardon, in 1557, which Nostradamus likens to that which was sent upon the world by Zeus and of which Deucalion and his wife were the sole survivors.

7

Le grand conflit qu'on apreste a
  Nancy,
L'Aemathien dira tout le soubmets,
J'Isle Britanne par vin, sel en
  soley,
Hem. mi. deux Phi. long temps ne
  tiendra Mets.

A great war is in preparation at
  Nancy,
The Aemathien shall say, submit to
  all, to me,
The British Isle shall be put in
  want for salt and wine,
The two bloody friends shall keep
  Metz long.

A war between France and Germany, instigated by the arrogant demands on the part of the rulers of Germany, is forecast. The British Isles will be involved much to the distress and suffering of the English people. France will be occupied for some years by the "two bloody friends," but will finally be liberated by the joint efforts of her allies.

8

Index & Poulse parfondera le front,
De Senegalia le Compte a son fils
  propre,
La Myrnamee par plusieurs de
  plain front,
Trois dans sept jour blessez more.

Index and Poulse shall break the
  forehead,
Of the son of the Earl of Senegal,
The Myrnamee by many at a full
  bout,
Three within seven days shall be
  wounded to death.

The reference here seems to be almost purposely obscured by apparently meaningless names; nevertheless, it seems clear to me that it points directly to the situation in North Africa during the early days of World War II, especially pertaining to the death of Admiral Darlan.

9

De Castillon figuires jour de brune,
De femme infame naistra sou-
    verain prince,
Surnom de chausses per hume luy
    posthume,
Onc Roy ne fut si pire en sa
    province.

Out of Castilon, signalized on a
    misty day,
From an infamous woman shall be
    born a sovereign Prince,
His surname shall be from
    breeches, born after his father's
    death,
Never a King was worse in his
    province.

The story told in this and the following two stanzas concerns the illegitimate son of a woman of ill repute, born after the death of his father, who grows up to be a powerful and tyrannical figure in the politics of his day.

10

Tasche de murdre, enormes adul-
    tres,
Grand ennemy de tout le genre
    humain,
Que sera pire qu'ayeuls, oncles, ne
    peres.
En fer, feu, sanguin & inhumain.

Endeavor of murder, enormous
    adulteries,
A great enemy of all humanity,
That never saw worse grandfathers,
    uncles, or fathers,
In iron, water, bloody and inhu-
    mane.

Continuing the story told above, the infamous deeds of this tyrant are further described.

11

Dessous jonchere du dangereux
    passage,
Fera passer le Posthume sa bande,
Les monts Pyrens passer hors son
    bagage
De Paripignan couvrira Duc a
    Tende.

Below Jonchere a dangerous pas-
    sage,
The Posthume shall cause his army
    to go over,
And his baggage to go over the
    Pyrenean Mountains.
A Duke shall run from Perpignan
    to Tende.

Here we are told that the tyrant becomes the leader of an army, powerful enough to conquer Spain and cause other nations to fear him.

12

Esleu en Pape, d'esleu sera mocque,
Subit soudain, esmeu prompt &
    timide,
Par trop bon doux a mourir pro-
    voque,
Crainte estainte la nuit de sa mort
    guide.

Elected for a Pope, from elected
    shall be baffled,
Upon a sudden, moved promptly
    and fearful,
By too much sweetness provoked
    to die,
His fear being out in the night,
    shall make a guide.

After the death of Pope Innocent IX, Cardinal Santa Severina was
elected Pope. However, his election was declared illegal and Clement VIII
was chosen in his place, for which shortly after the deposed one died of
grief.

13

Soubs la pasture d'animaux rumi-
    nants,
Par eux conduicts au ventre Herbi-
    polique,
Soldats cachez, les armes bruit
    menants,
Non loing temptez de cite Anti-
    polique.

Under the pasture of cud-chewing
    animals,
Conducted by them to the Herbi-
    polique belly
Soldiers hidden, the weapons mak-
    ing a noise,
Shall be attempted not far from
    the Free City.

Soldiers, disguised as shepherds, shall attempt a surprise attack upon
an enemy town. Betrayed by the clanging of their weapons beneath their
cloaks, they shall be exposed and routed.

14

Urnel Vaucile sans conseil de soy
    mesmes,
Hardit timide, par crainte prins
    vaincu,
Accompagne de plusieurs putains
    blesmes,
A Barcellone aux Chartreux con-
    naincu.

Urnel-Vaucile, without advice of
    his own,
Stout and fearful, by fear taken and
    overcome,
Pale and in company of many
    whores,
Shall be convicted at Barcelona by
    the Charterhouse.

This stanza is a reading of the horoscope of a contemporary of Nostradamus, Urnel Vaucile.

15

Pere Duc vieux d'ans & de soif
  charge,
Au jour extreme fils desniant les
  guiere,
Dedans le puis vif mort viendra
  plonge,
Senat au fil la mort longue &
  legere.

A Father Duke aged and very
  thrifty,
In his extremity his son denying
  him the pail,
Alive into a well, where he shall be
  drowned,
The Senate shall give to the son a
  death sentence.

An ungrateful son shall lead his father to a well and drown him; he is
later put to death for the crime.

16

Heureux au Regne de France heureux de vie,
Ignorant sang, mort fureur, &
  rapine,
Par non flateurs seras mis en envie,
Roy desrobe, trop de foy en
  cuisine.

Happy in the Kingdom of France
  in his life,
Ignorant of blood, death, fury of
  taking by force,
By no flatterers shall be envied,
King robbed, too much faith in
  kitchens.

This prognostication concerns a King of France who, though happy in
his reign and given to no great vices, is yet envied and hated by his subjects,
and shall be betrayed by those of his own household.

17

La Reyne Ergaste voyant sa fille
  blesme,
Par un regret dans l'estomach
  enclos.
Crys lamentables seront lors
  d'Angolesme,
Et au germain mariage forclos.

Queen Ergast seeing her daughter
  pale,
By a regret contained in her breast,
Then shall lamentable cries come
  out of Angolesme,
And the marriage shall be denied
  to the German.

The French patriots shall lament and fight against the attempted union
with the Germans by the collaborationists.

18

Le rang Lorrain fera place a Van-
dosme,
Le haut mis bas, & le bas mis en
haut,
Le fils d'Hamon sera esleu dans
Rome,
Et les deux grands seront mis en
defaut.

The house of Lorraine shall give
place to Vendome,
The high pulled down, the low
raised up,
The sons of Haman shall be elected
in Rome,
And the two great ones shall not
appear.

The reference here is to the downfall and subsequent triumph of two
rival ruling Houses of France.

19

Jour que sera par Royne saluee,
Le jour apres le salut, la priere;
Le compte fait raison & valbuee,
Par avant humble oncques ne fut si
fiere.

The day that she shall be saluted
Queen,
The next day after the evening
prayer,
The account being settled and
paid,
She that was humble before, never
was so proud.

A woman of lowly birth shall become a Queen; and as soon as the
crown is placed upon her head she shall assume a regal and arrogant
manner.

20

Tous les amys qu'auront tenu
party,
Pour rude en lettres mis mort &
saccage
Biens publiez par fixe, grand
neanty,
Onc Romain peuple ne fut tant
outrage.

All the friends that shall have taken
the part,
Of the unlearned, put to death and
robbed,
Goods sold at public auction, great
emptiness,
Never Roman people were so much
outraged.

A period of oppression of liberals shall occur, accompanied by general
confiscation of their property.

21

Par le despit du Roy soustenant moindre	To spite the King, who took the part of the weaker,
Sera meurdry luy presentant les bagues,	He shall be murdered, presenting the jewels,
Le pere & fils voulant noblesse poindre,	The father and the son going to vex the nobility,
Fait comme a Perce jadis feirent les Magues.	It shall be done to them as the Magi did at Persia.

A King and his son, taking the part of the people against the nobility, shall be murdered by a method once used by the ancient Persians when they desired to dispose of their rulers.

22

Pour ne vouloir consentir au divorce,	For not consenting to the divorce,
Qui puis apres sera cogneu indigne,	Which afterwards shall be acknowledged unworthy,
Le Roy des Isles sera chasse par force,	The King of the Island shall be expelled by force,
Mis a son lieu que de Roy n'aura signe.	And another subrogated, who shall have no mark of the King.

On the occasion of King Charles I being beheaded, and Oliver Cromwell being raised in his place, this prophecy of Nostradamus was fulfilled.

23

Au peuple ingrat faictes les remonstrances,	The remonstrances being made to ingrates,
Par lors l'armee se saisira d'Antibe,	At the time the army shall seize Antibes,
Dans l'arc Monech feront les dolesances,	In the vault of Monaco, they shall make their complaints,
Et a Freius l'un l'autre prendra ribe.	And at Freius both of them shall take their share.

A period of unrest and inter-city warfare in Southern France is here described.

24

Le captif prince aux Itales vaincu,	The captive prince captured in Italy,
Passera Gennes par mer jusqu'a Marseilles.	Shall pass by sea through Genoa to Marseilles,
Par grand effort des forens survaincu,	By great efforts of foreign forces overcome,
Sauf coup de feu, barril liqueur d'abielle.	A barrel of honey shall save him from fire.

A prince, captured in Italy, shall be brought back to France for trial in Marseilles. His friends shall obtain his release by bribing the city officials.

25

Par Nebro ouvrir de Brisanne passage,	By Nebro to open the passage of Brisanne,
Bien esloignez el tago fara muestra,	A great way off, el tago fara muestra,
Dans Pelligouxe sera commis l'outrage,	In Pelligouxe the wrong shall be done,
De la grand dame assise sur l'orchestra.	On the great lady sitting in the orchestra.

The only clear reference here is to the "great lady sitting in the orchestra," which means a woman of noble birth. The interpretation of the rest of the verse is hard to come by, but we believe there is no greater significance than that some harm shall befall this woman.

26

Le successeur vengera son beau frere,	The successor shall avenge his brother-in-law,
Occuper regne soubs ombre de vengeance,	And rule under the pretense of revenge.
Occis ostacle son sang mort vitupere,	That obstacle killed, his dead blood vituperated,
Long temps Bretagne tiendra avec la France.	A long time shall Brittany hold with France.

The prognosticated event and the fact that it refers to a quarrel between Brittany and other provinces in France are clearly described in the verse itself.

27

Charle Cinquiesme & un grand Hercules,	Charles the Fifth and a great Hercules,
Viendront le temple ouvrir de main bellique,	Shall open the temple with a warlike hand,
Un Colonne, Jule & Ascans reculez,	One Colonne Julius and Ascan shall put back,
L'Espagne, clef, aigle, n'eurent onc si grand picque.	Spain, the key, and eagle never at such great pique.

It is here predicted that Charles V of Spain and Henry II of France will split the Church with their quarrels.

28

Second & tiers qui font prime musique	Second and third that make first music,
Sera par Roy en honneur sublimee,	Shall by the King be raised to high honors.
Par grasse & maigre presque a demy eticque,	By a fat one, and a lean one, and one emaciated,
Rapport de Venus faux rendra deprimee.	A false report of Venus shall pull her down.

Here we have a detailed prognostication of events and people involved in the French Revolution. Because of the hostility displayed by the nobility and clergy, two of the most powerful groups in France, toward the Tiers État, this "third estate" constituted itself as a National Assembly and took one of the most active parts in the fomenting of the Revolution. The King (Louis XVI), during this time, was retained as "ruler" of the country. Perhaps the most remarkable part of this prophecy is the clarity of the descriptions of Mirabeau (the fat one), Danton (the lean one), and Marat (the emaciated one), three of the leading figures in the Revolution.

29

De Pol Mansol dans caverne caprine,	From St. Paul's house in a goats' cavern,
Cache & prins extraict hors par la barbe,	Hidden and taken, drawn out by the beard,
Captif mene comme beste mastine,	Captive, like unto an accursed beast,
Par Begourdans amenee pres de Tarbe.	By Begourdane shall be brought near to Tarbe.

One shall seek sanctuary in the Cathedral of St. Paul, but he will be taken prisoner and subjected to great indignities.

30

Nepveu & sang du sainct nouveau venu,	Nephew and blood of the saint newly come,
Par le surnom soustient arc & couvert,	By the surname, upholds arches and covers,
Seront chassez mis a mort chassez nu,	They shall be driven, put to death, and chased out nude,
En rouge & noir convertiront leur vert.	They shall change their red and black to green.

The downfall of the totalitarian groups in Europe is here predicted; but there is also a warning that they will attempt to continue their operations even though they may change their "colors."

31

Le Sainct Empire viendra en Germaine,	The Holy Empire shall come into Germany,
Ismaelites trouveront lieux ouverts,	The Ismaelites shall find open places,
Asnes viendront aussie la Carmanie,	Asses shall also come out of Carmania,
Les soustenans de terre tous couverts.	Taking their part, and covering the earth.

The Germans, imbued with the spirit of barbarism, shall embark on a conquest of the world.

32

Le grand Empire chacun en devoit estre,	The great Empire, every one would want it,
Un sur les autres le viendra obtenir.	One above the rest shall obtain it;
Mais peu de temps sera son regne & estre,	But his time and reign shall last little,
Deux ans aux naves se pourra soustenir.	He may maintain himself two years in his shipping.

The struggle for the control of an empire is here described, and the prediction that the successful party will exercise its power for only two years.

33

La faction cruelle a robbe longue,
Viendra cacher souz les pointus
    poignards,
Saisir Florence, le Duc & le
    diphlongue,
Sa descouverte par immeurs &
    flangnards.

The cruel faction of the long robe,
Shall come and hide under the
    points of daggers,
Seize upon Florence, the Duke and
    the long skins,
The discovery of it shall be by vas-
    sals and serfs.

Temporal and spiritual conflict shall ensue in Florence, the city of culture.

34

Gaulois qu'empire par guerre occu-
    pera,
Par son beau-frere mineur sera
    trahy;
Par cheval rude voltigeant trainera,
De fait le frere long temps sera
    hay.

A Frenchman who shall occupy an
    empire by war,
Shall be betrayed by his brother-in-
    law, a pupil,
He shall be drawn by a rude
    prancing horse,
For which fact his brother shall
    be long hated.

A true picture, foreseen by Nostradamus, of Napoleon and his numerous relatives, whom he placed on the thrones of Europe.

35

Puisnay royal flagrant d'ardant
    libide,
Pour se jouyr de cousine Germaine,
Habit de femme au temple
    d'Artemide;
Allant murdry par incongeau du
    Marne.

The royal son, heated with ardent
    love,
For to enjoy his German cousin,
Shall in woman's clothes go to the
    temple of Artemis,
Going shall be murdered by an un-
    known du Marne.

This concerns the son of a King who, very much in love with his German cousin, disguises himself in woman's clothing in order to keep a rendezvous with her in a Church. While going to meet her he is murdered by a person named du Marne.

36

Apres le Roy du Sud guerres parlant,	After the King of the South shall have talked of wars,
L'Isle Harmotique le tiendra a mespris;	The Harmotic Island shall despise him,
Quelques ans bons rongeant un & pillant	Some good years gnawing and pillaging,
Par tyrannie a l'Isle changeant pris.	And tyranny shall change the price of the Island.

The direct implication in this verse concerns King Philip II and the defeat of his Spanish Armada by the English Fleet of Queen Elizabeth. It is further predicted that England will go on to greater glories during the reign of this Queen.

37

Grande asemblee pres du lac de Borget,	A great assembly of people near the lake of Borget,
Se ralleront pres de Montmelian;	Will go and gather themselves near Montmelian,
Passants plus outre pensifs, feront projet,	Going still further, they shall make a project,
Chambary, Moriant, combat Sainct-Julian.	Upon Chambary, Morienne, and shall fight at St. Julian.

Internal struggles shall cause great disturbances in the above-mentioned towns of France.

38

Amour alegre non loin pose le siege,	Cheerful love lays siege not far,
Au Sainct Barbar seront les garnisons.	At St. Barbar shall be the garrisons,
Ursins, Hadrie, pour Gaulois feront plaige,	Ursini, Hadria shall be sureties for the French,
Pour peut rendus de l'Armee, aux Grisons.	And many for fear shall go from the Army to the Grifons.

A general truce shall be declared between the French and Italians; but a period of general conscription, in France, is to follow, because of the large number of army deserters.

39

Premier fils veufve mal'heureux
    mariage,
Sans nuls enfans deux Isles en dis-
    cord,
Avant dixhuict incompetant aage,
De l'autre pres plus bas sera
    l'accord.

The first son will make an un-
    happy marriage and a widow,
Without any children, two Islands
    in discord,
Before eighteen, an incompetent
    age,
Of the other, lower shall be the
    agreement.

Francis II, King of France, was married to Mary Stuart at the age of fourteen; before he was eighteen he died, leaving her a widow.

40

La jeune nay au regne Britannique,
Qu'aura le pere mourant recom-
    mande,
Iceluy mort Londre donra topique,
Et a son fils le Regne demande.

The young man born to the King-
    dom of Britain,
Whom his father dying shall have
    recommended,
After his death, London shall give
    him a topic,
And shall ask the Kingdom away
    from his son.

This is a reiteration of a previous prophecy, namely, the abdication of Edward VIII of England, and the accession to the throne of his brother, George VI. This verse, however, enlarges on the subject and hints at the gossip which was directed at Edward VIII and his future wife.

41

En la frontiere de Caussade &
    Charlus,
Non gueres loing du fond de la
    valee,
De Ville Franche musique a son de
    luths,
Environnez combouls & grand
    myrtee.

On the borders of Caussade and
    Charlus,
Not far from the bottom of the
    valley,
Of Ville Franche shall be heard the
    music of lutes.
Great dancing and company of
    people met together.

Caussade, Charlus and Ville Franche are towns in Provence, all in the same general vicinity; and the event described is quite obviously a festival.

42

Le regne humain d'Angelique geni-
ture,
Fera son regne, paix union tenir,
Captive guerre demy de sa closture,
Long temps la paix leur fera main-
tenir.

The humane reign of an angelic off-
spring
Shall cause his reign to be in peace
and union,
Shall make war, captive shutting it
half up,
He shall cause them to keep peace
a great while.

A powerful sovereign, of great goodness, shall have a long reign of peace
and prosperity.

43

Le trop bon temps, trop de bonte
royale
Faicts & deffaicts prompt, subit,
negligence,
Leger croira faux, d'espouse loyale,
Luy mis a mort par sa benevolence.

The time too good, too much of
royal bounty,
Feats and prompt defeats, quick
negligence,
Fickle shall believe false of his loyal
spouse,
He shall be put to death for his
benevolence.

By trusting those about him, even believing false rumors about his
wife, a King shall be destroyed.

44

Par lors qu'un Roy sera contre les
siens,
Natif de Bloys subjugeura Ligures,
Mammel, Cordobe & les Dalma-
tiens,
Des sept puis l'ombre a Roy
estrennes & lemures.

At the time that a King shall be
against his own,
One born at Blois shall subdue the
Ligurians,
Mammel, Cordova and the Dal-
matians,
Shadow of the seven, both a Royal
present and spectre.

Many European countries shall be conquered by a great French leader,
but he shall not hold them long.

45

L'ombre du regne de Navarre non vray,
Fera la vie de sort illegitime;
La veu promis incertain de Cambray,
Roy d'Orleans donra mur ligitime.

The shadow of the reign of Navarre not true,
Shall make the life of illegitimate chance,
The uncertain allowance from Cambrai,
King of Orleans shall give a lawful wall.

This deals with the legitimist quarrels of the various contending families for the French throne.

46

Vie sort mort de l'or vilaine indigne,
Sera de Saxe non nouveau electeur;
De Brunsvick mandra d'amour signe,
Faux le rendant au peuple seducteur.

The living die of too much gold, an infamous villain,
Shall be of Saxony, not the new elector,
From Brunswick shall come a sign of love,
Rendering a false account, seducing the people.

Industrialists shall seduce the people of Germany, misleading them with many promises, on the strength of which they shall change their government.

47

De Bourze Ville a la Dame Gurlande,
L'on mettra sus par la trahison faicte,
Le grand prelat de Leon par Formande,
Faux pellerins & ravisseurs deffaicte.

From Bourze, City of the Lady Garland,
They shall by a set treason,
The great prelate of Leon by Formande,
False pilgrims and ravishers destroyed.

Paris, City of the Garlands, shall be threatened by a treasonable conspiracy, engineered by a Spanish Prelate.

48

Du plus profond de l'Espagne
ancienne,
Sortant du bout & des fins de
l'Europe,
Trouble passant aupres du pont
de Laigne,
Sera deffaicte par bande sa grand
troppe.

From the deepest part of old Spain,
Going out to the extremities of
Europe,
He that troubled the travelers by
the bridge of Laigne,
Shall have his great troop defeated
by another.

Nostradamus predicts the equipment by Spain of the Fascist Blue Division to fight alongside the Nazi Armies at the other extreme of Europe, and their defeat and annihilation at the hands of the Russians.

49

Jardin du Monde aupres de cite
neufue,
Dans le chemin des montagnes
cavees,
Sera saisi & plogne dans la cuve,
Beuvant par force eaux soulphre
envenimees.

Garden of the World, near the
New City,
In the way of the man-made moun-
tains,
Shall be seized on and plunged into
a ferment,
Being forced to drink sulphurous
poisoned waters.

This startling prophecy of a catastrophic event at a pleasure resort not far from the great new city, predicts a tremendous tidal wave of poisoned waters that shall sweep in from the resort and overwhelm the man-made mountain-like skyscrapers of the city.

50

La Meuse au jour terre de Luxem-
bourg,
Descouvrira Saturne & trois en
Lurne,
Montagne & plaine, ville, cite &
bourg,
Lorrain deluge, trahison par grand
hurne.

The Meuse by day in the land of
Luxembourg,
Shall discover Saturn and three in
the Lurne,
Mountains and plains, town, city
and country,
A Lorrain flood, treason by a great
Heron.

Commerce and learning shall be endangered by a "flood" of wars, affecting all the peoples of the world.

51

Des lieux plus bas du pays de Lor-
    raine,
	In the place of peace of lower Lor-
	    raine,

Seront des basses Allemagnes unis,	Shall be a basis of a German unity,

Par ceux du siege Picards, Nor-
    mans, du Maisne,
	By reason of the siege of Picards
	    and Normans from Maisne,

Et aux Cantons se seront reunis.	And in the Cantons they shall be reunited.

Germany shall endeavor to unify all Europe under her banners, but shall meet with resistance from all the nations.

52

Au lieu ou Laye & Scelde se
    marient,
	In the place where the rivers Laye
	    and Scelde unite,

Seront les nopces de long temps
    mainees,
	Shall the nuptials be, that were
	    long a doing,

Au lieu d'Anvers ou la grappe
    charient.
	In the place of Antwerp where they
	    draw the grape,

Jeune vieillesse conforte intaminee.	The young unsullied will comfort old age.

An era of peace in Belgium is foreshadowed.

53

Les trois pellices de loing s'entre-
    batron,
	The three harlots shall be long em-
	    battled,

La plus grand moindre demeurera
    a l'escoute;
	The greatest less shall remain
	    watching

Le grand Selin n'en sera plus
    patron,
	The great Selin shall be no more
	    their patron,

Le nommera feu, pelte, blanche,
    routte.
	And shall call it fire, pelt, white,
	    route.

Three corrupt nations shall be defeated; only the weakest of them shall survive even though it will suffer much privation.

54

Nee en ce monde par concubine furtive,
A deux halt mise par les tristes nouvelles.
Entre ennemis sera prinse captive,
Et amenee a Malines & Bruxelles.

Born in this world from a furtive concubine,
Set up at two heights by the sad news,
Shall be taken prisoner among the enemies,
And brought to Malines and Brussels.

This is the story of a noblewoman, born of a concubine, who, by the pretext of sad news, is brought to Brussels and there made captive by those who envied and resented her high position.

55

Les mal'heureuses nopces celebreront
En grande joye mais la fin mal'heureuse;
Mary & mere Nore desdaigneront,
Le Phybe mort, & Nore plus piteuse.

The unhappy nuptials shall be celebrated,
With great joy, but the end shall be unhappy,
Husband and wife shall disdain Nore,
The Phybe dead, and Nore most piteous.

This predicts the marriage, in 1572, of Henry IV, then King of Navarre, and Margaret of Valois. The tragedy of the Massacre of St. Bartholomew, in the same year, is also foreseen.

56

Prelat Royal son baissant trop tire,
Grand flux de sang sortis par sa bouche,
Le regne Anglique par regne respire,
Long temps mort vif en Tunis comme souche.

Royal Prelate bowing himself too much,
A great flood of blood shall come out of his mouth,
The English reign by reign restored,
A great while dead, alive in Tunis like a log.

Two separate and completely unrelated prophecies are contained in this stanza. One deals with the death of a dignitary of the Church by a hemorrhage of the throat. The other predicts the saving of the British Isles by the interference in their behalf of a distant nation.

57

Le subleve ne cognoistra son
   sceptre,
Les enfans jeunes des plus grands
   honnira,
Oncques ne fut un plus ort cruel
   estre,
Pour leurs espouses a mort noir
   bannira.

The exalted shall not know his
   sceptre,
He shall put to shame two young
   children of the greatest,
Never was one more dirty or cruel,
He shall put their spouses to the
   black death.

A great tyrant, raised to the dignity of King, shall misgovern greatly,
being especially harsh in his treatment of the poor.

58

Au temps du dueil que le Selin
   monarque,
Guerroyera le jeune Aemathien;
Gaule bransler, perecliter la barque,
Tenter Phossens au ponant entre-
   tien.

In the time of mourning, when
   the monarch Selin,
Shall make war against the young
   Aemathien,
France shall quake, the ship being
   in danger,
Phocens shall be tempted, the real
   danger in the west.

In the West the Germans shall make their strongest stand; France shall
be occupied by enemy forces.

59

Dedans Lyon vingt & cinq d'une
   haleine,
Cinq citoyens Germains, Bressans,
   Latins,
Par dessous noble conduiront
   longue traine,
Et descouvers par abbois de mas-
   tins.

In Lyons, five and twenty of one
   breadth,
Five citizens, Germans, Brescians
   and Latins,
Under noblemen shall conduct a
   long trail,
And shall be discovered by a bark-
   ing of mastiffs.

In a time of war, an underground conspiracy against France, fostered
by Germans and Italians, shall be shown to be in existence.

60

Je pleure Nisse, Monaco, Pise,
Gennes,
Savone, Sienne, Capue, Modene,
Malte,
Les dessus sang & glaive par
estrennes,
Feu, trembler terre, eau, mal'heu-
reusse nolte.

I bewail Nice, Monaco, Pisa,
Genoa,
Savona, Sienna, Copua, Modena,
Malta,
Upon them blood and sword for a
new year's gift,
Fire, earthquake, water, unhappy
ending.

All places mentioned are cities on the Mediterranean; great disasters
to befall them are foreseen.

61

Betta, Vienne, Comorre, Sacar-
bance,
Voudront livrer aux Barbares Pan-
none,
Par pique & feu, enorme violance,
Les conjurez descouverts par
matrone.

Betta, Vienna, Comorre, Sacar-
bance,
Shall endeavor to deliver Hungary
to the Barbarians,
By pike and fire, enormous violence,
The conspirators discovered by a
matron.

A conspiracy to betray and surrender Hungary to "barbarians" shall be
uncovered by an elderly woman.

62

Pres de Sorbin pour assaillir Hongrie,
L'herauld de Budes les viendra
advertir,
Chef Bizantin, Sallon de Sclavonie,
A loy d'Arabes les viendra con-
vertir.

Near Sorbin, to invade Hungary,
The herald of Buda, shall give
notice,
The chief Easterner, Sallon of
Sclavonia,
Shall convert them to the Asiatic
law.

This stanza has some bearing on the preceding one, inasmuch as it
portends the eventual surrender of Hungary to a "barbarian" form of
government.

63

Cydron, Raguse, la cite au Sainct Hieron,	Cydron, Ragusa, the city of St. Jerome,
Reverdira le medicant secours,	Shall revive again the medical help,
Mort fils de Roy par mort de deux heron,	The King's son dead, by the death of two herons,
L'Arabe, Hongrie, feront un mesme cours.	Oriental Hungary shall go the same way.

This predicts a plague that will fall on Hungary and which, because of the lack of doctors and medical supplies, will kill off great numbers of people, including the son of the King.

64

Pleure Milan, pleure Lucques, Florence,	Weep Milan, weep Lucques, and Florence,
Que ton grand Duc sur le Char montera,	When the great Duke shall go upon the Chariot,
Changer le siege pres de Venice s'advance,	To change the siege near Venice he advances,
Lors que Colonee a Rome changera.	When Colonee shall change at Rome.

An attempt to change the residence of the Pope from Rome to some place near Venice is predicted.

65

O vaste Rome ta ruyne s'approche,	Oh mighty Rome, thy ruin approaches,
Non de tes murs, de ton sang & substance;	Not of thy walls, but of thy blood and substance,
L'aspre par lettres fera si horrible coche,	The sharp by letters, shall make so horrid a notch,
Fer poinctu mis a tous jusques au manche.	Sharp iron thrust in all the way to the shaft.

Rome is doomed to destruction, not actually, but metaphorically by verbal and literary assault.

66

Le chef de Londres par regne
l'Americh,
L'Isle d'Escosse t'empiera par gelee;
Roy Reb auront un si faux Ante-
christ,
Que les mettra trestous dans la
meslee.

The chief of London by rule of
America,
The Island of Scotland shall be
tempered by frost,
Kings and Priests shall have one,
who is a false Anti-Christ,
Who will put them altogether in
discord.

British and American leaders, united in a political venture, shall set up
a dictator, who shall in the end betray both leaders and common people.

67

Le tremblement si fort au mois de
May,
Saturne, Caper, Jupiter, Mercure
au Boeuf;
Venus aussi, Cancer, Mars en Non-
nay,
Tombera gresle lors plus grosse
qu'un oeuf.

The earthquake shall be so great
in the month of May,
Saturn, Caper, Jupiter, Mercury in
Taurus,
Venus also, Cancer, Mars in Zero,
Then shall hail fall bigger than an
egg.

Confirmation of a previous prophecy, this again signifies May 10th as
a fateful day, when the earth shall tremble violently and be bombarded by
hitherto unknown weapons.

68

L'armee de mer devant cite tiendra,
Puis partira sans faire longue allee;
Citoyens grande proye en terre
prendra,
Retourner classe reprendre grande
emblee.

The marines shall stand before the
city,
Then shall go away for a little
while,
A citizen army shall then hold the
ground,
The fleet returning and recovering
a great deal.

France shall be blockaded both on land and sea, but a citizen's army
will break through on all lines.

69

Le fait luysant de neuf vieux esleve,
Seront si grands par midy Aquilon,
De sa soeur propre grandes alles
    leve;
Fuyant, meurdry au buisson d'Am-
    bellon.

The bright action of new old ex-
    alted,
Shall be so great throughout the
    North and South,
By his own sister great forces shall
    be raised,
Fleeing, murdered near the bush
    of Ambellon.

Political upheavals, following the French Revolution, are prognosticated.

70

L'oeil par object fera telle excrois-
    sance,
Tant & ardente que tombera la
    neige,
Champ arrouse viendra en decrois-
    sance,
Que le primat succombera a Rhege.

The eye of the object shall make
    such an excrescence,
Because so much, and so burning
    shall fall the snow,
The field watered shall come to de-
    cay,
That the primat shall succumb at
    Reggio.

A volcanic-like eruption at Reggio in Italy shall cause widespread destruction.

71

La terre & l'air geleront se grand
    eau,
Lors qu'on viendra pour Jeudy
    venerer;
Ce qui sera jamais ne feut si beau,
Des quatre parts le viendront hon-
    orer.

The earth and air shall freeze with
    so much water,
When they shall come to worship
    Thursday,
That which shall be, never was so
    fair,
From the four parts, they shall
    come to honour him.

Nostradamus here predicts the return of an "Ice Age," in other words,
a reversal of mankind to the worship of lowly gods.

72

L'an mil neuf cens nonante neuf
  sept mois,
Du ciel viendra un grand Roy d'effrayeur,
Resusciter le grand Roy d'Angol-
  mois,
Avant apres, Mars regner par bon
  heur.

In the year 1999 and seven months,
From the skies shall come an
  alarmingly powerful king,
To raise again the great King of
  the Jacquerie,
Before and after, Mars shall reign
  at will.

A tremendous world revolution is foretold to take place in the year
1999, with a complete upheaval of existing social orders, preceded by world-
wide wars.

73

Le temps present avec ques le
  passe,
Sera juge par grand jovialiste,
Le monde tard luy sera lasse,
Et desloyal par le clerge juriste.

The present time together with the
  past,
Shall be judged by a great jovialist,
The world shall at last be weary of
  him,
And shall be thought without faith
  by churchly critics.

This describes the influence of Rabelais on customs and manners during the time of Nostradamus.

74

Au revolu du grand nombre septiesme,
Apparoistra au temps ieux d'Hecatombe,
Non esloingne du grand age mil-
  liesme,
Que les entrez sortiront de leur
  tombe.

The year seven of the great number
  being past,
There shall be seen the sports of
  the ghostly sacrifice,
Not far from the great age of the
  millennium,
That the buried shall come out of
  their graves.

When the year 7000 is reached, then Judgment Day shall be pro-
nounced, and the dead shall rise out of their graves.

75

Tant attendu ne reviendra jamais,
Dedans l'Europe, en Asie apparoistra,
Un de la ligue yssu du grand Hermes,
Et sur tous Roy des Orients coistra.

So long expected shall never come,
Into Europe, in Asia shall appear,
One issued of the line of the great Hermes,
And shall be over all the Kings of the Orient.

A consolidation of nations of the East is forecast, under the leadership of a notable scientist.

76

Le grand Senat decernera la pompe,
A un qu'apres sera vaincu, chasse;
Des adherans seront a son de trompe,
Biens publiez, ennemy dechasse.

The great Senate will bestow a great honour,
To one who afterwards shall be vanquished and expelled,
The goods of his partners shall be,
Publicly sold, and the enemy shall be driven away.

A man, once held in high esteem by his countrymen, shall betray their interests and shall be exiled for his misdeeds.

77

Trente adherans de l'ordre des Quirettes,
Bannis, leurs biens donnez ses adversaires,
Tous leurs bienfaits seront pour demerites,
Classe espargie, delivrez aux corsaires.

Thirty adherents of the order of the Quirettes,
Banished, their goods shall be given to their adversaries,
All their good deeds shall be reputed to them as crimes,
The feet scattered, they shall fall in the hands of the corsairs.

This continues the preceding stanza, going on to relate the similar fate that was meted out to the followers of the above-mentioned traitor.

78

Subite joye en subite tristesse,	Sudden joy shall turn to sudden sadness,
Sera a Rome aux graces embrassees,	At Rome to the embraced graces,
Dueil, cris, pleurs, larm, sang, excelent liesse,	Mourning, cries, weeping, tears, blood, excellent mirth,
Contraires bandes surprinses & troulsees.	Contrary troops surprised and carried away.

Some newly married couples shall be surprised by a great disaster in the midst of their jollity.

79

Les vieux chemins seront tous embellis,	The old roads shall be made more beautiful,
L'on passera a Memphis somentrees,	There shall be a passage to Memphis summarily,
Le grand Mercure d'Hercules fleur de lys,	The great Mercury of Hercules, fleur de lys,
Faisant trembler terre, mer, & contrees.	Making the earth, the sea and the countries to quake.

This foretells the time of increased and varied means of communication between the countries of the world.

80

Au regne grand, du grand regne regnant,	In the great reign, of the great reign reigning,
Par force d'armes les grands portes d'arian,	By force of arms the great brass gates,
Fera ouvrir, le Roy & Duc joignant,	He shall cause to be open, the King being joined with the Duke.
Port demoly, nef a fons, jour serain.	Port demolished, ship sunk on a fair day.

This relates the story of a great naval victory that shall take place when a King and a Duke join forces.

81

Mis thresor temple, citadins Hes-
periques,
Dans iceluy retire en secret lieu
Le temple ouvrir les liens famil-
iques,
Reprens, ravis, proue horrible au
milieu.

A treasure put in a temple by Hes-
perian citizens,
In the same hid in a secret place,
The hungry serfs shall cause the
temple to be open,
And take again and ravish, a fearful
prey in the middle.

The Spanish shall put their trust in the Church, taking refuge within
it, but a fearful revolution shall make the temple a ravished place.

82

Cries, pleurs, larmes viendront avec
coteaux,
Semblanyt faux donront dernier assault,
L'entour parques planter profons
plateaux,
Vifs repoussez & meurdris de prin-
sault.

Cries, weeping, tears, shall come
with daggers,
With a false semblance they shall
give the last assault,
Set around they shall plant deep,
Beaten back alive, and murdered
upon a sudden.

This has a relation to the preceding stanza, with reference to a Spanish
revolution.

83

De batailler ne sera donne signe,
Du parc seront contraints de sortir
hors,
De Gand lantour sera cogneu l'enseigne,
Qui fera mettre de tous les siens a
mors.

Of battle there shall be no sign
given,
Out of the park they shall be compelled to come,
Round about Gand, shall be known
to the ensign,
That shall cause all his own to be
put to death.

A massacre of a surrendered garrison shall take place in a civil war, between two opposing armies of the same blood.

84

Le naturelle a si haut, haut non bas,	The natural to one so high, high not low,
Le tard retour fera marris contens,	The late return shall make the sad contented.
Le Recloing ne sera sans debats,	The Recloing shall not be without strife,
En emploiant & perdant tout son temps.	In employing and loosing all the time.

A person in high office shall give birth to a natural child, which event shall cause her opponents to rejoice.

85

Le vieil Tribun au point de la Tre-hemide,	The old Tribune, at the end of the Trehemide,
Sera pressee captif ne delivrer,	Shall be much entreated not to deliver the captain,
Le vueil non vueil, le mal parlant timide,	They will not will, the evil speaking timidly,
Par ligitime a ses amis livrer.	By legitimate to his friends shall deliver.

After three months of imprisonment, an old judge shall deliver the captive safely to his friends, in spite of contrary influences.

86

Comme un Gryphon viendra le Roy d'Europe,	As a Griffon shall come the King of Europe,
Accompagne de ceux d'Aquilon,	Accompanied by those of the North,
De rouges & blancs conduira grande troupe	Of reds and whites shall conduct a great troop,
Et iront contre le Roy de Babylon.	And then, shall go against the King of Babylon.

The Griffon, a mythical monster, half lion and half man, was supposed to keep watch over the gold of Russia. Nostradamus foretells a United States of Europe, under the leadership of Russia, opposing the forces of Mammon.

87

Grand roy viendra prendre port
    pres de Nice,
Le grand empire de la mort si en
    fera,
Aux Antipodes posera son genisse,
Par mer la Pille tout esvanoistra.

A great king shall land at Nice,
The great empire of death shall
    interpose with it,
In the Antipodes, he shall put his
    horse,
By sea all the pillage shall vanish.

An invasion of the southern coast of France shall take place. In the Antipodes (Japan), they shall put their trust in conquest, but they shall be defeated decisively by sea power and lose their ill-gotten empire.

88

Pieds & Cheval a la seconde veille,
Feront entree vastiant tout par la
    mer,
Dedans le port entrera de Mar-
    seille,
Pleurs, crys, & sang, onc nul temps
    si amer.

Foot and Horse upon the old
    watch,
Shall come in destroying all by sea,
They shall come into the harbor
    of Marseilles,
Tears, cries, and blood, never was
    so bitter a time.

An invasion of Marseilles by a great armada is indicated.

89

De brique en marbre serot les murs
    reduicts,
Sept & cinquante annees pacifique,
Joye aux humains, renove l'aque-
    duct,
Sante, grands fruits, joye & temps
    melifique.

The walls shall be turned from
    brick into marble,
There shall be peace for seven and
    fifty years,
Joy to mankind; the aqueduct shall
    be rebuilt,
Health, abundance of fruits, joys
    and a mellifluous time.

Nostradamus predicts a golden age for humanity after a great calamitous war among nations.

90

Cent fois mourra le tyran inhu-
  main,
Mis a son lieu scavant & debon-
  naire,
Tout le senat sera dessoubs sa main,
Fasche sera par malin temeraire.

The inhuman tyrant shall die a
  hundred times,
In his place shall be put a savant,
  a kindly disposed man,
All the senate shall be at his command,
He shall be made angry by a rash
  malicious person.

After the death of one of the world's greatest tyrants, a wise and kindly
man shall take his place, and shall fight against the evil laws laid down
by his predecessor.

91

Clerge Romain l'an mil six cens &
  neuf,
Au chef de l'an fera election,
D'un gris & noir de la Compagne
  yssu,
Qui onc ne fut si malin.

The Roman clergy in the year 1609,
In the beginning of the year shall
  make a choice,
Of gray and black, come out of the
  country,
Such a one never a worse was.

As stated before, Nostradamus dates all events from the Council of
Nicaea, A.D. 325. By adding 1609 to this date we have 1934, the year
Hitler was granted full power.

92

Devant le pere l'enfant sera tue,
Le pere apres entre cordes de jonc,
Genevois peuple sera esvertu,
Cisant le chef au milieu comme un
  tronc.

The child shall be killed before the
  father's eyes,
The father shall enter into ropes
  of rushes,
The people of Geneva shall not-
  ably stir themselves,
The chief lying in the middle like
  a log.

The League of Nations, its headquarters at Geneva, and its unhappy
career, are clearly foreshadowed by Nostradamus.

93

La barque neufue rescuera les voyages,
La & aupres transfereront l'empire,
Beaucaire, Arles, retiendront les hostages,
Pres deux colomnes trouvees de porphire.

The new ship shall make a voyage,
Into the place, and thereby transfer the empire,
Beaucaire, Arles, shall keep the hostages,
Near them shall be found two columns of porphyry.

A government shall change not only its political and economic structure, but shall move to a new city and establish new headquarters there.

94

De Nismes, d'Arles, & Vienne contemner,
N'obey tout a l'edict Hesperique;
Aux labouriez pour le grand condamner,
Six eschappez en habit seraphicque.

From Nismes, from Arles, and Vienna contempt,
They shall not obey the Spanish proclamation,
To the laboratories to condemn the great one,
Six escaped in a seraphical habit.

This predicts a rebellion of the cities mentioned against an edict issued by a tyrannical leader of the Spanish nation.

95

Dans les Espagnes viedra Roy trespuissant,
Par mer & terre subjugant au midy;
Ce mal sera, rabaissant le croisant,
Baisser les aesles a ceux du Vendredy.

A most potent King shall come into Spain,
Who by sea and land shall subjugate the south,
This evil shall beat down the horns of the crescent,
And lower the wings of those of Friday.

A powerful ruler shall embark from Spain to crush an Arab confederation.

96

Religion du nom des mers viendra,
Contre la secte fils Adaluncatif,
Secte obstinee deploree craindra,
Des deux blessez par Aleph &
    Aleph.

Religion of the name of the seas
    shall come,
Against the Sect of Caitifs of the
    Moon,
The deplorably obstinate sect, shall
    be afraid,
Of the two wounded by A. and A.

One must delve deeply into these cryptic words in order to grasp their full meaning. The "Caitifs of the Moon" indicates the Arab nation. The phrase "A. and A." means America. The sense then is that there will be a struggle between the opposing philosophies of the two groups.

97

Triremes pleines tout aage captifs,
Temps bon a mal, le doux pour
    amertume,
Proye a Barbares trop tost seront
    hastifs,
Cupide de voir plaindre au vent la
    plume.

Triremes full of captives of all ages,
Time good for evil, the sweet for
    the bitter,
Prey to the Barbarians, they shall
    be too hasty,
Desirous to see the feather com-
    plain in the wind.

A continuation of the preceding stanza, this relates the bitter struggles that will ensue.

98

La splendeur claire a pucelle jou-
    euse
Ne luyra plus long temps sera sans
    sel;
Avec marchans, ruffians, loups odi-
    euse,
Tous pesle mesle monstre uni-
    versal.

The clear splendour of the joyous
    maid,
Shall shine no more, she shall be
    a great time without salt,
With merchants, ruffians, wolves,
    odious,
All promiscuously, she shall see a
    universal monster.

France shall be closely associated for a while with nations of hitherto enemy status.

99

La fin le loup, le lyon, boeuf & l'asne,
Timide dama seront avec mastins,
Plus ne charra a eux la douce manne,
Plus vigilance & custode aux mastins.

At last the wolf, the lion, ox and ass,
The gentle doe, shall lie down with the mastiffs.
The manna shall no more fall to them,
There shall be no more watching and keeping of mastiffs.

This reiterates previous prognostications of a period of peace and plenty and elimination of war.

100

Le grand empire sera par Angleterre,
Le Pampotam des ans plus de trois cens,
Grandes copies passer par mer & terre,
Les Lusitains n'en seront pas contens.

The great empire shall be in England,
The Pempotan for more than three hundred years,
Great armies shall pass through land and sea,
The Lusitainians shall not be content therewith.

A period of great power for England, during which time her empire will reach to the far ends of the earth, is here predicted.

[There follow fragments of Centuries XI and XII, the remainder of which have been lost. The original numbering of the verses has been retained.]

91

Meysinier, Manthis & le tiers qui viendra,
Peste & nouveau insult, enclos troubler,
Aix & les lieux fureur dedans mordra,
Puis le Phocens viendrot leur mal doubler.

Meysinier, Manthi and the third that shall come,
Plague and new insult shall trouble them,
The fury of it shall bite in Aix and places nearby,
Then the Phocens shall come and double their misery.

This prognosticates not only the coming of a plague to the city of Aix, in Provence, but also implies that they will have trouble with the inhabitants of Marseilles (Phocens).

97

Par Ville-franche, mascon en desarroy,
Dans les fagots, seront soldats cachez,
Changer de temps enprime pour le Roy,
Par de chalon & moulins tous hachez.

By the Ville Franche, Mascon shall be in disorder,
In the fagots shall soldiers be hidden.
The time shall change in prime for the King,
By dragnets and mills they shall be hewed to pieces.

Civil war will bedevil France in a struggle between the rulers and the people.

5

Feu, flamme, faim, furt, farouche, fumee,
Fera faillir, froissant fort, foy faucher;
Fils de Deite! toute Provence humee,
Chasse de Regne, enrage sans crocher.

Fire, flame, hunger, theft, wild smoke,
Shall cause to fail, bruising hard to move faith,
Son of God! All Provence swallowed up,
Driven from the Kingdom, raging and without spitting.

Religious wars, having to do with the struggle for supremacy between faiths, are visualized by Nostradamus.

24

Le grand secours venu de la Guenne,
S'arrestera tout aupres de Poitiers.
Lyon rendu par Montluel & Vienne,
Et saccagez par tout gens de mestiers.

The great help that came from Gascony,
Shall stop suddenly at Poitiers,
Lyon surrendered by Montluel and Vienna,
And ransacked by all kinds of tradesmen.

Help for oppressed France shall be delayed; meanwhile German industrialists shall entrench themselves in the economic life of the nation.

36

Assault farouche en Cypre se prepare,
Larme a l'oeil, de ta ruine proche;
Byzance classe, Morisque, si grand
tare,
Deux differente, le grand vast par
la roche.

A savage assault is preparing in
Cyprus,
Tears in my eye, thy ruin ap-
proaches,
The fleet of Turkey and the Moors
so great damage,
Two opposing, the great waste by
the rock.

Many battles between Moslems and Christians are envisaged by Nostradamus.

52

Deux corps un chef, champs divisez
en deux,
Et puis respondre a quatre ouys,
Petits pour grands, a pertuis mal
pour eux,
Tour d'Aigues foudre, pire pour
Eussovis.

Two bodies, one head, fields divided into two,
And then answer to four unheard
ones,
Small for great ones, open evil for
them,
The tower of Aigues struck by
lightning, worse for Euffovis.

Two nations shall amalgamate, electing one ruler; they shall then be
challenged by four other nations, and shall prove their united strength.

55

Tristes consiels, desloyaux, cauteleux,
Aduis meschant, la loy sera trahie,
Le peuple esmeu, farouche, querel-
leux;
Tant bourg que ville, toute la paix
haye.

Sad councils, unfaithful and malicious,
By ill advice the law shall be betrayed,
The people shall be moved, wild
and quarrelsome,
Both in country and city the place
shall be hated.

Here is a picture of the consequences of bad laws and government,
and the ills that befall the people thereby.

56

Roy contre Roy & le Duc contre Prince,
Haine entre iceux, dissension horrible,
Rage & fureur sera tout province,
France grande guerre & changement terrible.

King against King, and Duke against Prince,
Hatred between them, horrid dissension,
Rage and fury shall be in every province,
Great wars in France and horrid changes.

Civil war in France is repeatedly predicted by Nostradamus.

59

L'accord & pache sera tu tout rompue;
Les amitiez polues par discorde,
L'haine euvieillie, tout foy corrompue,
Et l'esperance, Marseille sans concorde.

The accord and pact shall be broken to pieces,
The friendship polluted by discord
The hatred shall be old, all faith corrupted,
And hope also, Marseilles without concord.

A continuation of the preceding stanza this goes on to give the evil consequences of such debacles.

62

Guerres, debats, a Blois guerre & tumulte,
Divers aguets, adveux inopinables,
Entrer dedans Chasteau Trompette, insulte,
Chasteau du Ha, qui en seront coulpables.

War and debates, at Blois fighting and tumult,
Several lying in wait acknowledgment unexpected,
They shall get into the Chateau Trompette, by abuse,
And into the Chateau du Ha, who shall be culpable.

These last few verses show the concern and uneasiness with which Nostradamus viewed the France of his day, and the France which he foresaw. Here again he warns of the horror of internecine warfare.

65

A tenir fort par fureur contraindra,
Tout coeur trembler, Langon advent terrible,
Le coup de pied mille pied se rendra,
Guiront, Garon, ne furent plus
horribles.

He shall by fury compel them to
hold out,
Every heart shall tremble, Langon
shall have a terrible event
The kick shall return to thee a
thousand kicks,
Gironde, and Garonne rivers are
no more horrible.

The confusion within the League of Nations, and the role of France
in its final dissolution, is foretold.

69

Eiovas proche, esloigner Lac Le-
man,
Fort grands appreste, retour con-
fusion,
Loin des nepeuex, du feu grand
Supelman,
Tous de leur suyte.

Eiovas is near, yet seemeth far from
Lake Geneva,
Very great preparations, return
confusion,
Far from the nephews of the late
Supelman,
And all of their suite.

And in this stanza, Nostradamus looks far into the future to predict
the coming of a French leader, stern and unyielding, who shall lead his
people out of bondage.

71

Fleuves, rivieres de mal seront ob-
stacles,
La vieille flame d'ire non appaisee,
Courir en France, cecy comme
d'oracles,
Maisons, manoirs, palais, secte rasee.

Brooks and rivers, shall be a stop-
ping to evil,
The old flame of anger being not
yet appeased,
Shall run through France, take this
as an oracle,
Houses, manors, palaces, sects shall
be razed.

This final prediction by Nostradamus points to the fact that not until
complete political and economic equality is realized in France, shall there
be an end to the spirit of unrest.